# A CONFESSION IN WRITING

*Other Books by the Author:*

Both Ends of the Candle
Dearest Enemy
Hugo
Sarah: The Letters and Diaries of a Courtier's Wife, 1906-1936 (Editor)

# A CONFESSION

IN

# WRITING

Alfred Shaughnessy

TABB HOUSE
Padstow, Cornwall

First published 1997
Tabb House, 7 Church Street, Padstow
Cornwall, PL28 8BG



ISBN 1 873951 30 2



British Library Cataloguing-in-Publication Data:
A catalogue record of this title is available from the British Library.

Printed and bound by: Short Run Press Ltd, Exeter

To the Writers' Guild of Great Britain

with gratitude

# CONTENTS

| | Page |
|---|---|
| List of Illustrations | viii |
| * * | |
| Early Days | 1 |
| Writing for Revue | 23 |
| Writing for the Cinema | 34 |
| Repair Jobs | 52 |
| Directing for the Cinema | 60 |
| Writing for Television | 83 |
| Writing for *Upstairs, Downstairs* | 117 |
| The Fruits of Success | 134 |
| Writing Stage Plays | 159 |
| The Elusive West End | 181 |
| Adaptation | 194 |
| Writing Books | 209 |
| * * | |
| Index | 221 |

# LIST OF ILLUSTRATIONS


| | | Between pp. |
|---|---|---|
| 1 | The Author's first short story as it appears in *Affinity* magazine. | 86 & 87 |
| 2 | T.B. Clarke at work on his script for *The Lavender Hill Mob* with the author at Ealing Studios, 1949. | |
| 3 | James Donald and the author's wife Jean Lodge on location for *Brandy for the Parson*, with Torquay doubling for Brittany. | |
| 4 | Ronald Squire, Andrew Keir and Kathleen Ryan in the film *Laxdale Hall*. | |
| 5 | Fulton McKay and Prunella Scales in her first film, *Laxdale Hall*. | |
| 6 | L. to R: Richard Warner, Anouska Hempel and Eric Pohlmann, (at back Ivor Salter) in the film *Tiffany Jones*. | |
| 7 | A scene from the film *Room in the House* with, L. to R, Hubert Gregg, Josephine Griffin and Marjorie Rhodes. | |
| 8 | Barbara Shelley in the film *Cat Girl*. | |
| 9 | Petula Clark sings 'Baby Lover' in *Six-Five Special*. | |
| 10 | Yvonne Ball as Principal Boy and John Salew as the Pantomime Dame in the film *The Impersonator*. | 118 & 119 |
| 11 | Honor Blackman and Patrick Holt in the film *Suspended Alibi*. | |
| 12 | The author on location for *The End of the Road* with, L. to R: Finlay Currie, Duncan Lamont, and director Wolf Rilla. | |
| 13 | Charles Gray, Dan Ogilvey and Nicola Pagett in a scene from *Upstairs, Downstairs*. | |

14 David Langton and Rachel Gurney with Gordon Jackson in a scene from *Upstairs, Downstairs*
15 and with Lesley-Anne Down and the author at a summer fête.
16 The author receives a Writers' Guild Award on behalf of the *Upstairs, Downstairs* team from Sir Michael Balcon, with Susannah York.
17 L. to R: Jeanne Moreau, Anthony Higgins and Norma West at a rehearsal for the TV play 'The Last Seance'.
18 Margaret Leighton and Anthony Forwood in the TV production of *Release.* 198 & 199
19 Paul Daneman and Christine Finn in the Birmingham Repertory production of *Release.*
20 The German version of 'The Tea Cosy', 'Die Teepuppe'. Left is Helen Thiemig, actress wife of Professor Max Rienhardt.
21 Roger Hume as Old Herbaceous.
22 L. to R: Michael Davis, Frank Lawton, Elizabeth Counsell and Marjorie Stewart in the Theatre Royal, Windsor première of *The Heat of the Moment* in 1965.
23 Robin Sachs, Sian Philips and Moray Watson in the play *Love Affair.*
24 Working at home.

# EARLY DAYS

THERE cannot be many writers who do not remember the tingle of pride aroused by the first payment for their work, through which they achieved the goal of professional status.

To recapture that tingle I have to cast my mind back to 1934 when I was sweating it out as a cadet at the Royal Military College, Sandhurst. That may not sound like an ideal training ground for a professional writer, and it wasn't. So what was I doing there?

When it was time for me to leave school and study for some respectable profession I had found myself in an awkward dilemma. As a schoolboy I had been taken frequently to the theatre and the cinema, because it was for my parents the simplest and most agreeable solution to the problem of what to do with bored children on weekend leave or during the holidays. Thus, at every long-leave or on the first and last night of every school holidays my heart used to race with excitement as my brother, sister and I, with our mother and stepfather, climbed into a waiting taxi outside our home in a London square and were whisked off to some West End theatre, there to sit in the dark, wide-eyed and clutching a programme, as the curtain rose on a warmly lit world of magical make-belief.

After a period of seeing childrens' plays such as *Peter Pan*, *The Rose And The Ring* and *Treasure Island* we were upgraded to musical comedies, farces and thrillers. As we grew older still we were taken to some of the more serious, educational plays like Gordon Daviot's *Richard Of Bordeaux* and Shaw's

*St Joan,* and by the time I came to 'hang up my top-hat' and leave Eton I was totally and irrevocably stage-struck. Although I had seen numerous shows with music by Coward, Novello, Gershwin, Kern and Rodgers and endless thrillers by Edgar Wallace and Agatha Christie it had not yet occurred to me to try to write plays or compose music myself. It is true that I had also acquired, while at my preparatory school, a fondness for literature through exposure to the novels of Baroness Orczy, Charles Dickens, Robert Louis Stevenson, Joseph Conrad, Percy. F. Westerman, P. G. Wodehouse, 'Sapper', John Buchan and others. This was partly due to being read to aloud by a master at bedtime in the dormitory before 'lights out', partly as a result of being required to study such works for a 'holiday task'. But the taste for books did not immediately fire me with a desire to write novels.

At the stage in my life when I left school my ambition was to be involved, somehow, in the world of the theatre and films and no other profession would do. My elder brother Tom had conformed by reading Law at Oxford. My sister had also conformed by getting married and having children. But I was in a spot for, in those days, the idea of a career in show business was quite unthinkable; "Not at all," as one of my aunts pointed out, "a suitable occupation for a gentleman". I was caught at that crucial moment with absolutely no idea of what else to do with my life but soon, as a result of my dithering, matters were taken out of my hands and a decision was made for me. I was to join my stepfather Sir Piers Legh's old regiment, the Grenadier Guards.

So it was that I sat the absurdly easy Army Entrance Exam and found myself in the Spring of 1934, my head close-shaven and wearing heavy boots and puttees, square-bashing under ferocious Drill-Sergeants as Gentleman

-Cadet A. J. Shaughnessy of No. 1. Company, the Royal Military College, Sandhurst. But I was now eighteen and just starting to nurse a secret ambition to become a writer. It seemed to me a possible route to a life in the theatre and a noble way of avoiding a career in the Army, which would involve, as I saw it in 1934, spending my life in the ignoble business of learning how to kill human beings.

During my second term at the RMC and inspired by the works of W. Somerset Maugham I began to write. My first piece was a short story conceived one hot summer night when I could not sleep and I scribbled it down with a fountain pen in a lined Army Issue Exercise Book.

The story was entitled 'Shop Window Bride' and it proves that my mind was not at that time in any way focused on military matters:

A young girl assistant in a dress shop is engaged to be married but her parents cannot afford a proper wedding-dress. There is a gorgeous one on display in the shop window. Eager to try it on, the girl stays behind when the shop closes for the night, steps into the window and puts on the dress. She hears intruders break into the shop and, scared of being attacked, she freezes into what appears to be a lifeless wax dummy bride. As she feels rough hands attempting to unzip the wedding dress from her back, the girl quickly seizes a wooden stand and hurls it at the shop window which shatters the glass and sets off the alarm. The thieves run for it, the police arrive and later the girl's employer, Madame Buchet, whose real name is Mrs Cohen, rewards the young assistant for her courage by giving her the dress for her wedding.

After parade one day I cycled into Camberley and visited the Public Library where I searched through a copy of the *Writers and Artists' Yearbook*. Dozens of magazines were listed in it, with information on the length and type of article or work of fiction that each magazine would consider – plus the fee offered per hundred words. I found a publication called *Affinity* which sought 'romantic material for the younger unsophisticated female reader', sent in 'Shop Window Bride' and waited. To my astonishment a letter arrived within a fortnight from the fiction editress of *Affinity* enclosing a cheque for one guinea. My story would (and did) appear in their next issue. I realized that *Affinity* was the kind of magazine that was read mainly by young girls of limited intellect but I did not care. I was an author. I showed my published literary masterpiece to those of my fellow-cadets I could trust not to howl with laughter. They numbered only two, but fortunately were both quite impressed. Thus encouraged, I wrote another short story called 'The Ninth Knife'. This was about a young girl, brought up in a convent, who is forced to renounce her vows when her mother dies after an accident on the stage, and take her mother's place in her stepfather's variety act. The story describes the girl's terror as she has to stand in front of an audience under bright lights while her stepfather, dressed as a Western cowboy, throws ten knives in a pattern round her scantily clad body and flicks cigarettes out of her mouth with a large stockwhip.

I sent this one to another magazine group listed in the *Writers and Artists Yearbook* and was once again thrilled to receive acceptance and a cheque, this time for two guineas. But 'The Ninth Knife' found its way into a monthly magazine called *London Life* and when my complimentary copy arrived with my story in it plus the cheque, I glanced through it with mounting embarrassment. There were stories about women with one leg; ladies in chains and a special feature on high-heeled shoes for foot-fetishists. In one memorable letter in the correspondence column the writer described a journey in a bus seated opposite a lovely girl wearing long drop-earrings which swung to and fro, catching the street lights and glittering on her beautiful lobes, and went on to reveal the passionate emotions this sight aroused in him. It ended 'I would be glad to hear from any of your readers who has had a similar experience, Yours Sincerely, Ear-ring Fan, Watford.'

BY 1935 when I had completed the first of the three terms of my course at Sandhurst I had been promoted to the rank of Intermediate Corporal and was appointed one of the Commandant's pair of Orderlies. Our role was to escort the General up to the Saluting Base for Sunday morning Church Parade, wearing a special buckskin belt and pouch and carrying a silver-knobbed stick. But during that Intermediate Term I had been reading Beverley Nichols' classic anti-war book, *Cry Havoc,* which finally caused me, before starting on my third and final term, to become a convinced pacifist. I marched myself into the office of the Commandant, General Bertie Fisher, and told him that I wished to resign from the RMC on the grounds of conscience. Both the Commandant and my parents showed commendable understanding and sympathy.

My stepfather then steered me towards a job in the City as a stockbroker's clerk in a firm run by one of his friends.

The following year of 1936, my twentieth, proved to be indirectly vital to my future. For in that year I was asked by an old schoolfriend Michael Killanin, who was working for Lord Beaverbrook as a journalist, if I could help to raise part of the finance for a lavish revue to be staged the following year – Coronation Year, 1937 – at the Saville Theatre in London.

The show, entitled *Floodlight*, starring Frances Day, John Mills and Hermione Baddeley, had been written, words and music, by Michael's friend and my hero, Beverley Nichols, in an attempt to out-do his friend Nöel Coward. To compete with Coward's song 'A Room With A View' from *This Year*

*Of Grace*, Beverley had written for Frances Day and Johnny Mills a similar, although inferior, bouncy little duet called 'We Want A Little White Room'.

*Floodlight* was to be a big show with chorus and full orchestra under Benjamin Frankel; sets and costumes were by the famous Paris-Hollywood designer, René Hubert; tap-dances were to be staged by Buddy Bradley and the ballets would be choreographed by a young and eager Freddy Ashton. Years later he told me that he never got paid for the job. This did not surprise me as there had been no firm control over the finances, no C. B. Cochran to keep a proper grip on things. We were just a bunch of amateur enthusiasts which a profligate, self-indulgent director. However, at the time, I was determined to become involved and I told Michael I would do my best. I managed to coax investments in the show from a handful of rich young friends in the City by dangling before them the prospect of taking the chorus girls out for dining and dancing during the run. I myself invested £300 of my own money, the inevitable loss of which I did not mention to my family but put down to experience.

Although he was not wildly enthusiastic about Beverley, Nöel Coward graced our first night and went backstage afterwards to dispense his usual charming but often barbed compliments to the cast. Cochran came too and Lady Cunard, the Duff Coopers, the Carisbrookes, an ambassador or two and other celebrities of the day.

After a week's try-out at the Opera House, Blackpool, while *Floodlight* was running at the Saville Theatre in London, I was still employed as a clerk, spending my days seated on a high stool at a Dickensian desk in the offices of the stockbrokers, Nathan and Rosselli, entering share transactions in a ledger. Since I had raised half the finance for *Floodlight* and was representing my syndicate of backers, I was billed as co-presenter of the show. Thus, I could see from my office window buses going by in the street below with placards on their sides announcing: 'Richard. D. Rose and A. J. Shaughnessy present Frances Day and John Mills with Hermione Baddeley in *Floodlight*, a New Revue with Words and Music by Beverley Nichols'. I suspect that at the age of twenty-one I was the youngest City clerk to have a big musical show running in the West End.

Johnny Mills was a great trouper, as he demonstrated during the run of *Floodlight*. The First Act finale of the show was a colourful scene representing the Duchess of Richmond's Ball before Waterloo. The chorus of officers in scarlet and gold uniforms and ladies in Regency dresses were frenziedly waltzing in a glittering ballroom, to choreography by Freddy Ashton, when suddenly a bugle sounded outside and the officers dashed off through the French windows to fight Napoleon. They were followed by their ladies, leaving the stage clear for Johnny as a young subaltern, who was supposed to come back into the ballroom to meet the girl he loved, Frances Day. She would then sing of her anxiety for him in the forthcoming battle.

One night Johnny came on but Frances did not. Whether she was busy in her dressing-room with a visitor and did not hear her call was never established. But Johnny came on to the empty stage, saw Frances was not there and started to search for her, peering behind the furniture, pulling back curtains, looking into the wings . . . everywhere, while the orchestra desperately reprised and reprised the intro. to the song until at last Frances appeared, dishevelled, out of breath and on the wrong side of the stage.

Johnny saw her and with undisguised relief cried out over the music and strictly in his Regency character, "Heaven be praised, Madam, for I was afeared I had lost you forever!" This was not quite the line that Frances was expecting to hear so she 'corpsed' completely, shaking convulsively.

Johnny clasped her quickly to his bosom and patted the top of her head consolingly, in a desperate attempt to convince the audience that she was meant to be sobbing, which she was not. At last Frances got control of her giggles and somehow managed to start singing, with great charm and emotion, Beverley's lovely waltz song 'I Will Pray'.

To improvise a line like that in a crisis showed more than ordinary stage sense.

*FLOODLIGHT* was not totally successful but my involvement in it had taken me into the real world of the theatre.

One Saturday morning, sitting in the stalls at rehearsals, I was chatting to the publicist for the show, Robert Ellison, an ex-*Daily Express* dramatic critic and showbiz columnist. He and a musician friend of his, Dennis van Thal, had formed a small publicity and theatrical agency. Bob Ellison and I had become close friends and talked a lot about the theatre and playwriting. I was now persuaded by him to use a little of some capital I had recently inherited from my grandfather's trust in Canada to quit my clerk's job in the City and invest in and join the firm of Ellison and van Thal.

My family decided that I had taken leave of my senses but at twenty-one I had 'come of age', with my own money in the bank, and I knew I was moving in the right direction.

With an office in Burlington Gardens, Ellison, van Thal and Shaughnessy Ltd managed a number of artistes, including the promising young song-and-dance man, Graham Payn, who years later became Nöel Coward's constant companion. When Coward died he left the bulk of his fortune to be divided between Graham and his secretary, Cole Lesley. When 'Coley' died Graham Payn became immensely rich, owning all the copyright in Nöel Coward's plays and music. As his one-time agent, I wish I still had 10% of him!

Ellison, van Thal and Shaughnessy also represented a few playwrights and songwriters and found the money to co-present one or two West End shows. Among these was a play by the Czech playwright Karel Capek called *The Power And The Glory* at the Savoy, which starred Oscar Homolka and was not very successful. One of our larger productions was a bizarre, avant-garde play with music, adapted from the Danish, called *The Melody That Got Lost*. For our sins we presented that enigmatic piece at the Phoenix Theatre in 1938 with an interesting cast including Esmond Knight, the actor who was later to be blinded in a naval action during the war; the lovely Dorothy Hyson, daughter of Dorothy Dickson; Margaret Rutherford, then relatively unknown for she had not yet appeared in *Spring Meeting* or as Madame Arcati in Nöel Coward's *Blithe Spirit*; and Viola Tree, the character actress daughter of Sir Herbert Beerbohm Tree and mother of my close school friend, David Parsons.

*The Melody That Got Lost*, though highly original, went well over budget as well as over the heads of audience and critics alike; the *Daily Mail* review was headed 'Actors and Melody Get Lost In A Symbolic Fog'. We were off in six weeks.

All the same, I had managed to persuade my partners to allow me to contribute to that show by writing for it the words and music of one song, and a short extra scene for Viola Tree. In it a young couple, searching for a certain tune, symbolic of the lost melody of life, arrive at the Stage Door of the Covent Garden Opera House and ask to speak to a famous *diva* who is inside rehearsing Brunnhilde. The diva emerges in full Wagnerian costume with horned helmet and armour and they ask her where they can find the elusive melody that they are seeking. After a certain amount of sentimental chat when Viola says "the melody you are searching for, my dears, is not to be found in crotchets and quavers but deep in your own hearts", she goes on to tell them how every time she takes a high, sustained F-sharp at rehearsals "all the fruit porters in the market knock off, thinking it's the dinner whistle".

The following laughter was the first experience I ever had of a theatre audience responding in that way to something I had written. I realized later they were really laughing at Viola's comic appearance as Brunnhilde, for she was a very funny woman, but at the time it was a thrill for me to get that laugh.

After we had recovered from the shock of *The Melody That Got Lost* we signed a contract with the Eastbourne Corporation to produce a Summer Show at the Winter Gardens Theatre for the 1938 season. It was to be a long-running 'West End Revue By The Sea,' built round the well-known comedian Charles Heslop, and it was entitled *The Pleasure Of Your Company*. This production gave me the chance I had been waiting for, to write a number of songs and sketches for it myself, because the material for the revue had to be changed every week throughout the summer season.

In the following autumn of 1938, Munich Crisis time, Dennis Van Thal left us to join a larger agency, Christopher Mann Ltd, but Robert Ellison and I decided to soldier on together, an unfortunate phrase as things turned out. But more about that later.

We decided to devise and write an intimate revue of our own and present it in the West End of London. It was now Spring 1939 and we had plenty of sketches and songs which we had tried out the previous summer at Eastbourne, so we put a show together and called it *Fiddlesticks*. By July we had raised the finance, signed a deal with the Whitehall Theatre and engaged a company of young artistes, some of whom were our own clients. Our leading player once again was to be Charles Heslop and the show would open in the first week of October 1939.

Towards the end of July our work on *Fiddlesticks* was complete so Bob and I decided to take a fortnight's break in Monte Carlo before rehearsals began on August 27th. By then, alas, the war clouds were gathering over Europe and the atmosphere of Monte Carlo that summer was electric. The place was full of luxury yachts and rich people all having a last fling before the inevitable Armageddon broke out.

While we were on our way back from Monaco to London Hitler and Stalin signed their notorious non-aggression pact, and on the morning of September 1st, when I arrived for rehearsals at the Whitehall Theatre, the old stage door keeper, who was in his cubby hole listening to the wireless, muttered to me "Old 'Itler's marched into Poland. That's torn it, eh?" And I was inclined to agree with him.

Inside the theatre I found the cast standing about on the stage in little groups, anxiously whispering and muttering to each other in an atmosphere of intense gloom. Two of the girls in the cast were in tears. After a while Elsie April, our musical arranger, came over from the Haymarket Theatre where she was dividing her time between my music for *Fiddlesticks* and Coward's medley of his songs to be played by a small pit orchestra for his twin productions of *This Happy Breed* and *Present Laughter*.

Elsie April, who had arranged Beverley Nichols' music for *Floodlight*, was a birdlike little woman who might be taken for the piano teacher at a girl's school. But she was a musical genius. As the rehearsal pianist for auditions she could sight-read a piece of music and transpose it into another key while actually playing it. And she could enrich orthodox harmonies to make a song sound infinitely better then it really was. Working closely with her on my own songs, I was able to learn how much Nöel Coward who, like me, played the piano by ear mainly in E Flat, really owed to her.

Once when working with me on my music she said, rather indiscreetly, "Nöel got himself into such a mess with the intro. for 'Nevermore' in *Conversation Piece* that I had to get him out of F Sharp and back into E Flat with a little bridge – like this".

Or she would play great chunks of wonderfully harmonized stuff leading from one song into another, a sort of Intermezzo for *Bitter Sweet*.

That September morning in 1939 Elsie came down the aisle at the Whitehall into the front stalls with a long face, to say "Nöel's just telephoned Anthony Eden, who told him that war is now inevitable, so he's cancelled his rehearsals and strongly advises you to do the same."

Well, who was I to argue with Nöel Coward? So we sent our cast home for the weekend and promised to contact them if there was any news on the Monday morning. But Bob and I knew in our hearts that *Fiddlesticks* was doomed.

Charles Heslop, who had fought in the First World War, declared that he was "ready to fight the Hun again if they'd take him" and swept dramatically out of the theatre.

I myself realized that as I was now a member of the Royal Army Reserve of Officers I would have to report for duty at any moment. My pacifism had long since evaporated: three years earlier I had witnessed an incident in the streets of Hamburg when a group of S. A. Brownshirts had ordered some Jews off a tram and kicked them brutally on the pavement. Now I couldn't wait to go to war against Hitler.

So the *Fiddlesticks* company dispersed and our revue never saw the light of day. It was tragic. But a lot of my songs and sketches found their way into other revues over the next few years, which was some consolation. One sketch called 'Pick Up', in which a young man tries to seduce a girl in his flat while she conducts an endless telephone conversation with her mother, was performed by Betty Ann Davies and Bill Fraser in a show called *New Faces* at the Comedy and later had the honour of being revived by Eric Maschwitz in an all-star ENSA show in Brussels for Laurence Olivier and Vivien Leigh.

Other sketches of mine appeared in wartime revues such as *Diversion* at Wyndham's in which Edith Evans appeared and *Between Ourselves* at the Playhouse, and I was able to see some of them performed while I was on leave in London. One of my numbers intended for *Fiddlesticks* that I never saw done on the stage was a rather camp song called 'The Oldest Chorus Boy In London'. It was eventually performed by Cyril Ritchard for a revue called *Up And Doing* at the Saville Theatre. But the show opened in 1944 at just about the time that I was busy landing with the Guards Armoured Division on 'Juno' Beach in the Normandy bridgehead. So I never saw Cyril perform 'Chorus Boy' live on the stage and had to settle for the gramophone record he made of the song, accompanied by Carroll Gibbons and his Orchestra.

The person to derive most benefit from the demise of our ill-fated revue was the striptease artiste, Phyllis Dixey. For *Fiddlesticks* Bob and I had planned a small orchestra and had thus been forced to have an orchestra pit built into the Whitehall Theatre, which did not then have one. So two rows of stalls were removed and the pit was installed at a cost to us of some £300. Later, after our revue had been abandoned, that same orchestra pit was put to good use by Miss Dixey for the band that accompanied her famous Fan Dance and other erotic cavortings which delighted the troops on leave in London through most of the war.

As it turned out, my sketch-writing continued in the Army. Between training exercises and battles I became involved in writing and staging shows for the troops, in farm buildings of all sorts, tents in camps, shell-torn and burnt-out *chateaux* and *schlosses* in Normandy, Holland, Belgium and Germany, or wherever the Guards Armoured Division found itself.

Many of these productions were built round Brian Johnston, the well-known cricket commentator and radio personality, for 'Johnners' and I were in the 5th Guards Armoured Brigade through most of the war and were able to work together on the shows. Brian, a brilliant stand-up comedian, fronted the revues as compère. I was the author and director.

Shortly before D-Day we did a show called *It's All Laid On* at a camp on the Yorkshire Wolds. There was a certain Guardsman O'Brien in our Brigade with a fine tenor voice, so we decided to give him a 'spot' in the show. I placed O'Brien centre-stage in a pool of light, wearing tattered battledress and hemmed in behind barbed wire to denote a German prisoner-of-war camp, in order to sing Ivor Novello's lovely song 'Shine Through My Dreams' from *Glamorous Night*. He performed it with such feeling that there was not a dry eye in the house, as they say. But one night, as the number ended, our stage manager, a subaltern called Hugh Burge, suddenly realized that he ought to be on the prompt side of the stage ready for the next item. So, as the lights faded on Guardsman O'Brien, Hugh charged across the stage until he came to an abrupt halt, in the black-out having become entangled in the barbed wire. The ASM and a stage-hand rushed to his assistance but they too became caught up in the wire and meanwhile Guardsman O'Brien had also become trapped while trying to get off, so that we had four people on stage struggling like rabbits in a snare. The show was held up and someone made a speech while a soldier was dispatched to the Company Stores for wire-cutters with which to free the four men.

The speech of apology was greeted with gales of laughter

and applause because during it the audience were able to follow the wire-cutting operation through a gap in the curtain.

Soon after that light-hearted evening in Yorkshire most of us in The Guards Armoured Division developed a more serious sense of purpose when we were moved south to spend the last weeks before the invasion in a state of readiness at Brighton and Hove. It was here that on June 6th we heard that Operation Overlord had begun. Shortly after that we moved to Tilbury Docks, bound for Normandy. Soon after we embarked came the great storm which almost destroyed the Mulberry Harbour and which held us up for forty-eight hours off Southend Pier, where the time was spent drinking gallons of tea and watching the 'doodlebugs' flying over on their way to London. Then came the order to sail and we were off.

As we ploughed our way across the Channel aboard an American Liberty ship, our convoy was escorted by a Hunt class destroyer *Holderness*, which kept station a few hundred yards off our starboard quarter. Its commander, a young and glamorous Captain D had obviously been to see Nöel Coward in his film *In Which We Serve*.

All the way over to France this young officer kept up an impressive imitation of 'The Master', as he spoke into the ship's telephone:

"Keep her steady quartermaster . . . send Number One to see me on the bridge . . . stand by guns . . . watch out for possible air attack . . ."

We all lined the deck rail, enjoying this performance until we reached Juno beach when *Holderness* wheeled away to go back for another convoy.

As she turned to sail back to England, the Captain D called out through his loud hailer in a clipped Nöel Coward voice, "Good luck, soldiers!"

At this I'm afraid that some of our guardsmen ungraciously jeered and made rude gestures, but I don't think the Capt. D heard them.

Our arrival on French soil was something of an anti-climax. Fearing a high tide which would force us to 'swim ashore' in deep water our tanks, carriers, armoured cars, half-tracks, and so on, many weeks had been spent in the UK waterproofing all carburettors and vital engine parts with bostick, fixing high funnels to exhaust pipes well clear of the water and trying out the results by driving the vehicles in and out of an open-air swimming pool in Brighton, watched by astonished crowds of schoolchildren. As Technical Adjutants of our respective Battalions, Brian Johnston and I had been responsible for this complicated task and both of us had experienced nightmares of all our vehicles going down the ramp to vanish under the water in a sea of bubbles. But when the ramps of our transport ships finally went down on the day, the tide was miles out, enabling us to motor happily ashore across a vast sandy beach, encountering nothing more hazardous than an occasional pool with a bit of seaweed and a jelly fish. All those months of waterproofing went for nothing. But it was a wise precaution.

DURING our spell of occupation on the Rhine, after the fighting had ended, I devised and wrote a big revue for the troops entitled – after the Guards Armoured Division's sign – *The Eyes Have It*. The show opened in a large white building on the banks of the Rhine at Bonn, which later became the official building for the West German Government of Dr Adenauer. Apart from Brian Johnston as the star presenter, we had a dance band, a number of talented soldiers – some of whom had been on the stage in peacetime – and three show-girls borrowed from a nightclub in Brussels. It was quite a lavish production.

A strange incident occurred later involving the poet, Stephen Spender. In his book *European Witness* he described a visit to post-war Germany, with an emphasis on its miseries such as the rubble and the tragedy of the Displaced Persons. He then reported seeing in Bonn the Guards Division Revue, *The Eyes Have It*, and drew an unfavourable comparison between it and an entertainment by a group of Polish DPs in a nearby camp. I did not see Spender's book until after returning from Bonn in 1946 when I was demobilized but I was so taken aback by his bias that I wrote to the author. I pointed out that *The Eyes Have It* was a show performed by a group of battle-scarred and weary soldiers for the enjoyment of their comrades who had been continuously under fire for a year and needed some light relief, and it was not intended for the amusement of itinerant poets travelling in the wake of the victorious army. I received in reply a postcard from Spender written in green ink. He said he took my point but stuck to his comments.

IN 1946 I was demobbed and set about trying to get myself a job. With the possibility in mind of joining forces again with my old colleague Robert Ellison, with whom I had lost touch, I telephoned his home at Worcester Park and was shattered to be told by his mother that he had joined up in 1943 and been killed in action in Holland, not many miles from Nijmegen where I had been involved in the capture of the famous bridge.

With a heavy heart I resumed my efforts to find employment for myself. I was ready to do anything I was offered, provided it was in the area of theatre, films or publishing. I sent off a barrage of letters to every theatrical firm, agency or film studio I could think of, and to the BBC, seeking interviews.

The first reply I received was from Michael Balcon, who

invited me down to see him at Ealing Studios.

I set out for Ealing Broadway by train and made my way to the modest little studios at Ealing Green where, because I had written some revue sketches and had a couple of short stories published in magazines (which I wisely did not show to Balcon) he gave me a job at £12 a week as an 'inside reader' in the Studio Scenario Department. I returned home to report the good news to my mother and stepfather, who were not too sure that it was appropriate for me to 'go into films'. But it was gainful employment and I, for my part, told them that I was thrilled to be working for the man who discovered Alfred Hitchcock. They nodded, although I was not sure that they knew who Alfred Hitchcock was.

On my first day at work in the Scenario Department one of the producers came into my room and deposited two enormously heavy books on my desk and asked me to do a synopsis of each of them by the weekend. One was Victor Hugo's *Toilers Of The Sea*, the other was Dostoevsky's *The Idiot*, each running to some 700 pages. It was a nightmare trying to grasp the plot and characters of these great works of literature in so short a time and then in addition having to make a short outline of the story, giving at the end my opinion as to the property's suitability as film material. But that was what I was being paid £15 a week to do and, at least, I had fulfilled an old childhood dream. I was a writer and I was in movies.

I soon moved on to other work, and while still a junior trainee at Ealing Studios I learned a great deal about film-making by working on the floor as an assistant director, in the cutting rooms and, mainly, in the Scenario Department.

Working with the great Angus MacPhail, Hitchcock's old writer at Gaumont-British, and top film writers like T. E. B. Clarke, John Dighton and W. P. Lipscombe, I learned much about scriptwriting. I wrote a screenplay of my short story 'The Ninth Knife', just to see if I could, and submitted it to Balcon and two of his producers. The producers were impressed but Balcon rejected it. It was frustrating, but I had to be patient and await my chance. In those days people with my kind of background were not expected to have any talent and when in 1956 I eventually directed my first feature film, *Suspended Alibi*, I was, I believe, only the second Old Etonian to have become a film director. As far as I know, the first was Penrose Tennyson who worked his way up as an Assistant Director at Denham Studios before directing three movies for Balcon in the late '30s. Nowadays, since Hugh Hudson made *Chariots Of Fire,* movie directors pour out of Eton as plentifully as Classical Scholars, Oarsmen and Cricketers.

At last, after two years, in 1948 I was taken under the wing of the witty and clever South Africa-born, Paris-educated, Jewish director, Henry Cornelius, and became his personal assistant on two pictures, *It Always Rains On Sunday* and *Passport To Pimlico*.

On the latter, which he directed, I sat in on all the original story conferences, contributing ideas, two of which plus four lines of my dialogue are to be found in the picture.

We had a drab location down the Lambeth Road on a street corner beside a bomb-site. It represented the anomalous state of Burgundy which had declared unilateral independence of the British Government and was under siege. In the film the people of South London were in sympathy with the rebellious cockney community in Pimlico and we had a scene in the script where a commuter-train passes over a viaduct overlooking the Burgundian street corner. As it rattles by, paper bags filled with sandwiches, meat pies and buns shower down from the train to be gathered up by the starving rebels below. This meant that a crowd of film extras, portraying the commuters, had to catch a local train out of Waterloo, armed with the paperbags, and at the right moment hurl them from the open train windows down towards the waiting camera below. They then got out at Vauxhall, crossed a bridge to catch the next train back to Waterloo, there to embark on the next train out, return to Lambeth and repeat the procedure until 'Corney' had a shot he was happy with. My job was to take the train with the extras and cue them to 'stand by' and 'throw buns' when I calculated we were passing over the camera. As I caught the seventh train out from Waterloo to Vauxhall on that pouring wet day, I remember thinking to myself 'If this is the glamorous, romantic film business I once dreamed about, I think I would rather drive a bus.'

As a dog's body at Ealing Studios I knew it would take time to reach producer or director status and exploit any creative gift I might have, so I embarked on a period of 'moonlighting'. With the reasonable security of a regular salary as well as the prestige of working in a movie studio, I proceeded to write more revue material and a stage play.

I contributed a sketch called 'Old Comrades' to *The Boltons Revue*, put together by and starring Billy Milton. The revue did well enough at the little Boltons Theatre to transfer to the late-lamented St James's Theatre, where it was seen one evening by Michael Balcon, who confronted me in the studio corridor the next day.

"What are you doing writing stuff for revues when you're supposed to be working for me?"

I was quick enough to say "Did it in my spare time, Mick, over the weekend." Otherwise Balcon might have claimed some share of the rights in my sketch, since he was at the time paying my salary.

From that moment on, although my next twenty years were spent for the most part in films, I became what can only be described as a 'journeyman writer'. The need to earn my living with my pen and other circumstances dictated that I would work throughout my writing life in nearly all the disciplines of the craft except poetry. But I believe the lyrics for songs to be a form of poetry so I shall delete the word 'except'.

Every job I have undertaken from 1934 to the present day has had its own special problems, provided a different experience and taught me a new lesson. Apart from the creative work he does, a 'journeyman writer', like a journeyman-carpenter or cabinet-maker, must also be prepared to do repair work. A cabinet-maker will make a new cabinet or chest of drawers for a customer but he must occasionally repair one made by somebody else, or mend one leg of one of a set of dining-room chairs or make and glue on a missing piece of a Regency sideboard.

Thus have I frequently been called in to mend, that is to say rewrite, a film script that has gone wrong, or devise an extra scene for a discontented star, or rewrite American dialogue into English, or redraw a character to suit a player who has been miscast. That kind of repair work can be very interesting and challenging. Later in my career I did quite a bit of script editing on television drama series and this often required the rewriting of other peoples' scripts, which can be a thankless, delicate business, writers being touchy people whose work is their brain-child.

My output as a writer has been very varied: books including two novels; plays for the theatre; screenplays for the cinema, some based on original stories of my own, many on source material; sketches, lyrics and music for revues; single television plays and episodes for television series and serials; radio plays and adaptations; and on one occasion the script for a pageant at the Royal Festival Hall.

It was the writing of revue material that involved me in

my first love, the live theatre, so let revue writing be the first discipline to be discussed in these pages.

# WRITING FOR REVUE

MOST theatre-goers of my generation deeply regret the passing of the revue, a stage art form that flourished throughout the '20s and '30s on both sides of the Atlantic. Some of the big shows came over from New York but London staged its own share of big revues under great producers such as Charles B. Cochran, Jack Hulbert, André Charlot and, later, John Murray Anderson, Robert Nesbitt and George Black. These shows were lavishly staged and dressed with large companies and a full orchestra in the pit. The material consisted of a variety of scenes, sketches, ballets, musical ensembles, single numbers, duets and sometimes quartets. Most items had some satirical comment to make on life, social habits, politics or current topical events of all kinds.

Sharp talents went into these shows with items written by playwrights such as Nöel Coward, A. P. Herbert, Ronald Jeans, Douglas Furber and others. Then, with *Nine Sharp* at the Little Theatre in the late '30s, there came into fashion the 'intimate revue', a more modest affair with a small gifted cast and two pianos. Writers like Herbert Farjeon, Diana Morgan and Robert MacDermott, Michael Trefford, Alan Melville and Nicholas Phipps provided these shows with sharply observed comment and satire of a very high order.

Apart from the originality and wit of the individual sketches and songs, a revue, being a kind of meal with varied courses, depended a lot for its overall effect on its 'running order'. The often complicated business of getting the songs and sketches into the right order depended partly on the technical necessity of the artistes involved having time to change their costumes, and on the artistic need to juxtapose the items in a suitable sequence of contrasts. For example, it would be unwise to follow a downbeat lament sung by a woman ("Mah man done left me . . .") with a satirical single of an undertaker in funeral clothes singing about his job. Better to follow the female blues singer with a bright quartet of fox-hunting squires or a lively ensemble in regency costume.

The revue sketch as such usually ends with a comic denouement, a funny line and a quick black-out. Brevity is desirable and I remember two extremely short sketches that amused me very much. The first might not now be considered politically correct. It was in Cochran's revue, *Streamline* and was by A. P. Herbert:

Two girls are at a table in a teashop, both pregnant and both weeping.

The waitress arrives with a tray and plonks the teapot down between them, saying cheerfully "Now then, which of you is going to be mother?"

Both girls in tears:

"Both of us."

Black out.

Another, in *The Punch Revue,* had no such *double entendre* but worked through a contrast of pomposity pierced by an unexpected whiff of frivolity.

An effete young man sitting over the cigars and port at a dinner table with an old buffer.

The old buffer gets up, saying "Come along now, my boy, let's go and join the ladies," whereupon the young man leaps up, clapping his hands excitedly and saying: "Oh, goody-goody, let's join all the ladies together and make one enormous lady".

In 1949 a sketch I had written called 'Non Compos Mentis' was included in a revue called *Sauce Piquante* at the Cambridge Theatre. In it a General in khaki uniform with red tabs is sitting in a railway compartment waiting for the train to start when the guard comes in to ask him if he would mind a 'special' passenger sharing his compartment, because the train is full. The guard adds in an undertone that the 'special' passenger is a mental case on his way to an asylum. The General reluctantly agrees and the mental case is led in by his keeper and told to sit in the corner and behave himself.

The train starts and the mental patient begins to ask the General odd questions, such as "Ere, why is your clothes that dirty, muddy colour?"

The General decides to humour the chap and replies "That's what we call khaki. We soldiers wear it in the field so that the enemy can't see us against the grass and the trees."

The lunatic ponders this, then asks "What are those red bits on your collar and round your cap?"

The General says "They denote my rank as a General so that people can see that I'm a highranking officer and salute me."

The lunatic says "But you just said you didn't want to be seen in the fields and that . . ."

Later, the lunatic asks "What are soldiers for?"

The General replies patiently "Soldiers are supposed to fight and kill their enemies."

So the lunatic says "If you're a soldier and get paid to kill people, what do you do when you're not killing people, like when yer on yer holidays?"

The General says patiently "When I'm on leave, my good fellow, I hunt and shoot and do a little fishing."

Lunatic: "What's that mean?"

General: "I chase foxes, shoot pheasants and kill salmon."

To this, the lunatic stares at the General in horror and says "Blimey, you're not safe to be in a railway carriage with, you aren't!" and climbs up into the luggage rack to get away from him.

In the end the train arrives at its destination. A chauffeur enters the compartment and asks "Which one of you gentlemen is for the asylum?"

The General gets up and says "I rather think I am."

Black Out.

In *Sauce Piquante* the General was played by Douglas Byng, the Guard by Bob Monkhouse and the lunatic by Norman Wisdom. And the showgirl who came on to announce the sketch was a young and dazzling Audrey Hepburn.

The dramatic critic of *The Star* A. E. Wilson lambasted me for that sketch, saying it was 'anti-militaristic and in very bad taste and should be cut from the show at once.'

But it wasn't cut and it got plenty of laughs. Looking back, I agree it might have been a bit tasteless to get laughs out of a lunatic but the lunatic won the argument and I thought the pompous General was fair game. Some years later I wrote a film for Norman Wisdom called *Just My Luck*. He told me one day on the set that he had enjoyed playing in 'Non Compos Mentis' and had not agreed with the critic of *The Star*.

During the run of *The Pleasure Of Your Company*, our summer show at Eastbourne, I came to realize that much of the art of creating revue material, apart from a talent for sketch-writing, lies in the art of rhyme. So much of revue consists of what are called 'point numbers'. These are in the main musically accompanied monologues in which an artiste portrays some bizarre character in a comically satirical way with a witty, pointed lyric, the laughs often coming from clever rhyming. Possibly one of the greatest exponents of this gift in my lifetime was the aforementioned Douglas Byng, known in his day as a 'female impersonator', who had his audience in stitches whenever he appeared in revue and cabaret as what today would be termed a 'drag queen'.

His *double entendres* were considered quite shocking when I was a boy and I was not allowed to see him in cabaret until I was grown-up, when I came to know him quite well. He was a very kind-hearted, modest and charming man.

At Eastbourne I wrote a rather tasteless point number for a comedienne in the company and called it 'My Pet Perversion'. The first verse ran:

On Wednesday night while dining with the Burtons
the conversation suddenly turned to vice;
we all discussed each others' pet perversions;
when they looked at me, I went as cold as ice.
Then the Applebys said *their* thing was tying each
  other up with string;
when they turned to me there was a dreadful hush . . .

It was considered unsuitable for performance at the Winter Gardens in Eastbourne in 1938 and later, after a brief discussion, it was eliminated from *Fiddlesticks* as well. But never one to waste an idea, I managed to sell the song in 1954 to Hermione Baddeley who, without turning a hair, sang it for three weeks in cabaret at Ciro's Club in London.

As a lyricist I am naturally fascinated by the lengths to which some lyric writers will go to get a rhyme. Some of Lorenz Hart's lyrics are startlingly ingenious, as for example, this verse of 'Manhattan':

Summer journeys to Niagra
and to other places aggra-
vate all our cares,
we'll save our fares.
I've a cosy little flat in
what is known as old Manhattan.
We'll settle down
right here in town . . .

Some of the great masters will occasionally come up with a horrendous line in a song that makes you imagine that they must have been very tired after a long day and settled for anything to finish off the job. In *The Sound of Music* the brilliant Oscar Hammerstein II follows the line 'to laugh like a brook when it trips and falls over stones on its way' with 'to sing through the night like a lark that is longing to pray'. Imagine a lark longing to pray!

Cole Porter in his classic 'Night And Day' only just gets away with 'Day and night under the hide of me there's an oh such a hungry yearning burning inside of me' because of the power and passion of the music.

In the immortal 'But Not For Me' Ira Gershwin must have been yawning and wanting his bed when he followed 'I was a fool to fall and get that way' with 'hi-ho, alas, and oh so lack-a-day'.

And my hero, Nöel Coward, who always wrote and spoke impeccable English wrote for *Operette* a beautiful song that began with 'Where are the songs we sung when love in our hearts was young'. He should have known that the past tense of sing is 'sang' and that 'sung' is the past participle of the verb. I suppose if he had written correctly 'Where are the songs we sang' the next line would have had to be 'when love in our hearts went bang'. Not half so romantic!

Another of my lyrics, lost to *Fiddlesticks* but later sung by three girls in the BBC Television Revue *Telescope*, was called 'Bobbysoxoffice Favourites' which reflects its year, 1947, when teenaged girl fans were called 'Bobbysoxers' and the romantic Gainsborough costume films were all the rage. One girl sang:

> I've a snap of James Mason
> by my washing basin
> I gaze at while cleaning my teeth
> being cruel to Pat Roc

in a transparent frock
and with not very much underneath.

The famous Windmill Theatre in Shaftesbury Avenue which 'never closed' during the war, a fact that gave birth to the old chestnut 'we never clothed', offered for many years a permanent show called *Revuedeville* because it was in a sense an amalgam of revue and vaudeville. The Windmill was for some time the only theatre in the country where the patrons could see totally naked young women on the stage. The girls were not allowed to move so posed on pedestals, pretending to be Greek statues. Many fine young British comedians started their careers at the Windmill and had to fight apathetic audiences of middle-aged men in macs impatient to get to the next scene when the undraped girls would be on again.

Another long-lost song of mine from *Fiddlesticks* once found its way into the programme at the Windmill. It was called 'One Square Foot Of Heaven' and was sung by a young girl looking out at the stars from the attic skylight of her small London flat. The girl, Betty Emery, sang it quite charmingly but, because it was the Windmill, she was required to deliver the number in a completely transparent nightdress, which must have distracted the men in macs from listening to my inspired words and music.

PROBABLY the most unusual assignment I ever had that required the ability to write short sketches were the two Royal Film Performances of 1948 and 1949 in the presence of the King and Queen. On both occasions I was engaged to write the scripts for the big stage shows that preceded the showing of the chosen film. This came about because in 1948 the chosen film was the Ealing Studios movie *Scott Of The Antarctic,* and Balcon wanted to make sure that the whole evening would be a success. So he fixed with the Cinematograph Trade Benevolent Fund authorities to engage Jack Hulbert, an old friend of his, to devise and direct the stage show. He also loaned me, as a former revue writer, to work with Jack and write the script for the show.

This meant providing a number of short sketches for the galaxy of Hollywood stars of the day who had come over to appear in the performance, intercast with some of our own British stars. With my experience of 'revue' this was no problem, so I started by cooking up a sketch with the unlikely cast of Rosalind Russell, Michael Wilding and Jean Kent as a cockney couple assisting an American tourist to find the British Museum; another sketch featured Myrna Loy, Elizabeth Taylor and Robert Taylor at rush hour in the London Underground.

One day, while Jack Hulbert and I were preparing the show, he told me the Motion Picture Association of America had cabled to say that we were to find a spot in the stage show for a B picture actor, of whom neither of us had ever heard, called Ronald Reagan. He had recently played a supporting part in a British-made movie called *The Hasty Heart,* starring Richard Todd, but was to be included in the party because he was President of the Screen Actors Guild, SAG. So I spent one memorable afternoon in a suite at the Dorchester Hotel watching Jack direct Virginia Mayo, Irene Dunne and a future President of the United States in my sketch about three Americans watching the Derby.

I remember sitting in the stalls at rehearsals one morning with Patricia Neale when Laurence and Vivien Olivier drifted in to do their bit. The effect was electrical: Miss Neale suddenly gasped "My God, look, its 'them'." They were glamour personified, those two at the time. I had written a speech for Vivien Leigh to make at the end of the show and I recall how nervous she was about it. She called me one evening at our Chesham Street flat and was on the phone for twently minutes, going through the speech paragraph by paragraph, making suggestions for new and altered phrases, all in a rather shrill, high-pitched voice. But she was immensely professional and efficient and like men the world over I was completely bowled over by her beauty and charm.

In 1949 the chosen Royal film was MGM's *The Forsythe Saga* and for the stage show we abandoned the revue format and used instead a satirical pantomime with a book by Phil Park and a cast consisting of Jean Simmons as Cinderella, Gregory Peck as Prince Charming, Moira Lister as the Fairy Godmother, Ralph Richardson as the Demon King and Dickie Attenborough as Buttons. The ball scene was an excuse for more sketches for the stars as they arrived and were announced as guests: Ann Sothern, Greer Garson, Walter Pidgeon and others.

At one point Ben Lyon, the compère, introduced an old retired technician from the early days of British films who had, he explained, come up for the evening from Chatham to be present as a guest of the Cinematograph Trade Benevolent Fund. When a seedy old creature in glasses and a moth-eaten dinner jacket appeared to be interviewed at the microphone, the audience listened to the veteran film technician with polite respect and never realized, until the old man had shuffled off, that it was Alec Guinness. I couldn't persuade Alec to unmask and reveal his identity on stage; he was far too modest for that.

The *Evening Standard* evidently appreciated our efforts for their critic wrote of the evening: 'After the film which ought to have been retitled *The Forsyte Sago* the stage show was a gay, nimble leg-pull. Full marks to scriptwriter, Alfred Shaughnessy and producer, Jack Hulbert.'

At a banquet at the Dorchester given by the Motion Picture Association of America following the first Royal

Film Performance in 1948 I found myself seated next to Rosalind Russell, with whom I had especially enjoyed working. She was sweet and tremendous fun and we had had a lot of laughs. When at dinner I asked her to sign my menu as a souvenir of our acquaintance, she wrote: 'To my other Freddy, love Roz.' This was quite a compliment to me as her main Freddy was her husband, the agent Freddy Brisson.

IN 1988, when Mrs Thatcher's popularity was just beginning to wane, I wrote the kind of song I imagined Nöel Coward would have written about her for a revue, had he still been living:

Colonel Hamish Drummond-Ife, a loyal Tory all his life,
who lived in Fife, informed his wife
he'd had a change of heart.
Not awfully keen to turn his coat, withdraw his vote
and rock the boat he wrote a note to Downing Street
his feelings to impart.
Trembling with unbridled rage he scribbled each successive page
till finally he reached the stage when all his ire was spent.
Then, mindful of the libel law and anxious to berate, not bore,
he read his letter through once more and this is how it went:

Dear Mrs Thatcher, much as we admire your guts, authority
and clout you've done your bit now
it's time to quit now
avoid a split now,
so just be sensible and wise before they cut you down to size
and go away.
Cher Madame Thatcher, much as we admire your hats, your
wardrobe and your 'chic' it's time to stop now
you're at the top now
so close the shop now
and just be big and realize that hanging on is most unwise –
call it a day.
Against your splendid leadership and flair it would be
little short of churlishness to grouse.

But let's be fair, while England has a reigning Queen
your place is Number Ten and not Buck House.

Signora Thatcher, think how cosy it would be
with Dennis on your knee to hang your hat up
or do a flat up,
not have to chat up
those foreign statesmen on the make
and take a break
from being discourteous to France.
Liebe Frau Thatcher,
we don't want to lose you but we think you ought to go.
We do beseech you –
no one can teach you –
how can we reach you
to say 'just vanish in the fog, go for a jog'
and you'll receive your just rewards?
Don't be so stubborn,
quit and be a hit as Countess Thatcher in the House of Lords.

Revue is a fascinating, challenging form of theatre and I dearly wish some enterprising West End management would take the plunge and revive it.

# WRITING FOR THE CINEMA

1951 was lucky for Winston Churchill and the Conservative Party, when they were returned to power; it was also lucky for me. In that same year my first stage play *Release* was produced in Birmingham, I had my first screenplay filmed and was in addition appointed to be Associate Producer on the picture.

My good fortune was that a new, experimental film company had been formed by the National Film Finance Corporation to make low budget pictures, giving young film makers a chance to develop their talents. For the first time, the Government would be funding the production of films.

The company was called Group Three and it was run by three men: John Grierson, the famous founder of Documentary Film; John Baxter, an old and highly experienced producer-director; and my Ealing Studios boss, Michael Balcon. Supervising the NFFC's money was its boss, the artistically inclined James Lawrie.

A young documentary director under contract at Ealing Studios called John Eldridge was at that time at a loose end in the studios with very little to do, as bored as I was. His main job was directing a Second Unit, getting documentary shots of the Thames for a Basil Dearden film called *The Pool Of London*. Meanwhile, I was acting as Personal Assistant to the director, Thorold Dickinson, on a film called *The Secret People*. One of my tasks on this picture was looking after the distinguished French actor, Serge Reggiani, who was in the film. He spoke very little English so I acted as interpreter for him on the set, explaining to him what the director wanted and the meaning of some of his lines. I was also charged at weekends with taking him sightseeing and to the theatre. On one occasions I was sent by Thorold to see Irene Worth, whom I happened to know, in her dressing-room at the theatre where she was appearing in T.S. Eliot's play, *The Cocktail Party*. My brief was to persuade her on Thorold's behalf to accept a part in *The Secret People*. Apart from those kind of chores I spent much of the picture giggling in quiet corners on the set with Lindsay Anderson, a young film journalist. He had been so rude about Ealing films in a waspish magazine he edited, called *Sequence*, that Balcon had invited him, in self-defence, to join the studios as an observer and watch the filming of *Secret People*. In the event Lindsay wrote a book about his experience, *A Film Is Made*, and before very long had himself become a distinguished, radical, if sometimes outrageous director of the 1960s' *nouvelle vague* school.

While in attendance on Thorold Dickinson every day on the set of *The Secret People* I had the task of getting a chair for the Italian star, Valentina Cortese, to sit on between 'takes' because she was pregnant. We had a little joke about it and whenever the director said "Cut" and I appeared with a chair for her, she would say "Here is my dear Mister Sitdown."

Forty years later in Venice I was taken to a drinks party given by Valentina Cortese in her elegant flat on the Giudecca. She was then the widow of a wealthy Italian property millionaire who had owned most of Milan. When I reminded her of my getting her chairs to sit on when she was pregnant, she laughed and said "And there is the baby I was expecting," and pointed to a very tall, handsome Italian in his forties who was approaching us: "my son, Giulio".

As soon as John Eldridge had finished working on *Pool Of*

*London* and I had seen Serge Reggiani off when he went back to Paris, we got together with the Ealing Studios story department and unearthed an old discarded subject called *Brandy For The Parson*.

This was a breezy little novel by Geoffrey Household, about a newly wed couple who on their honeymoon, yachting on the Devon coast, became involved with a young man secretly engaged in smuggling brandy from France in his motor launch.

John and I guessed that Balcon, who was boss of both Ealing and Group Three, would welcome the chance to off-load a dead Ealing subject on to the new Government-financed company and thus recoup from the tax-payer Ealing's original development costs on the subject – whilst at the same time being seen to give two eager young talents a chance to make a picture. So we went to see Mick Balcon and suggested to him that we should make *Brandy* into a movie for Group Three as Producer and Director. And Balcon gave us the go-ahead. I re-wrote the old Ealing script that had never gone into production but, being somewhat in awe of the two rather senior writers who had done the original screenplay, I rather over-modestly gave myself only a subsidiary credit – that old war-horse 'additional scenes and dialogue' – by Alfred Shaughnessy. But with my Associate Producer's credit on the screen as well, I was reasonably satisfied, although I realized that I was giving up the cosy security of Ealing Studios to take my chance in the outside world as a freelance film writer and producer. It was scary, but it was exciting to be on the brink of my first feature film when we started to cast *Brandy*.

While she was still in the studios we offered the part of the girl in *Brandy For The Parson*, Petronilla, to Audrey Hepburn whom I had got to know quite well while working with her on *The Secret People*. At that time she was just beginning to emerge as star material and John and I knew that we should grab her as soon as possible.

Audrey read my script over a weekend. In one scene I described Petronilla peering out of the porthole of a yacht and when Audrey handed the script back to me she asked with an impish grin if I really meant that. Someone in the typing-pool had omitted the letter 'r' from the word peering.

Although Audrey loved our script, she soon received another tempting offer of a musical picture to be shot in Monte Carlo and because our budget had not yet been agreed by the National Film Finance Corporation, my bosses, Group Three Films, would not allow me to contract her for *Brandy For The Parson.* So we lost one future star, but gained another, in the relatively unknown Kenneth More, who had his name over the title on *Brandy* for the first time in his career, which pleased him a lot.

We also cast James Donald for the young husband. He was rather highbrow and a bit choosy. Most of his career so far had been with Nöel Coward and David Lean and in cerebral French plays in the theatre. But when he heard the magic name 'John Grierson' he at once agreed to do the movie. The girl in the movie, Petronilla, was eventually played by the actress Jean Lodge, to whom I have now been happily married for forty-eight years. I hasten to add that she only got the part after testing for the director in competition with seven other girls. Jean was a busy actress in those days and when *Brandy For The Parson* was running at the prestigious Empire Cinema, Leicester Square, she was at the same time appearing at a little club theatre in Irving Street close by, in a revival of the Gate Revue, and being seen on TV in the drama series called *Douglas Fairbanks Presents . . .'*

The music for *Brandy* was composed by John Addison, whose first film score it was. He went on to compose movie music for the Boulting Brothers, and for Tony Richardson's films such as *Charge Of The Light Brigade*, *Tom Jones* and others, and later in Hollywood was responsible for the jaunty theme that precedes *Murder She Wrote* with Angela Lansbury. This bouncy little passage is very similar to the one Jock composed for the ponies trotting across the Downs with brandy barrels strapped on them in our film.

Before *Brandy* had been released in the cinemas (including an Art House in New York where it ran for twenty-three weeks) Eldridge and I had acquired yet another dead Ealing subject and once again persuaded Mick to sell it to Group Three and let us film it.

It had all begun with Charles Crichton, the Ealing director, wanting to make a film about salmon poaching in the Highlands of Scotland. To this end Balcon had invited the renowned Scottish author, Eric Linklater, to write a story outline. Linklater delivered it but Charles did not like it much, so the project went dead. But Linklater asked Balcon to sell him back the rights in his salmon poaching story so that he could turn it into a novel. Balcon agreed and Linklater wrote the book, *Laxdale Hall*. As an incentive he had offered Mick the film rights in the novel free. Mick accepted and John and I jumped hungrily on the novel, seeing it as our next film for Group Three. I did the script, to which Eric Linklater gave his blessing, and off we went to Locharron in the misty Highlands to start shooting. It was always fun to write a script for a film and then, as the producer, to work out the casting. From a close study of the original Linklater novel I was firm in my ideas as to how most of the parts should be cast. Many of the Highland characters in the story were easy to find from among the players at the Glasgow Citizens' Theatre. But for a time I could not think of anyone to play the wife of one of the English MPs, a blonde, middle-aged, ex-musical comedy star called Lucy Pettigrew. She was married in the story to a rather pompous MP, Sam Pettigrew, eventually played by my old friend Raymond Huntley.

Then an agent I consulted, Ronnie Waters of the Al Parker office, said to me, "Had you thought of Jean Colin?"

I said "Jean Colin is she still . . . well . . . with us?"

"Certainly," said Ronnie; "what's more she's still working. I'll send her down to the studios to see you tomorrow."

So onto the set the following morning came a plump, pretty middle-aged woman, whom I greeted with the words "This is such a thrill for me, you know, because I was deeply in love with you when I was thirteen years old."

Miss Colin laughed, and was not in the least offended. Of course she got the part, and was lovely in it. The point was that I had seen her back in 1929, in a musical comedy called *The Five O'Clock Girl* at the Hippodrome, co-starring with an actor called Ernest Truex who, incidentally, was understudied in the show by one of the chorus boys called John Mills. One evening on location I found a broken down old piano in the hotel at Lochcarron where the unit was staying and played for Jean Colin the number she had sung in *The Five O'Clock Girl* and captured my heart in 1929. It was called 'Thinking Of You'.

Another early casting problem on *Laxdale Hall* was that I couldn't find a leading lady for it. We needed an outdoor girl in her late twenties to take the part of Catriona, the daughter of the highland Scottish laird, who despite fierce opposition from John Grierson, was played by Ronald Squire in a kilt. Catriona would need a Hebridean accent and must be someone the public would have heard of – in other words what the Americans call a 'marquee name.'

One Sunday morning, as a devout Roman Catholic, I took my casting problem with me to Mass at the Brompton Oratory. As the choir was singing the Gloria a tall, dark young woman dressed in a tweed coat and skirt with a silk scarf over her head, who had arrived a bit late, edged her way into the pew in front. I could see her profile, which was somehow familiar. All through the Sermon and the Credo I fidgeted about, trying to get a proper glimpse of her but failing. At last when Holy Communion time came I saw her full face as she went up to the altar rails and returned to her seat. She was an Irish actress called Kathleen Ryan who had starred in Carol Reed's film *Odd Man Out* and Launder and Gilliatt's *Captain Boycott*. She would be perfect for Catriona Matheson in *Laxdale Hall* but I had a nasty feeling that someone had told me she had married a vet. in Dublin and given up films. I had to find out. As Mass ended I pursued her through the throng leaving the church and caught up with her outside on the steps.

Rather out of breath, I seized her by the arm and said "Excuse me but you are Kathleen Ryan, aren't you; and are you still acting in films and, if so, who is your agent?"

Miss Ryan smiled charmingly, said that she was, and that her agent was Ronnie Waters of the Al Parker office.

On the Monday morning I called Ronnie, who had already provided me with Jean Colin for Lucy Pettigrew, made a deal for Katie Ryan and told him the story. We both decided that seeing her at Mass the day before had been nothing short of a miracle in answer to my prayers. Maybe Kathleen Ryan had been praying, too, for a job.

As General Matheson, the laird of *Laxdale Hall*, Ronnie Squire used to amuse us with stories about his many appearances on the London stage in the '20s with Yvonne Arnaud. He looked splendid as a Highland laird in his kilt and bonnet striding across the moors in the drizzle and mist, a long way from the Earls and Dukes he so often played in the elegant drawing-room comedies of Frederick Lonsdale. Once we had signed Katie Ryan for the film Ronnie Waters, who was a smart agent, asked me if there was anything in the film for a very young, very promising actress whom Al Parker had recently signed up. I told him there was the nice part of a young village school teacher, also Highland Scottish, and he promptly sold me another of his clients, one Prunella Scales. It was her first film. As a brilliant mimic she soon mastered the Hebridean accent and gave a charming performance.

Whether by accident or design, it happened that three of the screenplays I wrote in the late '50s were vehicles for British comedians. In 1956 I was approached by the film producer Raymond Stross to write a comedy for Frankie Howerd, so I cooked up a story, the idea for which I pinched from a short French play called 'Le Petit Café' which I had acted in at school:

> The hall-porter of a smart London hotel wins a lot of money in a lottery and wants to give up his job. But the manager holds him to his contract because he is such a marvellous hallporter that to lose him would upset the regular guests and seriously damage the hotel's reputation. But, determined to get sacked, so that he can leave and spend his windfall in luxury, the hall-porter, Frankie Howerd, starts sending up the wrong trays to the wrong rooms, has wrong messages put through to the wrong people, calls guests an hour before they want to get up and causes such chaos that the manager is finally forced to dismiss him. Frankie fulfils his dream by going off to the South of France but soon gets bored and longs to be back in harness as a hall-porter. In the end he buys his old hotel in London which has since gone bust, re-employs himself as the hall-porter and is happy again.

I gave my script the title *The Revolving Door*. When I had finished it Stross told me that Frankie would like to discuss it with me and gave me a number to ring.

Frankie answered, saying "I'm in a madhouse, dear, but come down and have lunch in the pub. They let us out, you see." Evidently he had suffered from some kind of nervous breakdown and was in a rest home at Harrow, a Victorian red-brick institution with a cedar tree on the lawn and rather stressed-looking people walking about in the grounds.

We had lunch in the local pub, then we went back to the rest home to walk in the grounds and discuss my script, which had now been re-titled *A Touch Of The Sun*.

As we strolled on the lawn Frankie kept twitching and grinning and jumping about, miming some of the scenes in the script and making funny faces. I could see people up in the windows, doctors and nurses in white coats, looking down at us.

I said to Frankie "Go easy; there are people up there watching us. You could end up in a strait jacket!"

"Sod them, dear, they're all potty themselves. Much pottier than I am," was Frankie's reply. And he turned round and made a grotesque face up at the high windows. The doctors and nurses rapidly disappeared.

Later we went up to his sparsely furnished room where I noticed beside his bed a large signed photograph of Richard Burton. Frankie said simply, "I love that geyser".

THE movie was eventually made with a location in the South of France where Frankie took part in a fairly bizarre water-skiing sequence. The smooth hotel manager in the film was played by Dennis Price, who was quite a friend of Jean's and mine. There is a story which Dennis used to tell against himself. When, for some reason ostensibly to do with income tax, he attempted to take his own life by putting his head in the gas oven, he was saved in the nick of time. But someone must have tipped off the press, because by the time an ambulance arrived to take him to hospital the story was on the placards. On the way to St Stephen's, as he lay semi-conscious in the ambulance, Dennis became aware that they had stopped at the traffic lights and he could hear a newsvendor calling out, "*Standard, Evening Standard.* Famous actor attempts suicide, *Standard* . . ."

As Dennis put it himself: "I asked the ambulance man to hop out and get me an evening paper. Just had to read my notices."

THE following year an American producer, called Peter Cusick, told me he had a great idea for a comedy film. It was based on a racing story he had heard in Kentucky. A small-time punter had an 'accumulator' on a jockey for one day of a meeting. The jockey won his first five out of six rides. If he lost the sixth the punter would lose his money. But if the sixth mount was scratched the punter would clean up on the five races.

Over a number of expensive lunches at the Connaught and the Caprice Peter and I thrashed out the story. It ends with the punter realizing the sixth mount has no chance of winning but is to run anyway, so the punter has to find the owner and persuade him to scratch the horse.

I went to work on the script and called it *I Gotta Horse.* Peter was delighted with it and offered it to Columbia with George Cole (already a bankable star) as the punter; Robert Morley and Wilfrid Hyde-White as the two bookies who finally 'welsh' on the punter; and Margaret Rutherford as an eccentric Irish woman who owns Old Caspar, the horse that the jockey is to ride in the last race but which can't possibly win.

After much coming and going the project fell through. Then I heard that the script had fallen into the hands of Producer Hugh Stewart, at Pinewood, who had seized upon it instantly as a vehicle for Norman Wisdom.

The Rank Organization bought the property from Peter Cusick and the picture was made with a main location at

Goodwood races under someone else's new title of *Just My Luck*. The two bookies were played by Peter Copley and Leslie Phillips and the director was John Paddy Carstairs. Like all the Wisdom pictures it grossed big money world-wide and pops up on TV to this day. But I was sorry that a number of my wittier comedy scenes had been cut out to make room for 'Wis' to fall flat on his face or get tangled up in the starting gate at the racecourse. It would have been a much better film done straight with George Cole. All the same *Just My Luck* got its laughs. I went to see a sneak preview one evening at the giant Gaumont State Cinema in Kilburn High Road. Unlike the little cinemas within cinemas of today, which sometimes hold only a hundred people and where comedy lines receive little more than embarrassed titters from a small audience, a laugh in the packed Gaumont State, seating well over 1,200 people, was like a thunder clap. Quite a simple line such as Marjorie Rhodes saying to her son, Norman Wisdom,"Shut up and eat yer liver," was received with the sudden roar of a thousand plus people laughing simultaneously. It was quite a thrill for the writer.

The third comedian or rather funny actor for whom I designed a film script was David Tomlinson.

My old film producer friend, Thomas Clyde, had bought the rights in a very funny novel called *Photofinish,* written by the daughter of the famous actress Cathleen Nesbitt. She was called Jennifer Ramage. At the time there had been a few quite sensational defections from the Atomic Research Establishments by the likes of Pontecorvo and Klaus Fuchs. *Photofinish* was about a Central European atomic scientist called Dr Spiegel, who tries to defect to the Soviet Union from Harwell with a roll of microfilm revealing the secret work he has been doing. On the run from Harwell with the alarm bells ringing he jumps, unseen by its occupants, into the back of a horsebox on its way from nearby Lambourn to

Kempton Park races. Scared by the horse he finds inside the box, the scientist panics and drops his microfilm into the hay. Before he can recover it the racehorse eats it and an hour or so later is lined up under starter's orders at Kempton with this highly classified information in its belly.

I wrote the screenplay, and David Tomlinson was joined by a strong cast including Cecil Parker, Richard Wattis, Mary Peach who later married the producer and, in a small part, Arthur Lowe, later of *Dad's Army*.

Owing to a currently running stage play by Peter Ustinov called *Photofinish*, we had to find a new title and decided on *Follow That Horse!*

In the movie David Tomlinson plays Lanchester, a rather stupid junior Security Officer at the Research Establishment, who is answerable to a senior Government Minister called Garrod, played by Cecil Parker. Most writers remember an occasional 'good line' they have written in a stage or screen play long after the original work has been forgotten and Tomlinson's name in the story made me unable to resist an extremely obvious joke that stands out in my memory. Cecil Parker says to David: "Do you realize that if some fool dropped an atomic bomb on Manchester, Lanchester, they'd wipe out the whole place?"

Lanchester spends the whole film trying to catch up with the racehorse and prevent it from falling into the hands of the atom spies. But he fails to prevent it from running at Kempton and winning a Selling Plate. Thus, Tomlinson ends up desperately bidding for the animal on behalf of Her Majesty's Government, making his bids with one hand from a telephone box in the ring and at the same time trying to squeeze more money out of the Treasury official on the other end of the line.

I was particularly fond of another line in *Follow That Horse*:

Lanchester (David Tomlinson) and his staff driver Farrell (Sam Kydd) are trying to crawl under the barbed wire into the Research Station when they accidentally set off the alarms. Bells clang and the sound is heard of guard dogs being unleashed, barking and snarling, in the distance.
*Farrell*: The Police dogs! Quick, run for it, sir . . .
*Lanchester*: (nervously) They wouldn't eat a Civil Servant, would they?
*Farrell*: They'd eat anything.

Looking back over my career as a screenwriter in films, I find the list of my credits is punctuated every so often by movie scripts that I have written with what might be called 'tongue firmly in cheek', in other words writing jobs undertaken against my better judgement when money was short and I had to accept whatever was on offer in order to pay the rent. Some writers call this 'whoring', although quite often I found I had done something pretty skilled in the way of a clever line of dialogue, a twist in the plot or an effective scene so that I need not always hang my head in shame.

An example of this was a film called *Crescendo* that bears my name. It all began when a talented young director called Michael Reeves asked me to script a story he had cooked up. It involved twin brothers, one of them a brilliant but insane musician; and a sinister mother figure. I called the script *Apassionata*, and Mike Reeves put it up to some distributors, Compton Films, with a cast of Christopher Lee, Flora Robson and Susan Hampshire. Compton accepted it but at the last moment the deal fell through and not long after that Mike Reeves, having made a very good film called *Witchfinder General*, very sadly died. Some years later my script, after changing hands several times, came to Hammer Films with a new title, *Crescendo*. Hammer's producer Michael Carreras had set it up with Warner Brothers for a clever young Canadian director Alan Gibson, and I by chance heard that it had started shooting at the MGM Studios at Elstree. I discovered that in the interim changes had been made to the screenplay by Jimmy Sangster, Hammer's favoured writer. The cast had changed, too. Susan Hampshire had become Stephanie Powers, Chris Lee was now a minor Hollywood star called James Olsen and Flora Robson as the mother had become Margharetta Scott. In addition there were Joss Ackland as the mad brother's minder and in the South of France villa, where the story takes place, a French maid played by Jane Lapotaire who, it being an X-certificate film, was obliged to appear in the nude in the swimming pool. One compensation was a fine musical score by the Master of the Queen's Musick, Malcolm Williamson, which included an exciting piano concerto, one of those pseudo-Rachmaninoff pieces that have featured in so many British films over the years, for the mad twin musician to compose and play.

A friend of mine called Peter Walker made a number of similar X-pictures and came to my rescue on more than one occasion, when I was hard pressed to pay my sons' school fees, with the offer of a script job. One of Peter's films which I scripted for him was entitled *The Flesh And Blood Show* about violent murder and sexual activity in a theatre company on the end of a seaside pier. I came face to face with that one quite recently while watching one of the many cable channels at my son's house in Los Angeles. It was quite a shock. Then there was *Tiffany Jones*, based on a popular newspaper strip cartoon, which featured a staggeringly attractive girl called Anouska Hempel who spent much of the film very scantily, if at all, clothed. But she was sweet and uncomplaining and is now, I believe, a big tycoon in the hotel and fashion business. It was always fun to work with Peter Walker who is a generous, hospitable and amusing film maker and I was grateful for his patronage.

* * *

THE next film I scripted I also produced. This was an adaptation of a successful television play by the Welsh writer, E. Eynon Evans. It was called *Bless This House* and was offered to me by ACT Films, a production unit of the technicians' union, The Association of Cinematograph Technicians. Because of the somewhat corny song of the same name, favoured by baritones singing to old ladies in Winter Garden Floral Halls at seaside resorts, we changed the title to *Room In The House*.

This was an amusing, light-hearted story about a bossy widowed mother imposing herself on the homes of her three married sons, one after the other. The mother was played by the lovely Lancashire actress, Marjorie Rhodes, who had played Norman Wisdom's Mum in *Just My Luck*. Also in the cast were Patrick Barr, Rachel Gurney, Hubert Gregg and, in her first film role Billie Whitelaw, as a maid. The director was the veteran Maurice Elvey who had been making distinguished British films almost before I was born. One of them was the great silent classic, *Balaclava*.

On *Room In The House* I learned one important lesson for writers. We were shooting in the front hall of a house where one of the actresses, carrying a suitcase, had to play an important farewell scene at the foot of the stairs. Maurice Elvey, who was at the best of times a rather snappy, ill-tempered man, seemed unusually irritable and kept cutting in the middle of the scene and complaining about the suitcase. First he said it was too big, then he said it was too small and the wrong colour. The Prop man had to keep going off to fetch a succession of alternative suitcases. Elvey became more and more bad-tempered, making cutting remarks to the actress who was getting close to tears. I tried to calm things down. Eventually Maurice accepted a suitcase and we started shooting again. Once more he yelled "Cut".

I sat in my chair and glanced at the script. Reading through the scene we were shooting I saw with hideous clarity that it was flawed. There was a line missing that was needed to resolve something planted earlier, so that one of the actress's lines made no sense. I wrote in the missing line on the spot and explained it to Elvey, who saw the point and shot the scene once more. This time he got it right first take and everybody was happy. There was no further reference to the suitcase. The episode taught me that sometimes directors, producers and actors feel uneasy with what they are filming but cannot analyse the problem so that they blame it on the props. There is a story that Gabriel Pascal took Vivien Leigh up to eleven takes on a scene in *Caesar and Cleopatra*, when he had a parrot in a cage endlessly replaced with substitute parrots from a nearby petshop before he realized there was something wrong with the scene rather than the parrot.

There is a sense in which screenwriting can give a writer a great sense of power. I have always found it exciting to realize that what 'the script calls for' has to be provided. For example you could be sitting at your typewriter or word processor, working on a film script for a period picture, and you casually write: 'Ext. Town square night. Lights are blazing in the windows of the Palace where a ball is taking place. Outside a rioting mob with flaming torches is marching towards the Palace. A troop of cavalry charges into the square to disperse the crowd.'

With those few words you have committed the film company to an enormously expensive 'night shoot' with crowds of extras, horses and stunt riders who will have to be brought to the location in fleets of coaches and horse-boxes. The location town square will have to be sealed off by the police and traffic diverted; the streets of the town will be blocked by huge lamps, generators, prop vans, make-up and wardrobe caravans; a huge canteen van or 'chuck wagon' will be parked in a side street, dispensing hot food and coffee throughout the night; costumes, pitchforks and sticks for the rioting mob and uniforms for the cavalry will have to be checked and distributed to the extras in a crowd dressing-room, probably in a nearby school which must be specially opened up for the evening, and so on.

Of course, if your script calls for too many extravagant night location scenes or studio sets the producer will cut them and force you to set the big love scene in the back of a mock-up carriage in the studio. But writing big scenes gives a nice feeling, rather like playing God.

Secretly, I get the same sense of power from writing the dialogue in plays and scripts. Whatever words you choose to write down in your script some actor or actress, who may be a world-famous star, will be obliged to learn by heart and deliver. You are literally putting words into the mouths of the players. Or you may, with a few careless words of stage direction in a script, condemn a player to discomfort and embarrassment. In the TV Series *By The Sword Divided* a girl called Susan Protheroe, a cousin of the Royalist Lacey family, arrives at Arnescote late at night with a sick mother in a cart. She is looking for shelter from the Civil War but on arrival her mother dies of the Plague and is quickly buried. But Susan must be cleansed and disinfected. So the old family Goodwife takes charge, orders the girl to strip and be scrubbed and anointed with various herbs and ointments. This required the lovely Judy Buxton, as Susan, to spend two hours on the set sitting naked in a tub of warm water. It was in the script, so it had to be done. I probably ought to have apologized to the actress for subjecting her to such treatment but they are all used to it nowadays. And the director, Lord Pembroke, shot the scene with commendable discretion.

Writing parts for actors is the verbal equivalent of pulling the strings of a puppet, controlling its speech and behaviour.

But never, never, dear writer, let any actor hear you say that. The truth is that a line of dialogue or a piece of action in a script has no life, no existence *until* it is performed in its context by an actor. At that point it leaves the printed page and *exists*. So a performance is really a collaboration between writer and actor, as it is between the composer who writes down the notes on his score and the instrumentalist who plays them.

# REPAIR JOBS

FROM time to time during my long career my agent has got me assignments to rewrite screenplays that have gone wrong. Soon after *Brandy For The Parson* and *Laxdale Hall* my name began to appear on the screen in cinemas with those of other screenwriters, sharing the credits.

As a schoolboy sitting in a movie theatre and watching the opening credit titles on a film, for example 'Screenplay by Bob Schultz and Aaron Spieler', I used to envisage two cigar-chewing writers in their shirt-sleeves pacing about a small office in the Scenario Department of a Hollywood Studio and arguing about some story point until it was time to break off and go to the Commissary for lunch.

In later years, when I became a screenwriter myself, I realized that it was quite possible that Bob Schultz had never actually met Aaron Spieler, that neither even knew of the other's existence. A movie script can all too often pass through the hands of a dozen or more writers and end up a confused mess of widely disparate styles and ideas. The string of writers credited with a screenplay are more likely to be a succession of people mucking about with their predecessor's work rather than a smooth collaboration of like minds.

My first 'repair job' was on a film called *The High Terrace* for RKO, which starred the Hollywood cowboy actor, Dale Robertson, who was oddly cast in it as a smooth Broadway theatre producer, in a tuxedo that did not suit him at all. It was a backstage murder story, one of a number of Anglo-American films made here in the '50s with imported

American stars for the British 'quota'. The female lead was Lois Maxwell, later to make her name as Miss Moneypenny in the James Bond pictures. I rewrote parts of this script and shared the credit with Norman Hudis.

Another project I was brought in on involved working with Rex Harrison and Lilli Palmer. I had become acquainted with Rex back in 1938 while Bob Ellison and I were preparing our ill-fated revue *Fiddlesticks*. I was in a Soho nightclub, or rather at a bottle-party in a place called The Slippin, one evening with Rex and a mutual friend of ours, Iris Mountbatten. Rex was playing Leo with Diana Wynyard and Anton Walbrook in Nöel Coward's comedy *Design For Living* at the Haymarket Theatre and Iris and I had picked him up to go to the nightclub, where we were drinking gin and listening to Ike Hatch's marvellous black band. Rex was a great jazz fan and already a pretty big star. At some point in the evening I asked him if he would ever consider appearing in an intimate revue. I had my show *Fiddlesticks* in mind, of course.

"Certainly, old boy," said Rex, slightly pissed; "always wanted to do a revue, you know. I could tear 'em up in the sketches and get by with the odd song."

I was delighted, because I knew his name would be a huge asset to our revue. But when I called his agent the following morning to fix a deal, I was told in so many words to get stuffed.

"Mr Harrison has two films lined up for Korda as soon as *Design For Living* comes off," his agent told me haughtily, "and he would never consider doing a revue, anyway, because he can't sing." And that was that.

Now, twelve years later, I was asked by an actor-film producer friend, Anthony Bushell, to do some rewriting on *The Long Dark Hall*, a script by the famous Hollywood writer Nunnally Johnson. Mr Johnson had written what was frankly a poor thriller about a murderer being saved from the gallows at the last minute, and the dialogue needed to be anglicised and put right vis-à-vis the British legal system and the court procedures for a murder trial at the Old Bailey. The picture was being financed by Five Oceans Films and the attraction of it to Rex and his wife Lilli Palmer, who would co-star with him, was that the international company was prepared to pay them in Italian lire so that they could dodge the currency export regulations and build their dream villa at Portofino.

At the various script conferences in the director Tony Bushell's flat, conveniently just opposite mine in Chesham Street, Belgravia, I found Rex far less fun to be with than he had been as a young man before the war. He had become spoilt, and rather arrogant and obstructive. He could not seem to grasp that a Hollywood screenwriter of Nunally Johnson's huge reputation could do anything wrong. Lilli, on the contrary, was full of good ideas about the script. At one point we were arguing about how the judge at the Old Bailey would deal with Counsel on a certain point of law when Rex said snappily, "I don't know why we're arguing about this. All I have to do is call my brother-in-law; he'll soon settle it. Now for God's sake, let's get on with the next scene." Rex Harrison's brother-in-law at the time was Sir David Maxwell-Fyfe, the Attorney-General, later Lord Kilmuir.

*The Long Dark Hall* was eventually made and the screenplay credit divided between Nunally Johnson and W. E. C. Fairchild, an old friend of mine. Bill Fairchild must have been called in to rewrite my rewrites for what was considered by the Press and by Rex himself – quite rightly – to be the worst film he ever appeared in. But it was not really mine or Bill's fault. It had been a ridiculous story in the first place and pretty well unsalvageable. But it did no damage to Rex's brilliant career and I was modestly paid for my contribution.

Another repair job brought me into contact for a few days with the legendary Marlon Brando. In 1985 he had become interested in a script, set in eighteenth-century Ireland, called *The Last King*. Brando would play an English General of King George III's army, brutal and ruthless but with a certain nobility of spirit. He would be seen galloping around the Irish countryside, burning the farms and crops and ill-treating the wretched peasants. I think Brando felt as strongly about the English treatment of the Irish as he does about the American settlers' treatment of the Red Indians and he probably saw *The Last King* as a chance to speak out for the Irish Republican cause. I had recently written some scripts for the TV series *The Irish R.M*, which Brando had seen in the States and liked, so I was hired by a London-based company, British United Artistes, to rewrite the script of *The Last King*. This meant flying out to Hollywood with the producer Peter Shaw to meet up with the director designate, Fred Schepisi, who was already out there, and discuss the project with Brando. On arrival in my hotel in Los Angeles I found awaiting me a beribboned basket of caviar, preserves, a bottle of champagne and other goodies with a card which read 'Welcome to our dirty city, looking forward to our deliberations, Yours Marlon Brando.' Having never met the guy, I felt that was a good start.

The next morning we all drove up in a stretch-limousine to a large bungalow high up in the Encino Hills on Mulholland Drive, a kind of eyrie overlooking the San Fernando Valley. Here awaiting us on the steps, rather like Hitler greeting his guests at Berchtesgaden, was Brando himself. He had grown unbelievably fat and looking as he did like Teddy Brown, the famous xylophonist of the '30s, I could not see how he could possibly be contemplating a film in which he would be required to spend most of his time galloping about on horseback. However, Brando greeted us warmly and led us up the steps into a room where we all sat down and started to confer. After learning that Brando had enjoyed the TV version of *The Irish R.M.*, I had concluded that he imagined from my name that I was some kind of wild, eccentric Irish writer; a whisky-sodden bearded poet and rebel in the Brendan Behan mould, perhaps. He must have been a bit surprised to be confronted by a rather 'La-di-da' Old Etonian with a posh English accent. But he was very pleasant to me and quite complimentary.

Half way through the conference there was a hell of a noise outside the window. Someone was using a chain-saw.

Marlon got up and went to the window to yell out "Stop that fucking noise!"

A head appeared at the window. It was an unshaven, scruffy youth in a baseball cap who said "Sorry, Dad," and disappeared again.

Marlon came back to the table muttering "My son, Christian."

A few months later the lad shot his sister's boyfriend and so hit the world's headlines.

When our rather unproductive script meetings on *The Last King* were over and Peter Shaw flew back to London, I remained in Los Angeles for a day and a night because I was due to join Jean in Washington for a week, before returning to LA to stay with our two sons who live there. So Brando asked me to hang around and talk to him. I think he was lonely and wanted company. He told me he had bought the bungalow from Howard Hughes, who evidently entertained girls there away from his proper home, and he described the place as "Howard Hughes's whorehouse". We ate and drank, waited on by his petite Polynesian wife, or lady-companion, who shuffled silently and deferentially about the villa in a sarong like Tondelayo in *White Cargo*. We played music and chatted about almost everything from American and Irish history and politics to the Arts in general, books, movies, directors and the theatre. It transpired that he had no time for any of the directors he had worked with in movies except Elia Kazan, who brought him from the Broadway stage to do Kowalski in *Streetcar*. When I mentioned his admirable performance as Mark Anthony in *Julius Caesar* I was surprised that he was not particularly complimentary about Joseph L. Mankiewicz. But he did have the grace to acknowledge his debt on that occasion to John Gielgud, who played Cassius and evidently helped him a lot with the text.

Brando liked to talk and was inclined to lecture and show off his knowledge, which was considerable. But I enjoyed one moment when he was banging on about British Imperialism and I was able to point out that my ancestor on my mother's side, James Knox Polk, who was the 11th President of the United States, had plunged America into war with Mexico and had the USA annexe California from the Spanish. And he was suitably intrigued when I told him that my grandfather on my father's side had been a staunch Republican and a supporter of Home Rule for Ireland, was a friend of Mr Redmond and had made impassioned speeches on the Irish Question in the House of Lords.

On my eventual return to London I worked hard on the script for *The Last King* and was well paid for what I did, but sadly, as is so often the case, the movie never got off the ground. But it was a compensating experience to have spent a day and an evening with the legendary Marlon Brando.

Another minor rewrite job came my way earlier while I was under contract to the Rank Organization at Pinewood but working on and off for Sydney Box's family film empire. This company consisted of Sydney himself as emperor; his wife Muriel, a kind of Poppaea behind the throne; his sister Betty Box, who was married to Peter Rogers but made pictures with Ralph Thomas, whose brother Gerald was a film editor; and the producer, William MacQuitty.

I had been 'borrowed' previously from the Rank Organisation by the Box Organisation to produce a film called *Heart Of A Child*, directed by Clive Donner, with locations in the Austrian Tyrol. Soon after *Heart Of A Child* was finished Peter Rogers had asked me to rewrite a comedy script called *The Bull Boys* which was in a mess. It was from a story by R. F. Delderfield and concerned a group of awkward squaddies in a training depot. National Service was in force at the time and there was already a popular TV series running called *Bootsie and Snudge*, about army life. Peter knew I was keen to direct pictures and told me that, if I could get this army script right, it was mine to direct. I read it with mounting unease because it was not my cup of tea. However much it could be improved, it remained basically a broad army farce, with recruits dropping their rifles on the drill sergeant's foot and comic scenes in the barrack room and in the mess. It was to be retitled *Carry On, Sergeant* and was the first of what was to become the long and successful *Carry On* film comedy series.

Unhappy to turn down a directing job, I nevertheless declined.

Peter told me not to worry too much as he had an Anglo-American X-certificate picture for me to rewrite and direct for him called *Cat Girl*. That sounded much more interesting and I was genuinely relieved to hear that he had found a director for *Carry On, Sergeant*. This was Ralph Thomas's film editor brother, Gerry, who was anxious to leave his movieola in the cutting rooms for a director's chair on the set. *Carry On, Sergeant* was a smash hit and a couple of weeks before I started to work on the script for *Cat Girl* Peter Rogers came into my room at Pinewood with another script under his arm. This one was called *Carry On, Nurse* and was to be the next 'Carry On', but again there were problems with the script. For one thing neither Wilfrid Hyde-White, cast as a racing-mad hospital patient, nor Hattie Jacques as the formidable hospital Matron, were happy with their parts. They both needed better dialogue and a more interesting relationship. Also, the end of the picture did not work. It needed a stronger 'last reel'.

I agreed to work on the screenplay and Peter suggested that I should have an 'additional scenes and dialogue' credit on the picture but I have to admit that most of the script struck me as so vulgar and tasteless, including a scene where a patient has a daffodil stuck up his backside, that I went all prudish and declined to have my name on the film at all.

But I worked hard on the script and added a new set-up in the hospital whereby Hyde-White opens a secret book so that all the patients can have a bet each day by putting their money on the exact time of the Matron's arrival in the ward. I improved (I hope) the dialogue and, finally, invented a new end sequence wherein the patients of one ward, feeling sorry for one of their number whose operation for a carbuncle on his foot has been endlessly put off, get up secretly in the night, take over the operating theatre and attempt to carry out a sort of 'Do It Yourself' operation on their friend. This end sequence went down very well with audiences and got big laughs in the cinema.

I was paid only £200 for my work on *Carry On, Nurse* but if I had asked for a percentage of the picture and had agreed to direct *Carry On, Sergeant* my future would have been secure.

# DIRECTING FOR THE CINEMA

SINCE 'talkies' came in, the origin of every film that tells a story has been a long and detailed list of scenes to be photographed and recorded on sound in the order in which they must later be cut together and screened in the cinema. This list is called the screenplay or scenario and it is normally written by a screenwriter.

But also, ever since the film director – often wearing riding-boots, a monocle and carrying a megaphone – told the first comic when to throw the custard pie at the second comic in front of a hand-cranked camera, the director has always been in charge of and has supervised the photography of that list of scenes. In silent days the director improvised the action while a 'script girl' sat beside him taking notes of what happened and making sure that the comics wore the same clothes from shot to shot. This was the forerunner of today's continuity girl.

But when 'talkies' arrived the actors had to be provided with dialogue to speak and many of the literate few in the studio, who up until then had been creating those stirring sub-titles like 'Came the dawn' and 'Unhand that woman, curse you,' started to write talking screenplays. From then on, Directors were obliged either to collaborate with the writers or do the job themselves. This sometimes makes it hard to know whether a sequence in a film has been dreamed up by the writer or the director or both.

Imagine that a script sequence reads:

*Ext. Railway carriage step. Day*
As the train races along the track at top speed MASON is outside on the step, desperately clinging on to a doorhandle by the coach-divide and perilously working his way along towards the first compartment window. The wind is tearing at his hair and jacket as he reaches the edge of the window and by leaning over, he manages to look in. He sees:
*Int. Compartment. Day*
Mason's pov. (Point of View) through the glass.

Two chattering women and a man are seated inside. The man is asleep.
*Ext. Railway carriage step. Day*
Mason leans forward again and, not daring to let go, just manages to tap with his head on the window hoping to attract attention. But the roar of the train renders this almost inaudible. But he sees:
*Int. Compartment. Day*
Mason's pov through glass.

The two women pause in their chatter. One of them seems to have heard something, looks up into the rack and about her but shrugs and they go on talking.
*Ext. Railway carriage. Day*
Mason is becoming exhausted and almost losing his grip. He desperately tries once more to tap the glass window with his head.
*Int. Compartment. Day*
Mason's pov through glass.

The two women continue to chatter. The sleeping man now wakes up, looks at his watch, starts to get up from his seat . . .
*Ext. Railway carriage. Day*
Mason looks suddenly hopeful. He again tries to bang the glass window with his head. He looks in again and sees:
*Int. Compartment. Day*
Mason's pov.

The man almost turns towards the window but appears to change his mind. He sits down again and nods off to sleep.
*Ext. Railway carriage. Day*
Mason is in despair. He closes his eyes as:
*Ext. Train. Day*
Its whistle screeches as the train roars into a tunnel.

This simple and orthodox suspense sequence might be in a script that would have been handed by a screenwriter to a director to direct. The director might ultimately have changed it to suit his taste. He might have preferred the compartment to contain two men and one woman or to have had Mason fall from the train earlier. Who knows? But the cinematic suspense sequence would be worked out and written into the script by the screenwriter. It would not be the director's concept.

In the film business bitter quarrels between directors and writers occur with sickening frequency and the conflicting parties often seek the help of the professional bodies or trade unions to whom they belong. As a Councillor of The Writers Guild Of Great Britain I was once co-opted to arbitrate in a row about screen credits between a distinguished British writer and a famous Hollywood producer-director, both of whom must remain anonymous. I shall call the writer Frank Mills and the director-producer Martin Barber. The battleground was the film version of a well-known novel which was out of copyright.

When the Guild delivered to me for examination a mountain of outlines, treatments, first, second and third-draft screenplays, rewrite notes, memos and correspondence, I thought I was in for a tedious few weeks, but I was wrong. What I read and found fascinating was not so much the story variations in the different versions of the projected movie but the tragicomedy which unfolded before my eyes, illustrating the gradual breakdown of a promising partnership between two talented men – a writer and a director. It all began happily with an exchange of letters in January, the gist of which follows:

Dear Frank Mills,

Just a line to say how much I enjoyed meeting you and your agent at lunch today and how delighted I am that you have agreed to do the screenplay. I look forward to working with such a distinguished writer as yourself and I am sure our collaboration will be as fruitful as it will be enjoyable.

Yours sincerely,
Martin Barber

Dear Martin Barber,

Thank you for your kind letter. I look forward equally to working with a director whose work I have long admired.

Yours sincerely,
Frank Mills

In April Mills delivered his treatment to Barber.

Dear Martin,

Here is the treatment on time. I look forward to getting my teeth into the script. Can't see any problems.

Yours Frank

Dear Frank,

Thanks for the treatment. It seems fine. My only reservation is the ending. I don't quite see why you have altered the ending of the novel so radically. I think we ought to discuss this at a meeting. So enjoyed our evening out and meeting your charming wife.

All the best, Martin

Dear Martin,

Thanks for your note. I'm glad you enjoyed our dinner at Marco's. Pat send her regards. The end of the novel is plainly unacceptable in film terms. I think it best if you wait and see how it works out in the first draft screenplay. Then we can discuss it.

All the best,
Yours Frank

Dear Frank,

OK. Let's see script.

Yours Martin

In early June Mills delivered his first draft screenplay to Martin:

Here it is. I feel it's worked out pretty well, especially my new ending. Call me when you've read it and we'll have lunch.

Yours Frank

Dear Frank,

Although I can see what you are trying to do, I honestly don't think your screenplay really works at present. For a start I suggest that we go back to the novel's original ending, as I wanted to in the first place. To save time and trouble I enclose the last fourteen pages of the script as I see them.

Yours Martin

Dear Frank,

Much as I appreciate your concern for our script, I do not think it proper for a director, under any circumstances, to cut pages out of the original novel and paste them into a writer's draft screenplay before returning it to him. I must remind you that I am the writer whose job is to write the movie and you are the director whose job is to interpret my work in pictures on the screen. I will, however, make some of the minor alterations you mention. I am returning the pages from the novel which have come unstuck anyway, since they are really not relevant.

Yours Frank

Dear Frank,

I have now read your revised script and note that you have put back your ending as before. I regret to say that I feel we are at cross purposes here. We really ought to be working far more closely on this project. I suggest a proper collaboration from now on, with a shared screenplay credit. Only in this way will we end up with the movie I believe we both envisage. Let me know when and where we can get together.

Two weeks elapsed. Then:

Dear Mr Barber,

As the agent representing Mr Frank Mills I am writing to say that my client takes the greatest exception to your suggestion of a form of writing collaboration and a shared credit on his script and must ask you to allow him to complete his contracted work for you without further interruption. The third draft will be delivered to you as contracted at the end of the month.

Dear Frank,

I am surprised that you found it necessary to involve your agent in our mild disagreement over the script. I have just read your third draft screenplay which is, in my opinion, a considerable improvement on the last draft – owing mainly to my own contributions e.g. the new beach scene I have written in, the quarrel in the woods and the far more dramatic ending on board ship, which you will remember I originally suggested. As far as I'm concerned we can go ahead on this basis but I must make it quite clear that I shall expect a shared screenplay credit.

Sincerely Martin Barber

In late August, after a silence of some weeks, Martin Barber received a letter:

From Messrs. Wargrave, Mason and Cubitt
107, Lincoln's Inn Fields, WC2
Dear Mr Barber,

I am writing on behalf of our client, Mr Frank Mills, for whom we act. I am instructed to say that in our opinion your attempts to rewrite our client's work and the demands you have made on him regarding the eventual allocation of screen credits for the work are in breach of the contract he signed with your company. We shall, therefore, expect a letter from your good self at the earliest date retracting your intentions and undertaking to restore our client's original work in the said screenplay.

Yours faithfully,
Arnold Wargrave

From Messrs Simpson, Ward & Co
High Holborn, WC2
Dear Mr Mills,

My client, Mr Martin Barber, has consulted me about the contents of the letter, dated 12th inst., which he has receive from Messrs Wargrave, Mason and Cubitt regarding your collaboration with my client on a screenplay and I am instructed to say that he is not willing to comply with your request for a letter of retraction, as demanded. I await your comments.

Yours faithfully,
Philip Simpson

After some weeks of similar correspondence between the solicitors, Martin Barber received a letter from the Writers Guild of Great Britain:

Dear Mr Barber,

Our member, Mr Frank Mills, has drawn our attention to a dispute between himself and your company regarding the allocation of screenplay credits on the above film. I am writing to say that, in the Guild's opinion, this matter can best be settled by arbitration. If you are agreeable to this arrangement, perhaps you would be good enough to forward to this office copies or originals of any drafts of the treatment and screenplay together with all relevant notes, memos, correspondence and records of telephone conversations etc. so that our arbitrator can assess the dispute and make his findings known to the Executive Council.

Yours sincerely . . .

As the Writers Guild-appointed Arbitrator I eventually found in favour of the writer.

In the following summer Martin Barber and Frank Mills both happened to attend the Cannes Film Festival. When the two men came face to face at a screening they were seen to turn their backs on each other and are said to have neither spoken nor communicated since.

THERE are, of course, total film-makers about. The French call them *auteurs*. They are those who control every single word that goes into the script and work as one mind with the writer of the scenario, if there is one. Others first write, then direct the film. Orson Welles was such a film maker.

Other master directors such as David Lean and Carol

Reed made such reputations as directors that they tend to be more identified with their films than their often renowned story writers such as Robert Bolt, Charles Dickens, Graham Greene and Nöel Coward.

Just as every private soldier is said to carry a field-marshal's baton in his knapsack, so does every film technician and many a writer carry a director's view-finder in his brief-case. I myself was no exception and had cherished an ambition to direct films ever since I was taken down to the old BIP studios at Elstree as a schoolboy in 1930 and watched a film being made. It was called *Fascination* and was directed by Miles Mander with Kay Hammond in the cast. In those days the mystique of film-making was carefully kept from public scrutiny. Techniques such as 'back-projection', 'foreground miniatures' (sometimes known as the Schufftan process) and 'travelling matter' were closely-guarded trade secrets; today because of TV programmes such as *How Do They Do It?* filming techniques have become common knowledge.

Most people are also aware nowadays of the difference between a director and a producer. In films a director is in charge of the actual filming, planning the composition of each shot, instructing the actors, deciding which 'take' to print, and so on, whereas the producer spends his time between the office and the studio floor or the location, worrying about the budget and the shooting schedule and supervising the overall administration of the production.

BY 1950 my years at Ealing Studios had taught me the theory and technical aspect of making pictures and, when my chance came to direct, I felt that I was qualified to do so. It happened that my reputation for fixing flawed scripts got me my first job as a film director. In 1954 I had adapted and produced *Room In The House* for ACT Films. In 1956 I was approached by the same company with a script for a thriller called *Suspended Alibi*, which needed a lot of work to be done on it. Again I was asked to rewrite the script and produce the film. But this time, I had a bit of extra power in my hands. I knew that they had already booked studio space at Walton Studios and had a start date fixed but they had not yet engaged a director. Time was short. So I made it a condition for fixing the script that I should direct the movie.

There was a slight pause, then Ralph Bond, who ran ACT Films, said he would "have to go into it".

I lobbied 'Puffin' Asquith who was both a personal friend and President of ACT, and I suspect that he put in a word for me. In any case, I got my way and directed my first of four feature films.

*Suspended Alibi* was a very routine thriller, made on a small budget, but I had the lovely Honor Blackman as my star and the movie was well reviewed in the Trade papers and booked on the Rank circuit as a second-feature attraction.

The film includes a scene in a newspaper office where a bright young reporter breezes in to see his editor:

*Larry*: How'd you like to buy a terrific idea for a series?
*Editor*: (Wearily) What is it this time? Notting Hill Gate with the lid off?
*Larry*: Not quite, chief. Nights of vice in Budleigh Salterton.

Soon after my script had been passed round the Rank Organization for approval I received a memo from Earl St John's office asking me to delete the reference to Budleigh Salterton. I was amazed, until I heard that the complaint had been made by the Rank Publicity Department. At the time they were busy promoting a divine-looking young contract starlet called Belinda Lee who happened to come from Budleigh Salterton. The studio feared the joke might indirectly damage Belinda Lee's image. However, in the end the line was left in. Tragically this delightful young actress was killed in a car crash at the beginning of what might have been a great career.

BUDLEIGH Salterton raises the point about using 'funny place names', a terrible habit which many writers (me included) find hard to resist.

In one of Nöel Coward's plays, I forget which one, somebody says to the comedy charlady: "Ah, so you've been married twice . . . "

*Charlady*: "That's right. One's dead and one's in Liverpool." It brings the house down.

You can always get a laugh with a place name. If a character in a play says "My brother's a vicar in Nether Wallop," the audience will laugh but if you write "My brother's a vicar in Folkestone," they won't.

The Americans love comically named towns with the State attached. Thus Judy Garland in *A Star Is Born* sings "I was born in a trunk at the Prince's Theatre in Pocatella, Idaho", and it's funny. I remember a song in some movie of which the punch line was 'when the leaves are falling in Kokomo, Indiana', and Robert Sherwood got a laugh (or rather Raymond Massey did) when the character of Harry Van said to Irene in Sherwood's play *Idiot's Delight*, "You can't deny the fact that you slept with me in the fall of 1925 at the Governor Bryan Hotel, Omaha, Nebraska." The audience loved that.

THE next two movies I directed were for the Sydney Box empire while I was under contract to Rank at Pinewood. The first was Peter Rogers' promised X-certificate film for American International and Anglo-Amalgamated, *Cat Girl*. I worked hard on the rather ludicrous American script for this film and spent an afternoon with the Hollywood writer of it, Lou Rusoff, who had flown over and was staying at the Mount Royal Hotel at Marble Arch. I was anxious to persuade him that the movie would be all the more effective and less open to accusations of hokum if the girl, instead of actually changing into a leopard on dark nights in the woods, simply imagined she was a leopard owing to a deep psychological disorder. Rusoff listened patiently to my arguments but it soon became clear that he could not care less what I did with his script. He had been paid for it, and was mainly interested in getting his 'first day of principal photography' money and enjoying his trip to London, away from Mrs Rusoff, at the expense of American International Pictures Corporation.

So, after a while he asked me about joints in London where a guy could get a girl for the evening. I advised him to consult the Hall Porter at the Mount Royal and left him to get on with his sex life while I rewrote his script.

We started shooting *Cat Girl* at Beaconsfield Studios. One of the important props on the picture was a leopard which had to be handled on the set by its trainer, a circus man, armed with a loaded revolver in case of trouble. The animal was called Chiefie and though seemingly docile it was obviously capable of turning nasty, if provoked. Our leading lady, Barbara Shelley, was supposed in the film to have some weird affinity with the creature and tore her lovers to pieces with claws which she suddenly grew in a series of matching dissolves, as she took on the leopard's identity. But Barbara adored Chiefie and insisted on playing with him on the set as though she was fondling a pet kitten. I reckoned it was only a matter of time before the leopard ate Barbara Shelley, but happily it never did. Another member of the cast, Ernest Milton, the famous old Shakespearean actor, whom I had seen play Shylock at the Old Vic when I was a boy, adopted a more cautious attitude towards Chiefie.

I had cast Ernest as the sinister, evil Count in the story and when I asked him to move across the set for one shot with the leopard following obediently at his heels, Ernest protested in his high-pitched, rather precious voice, "Oh, but I daren't do that, my dear. If the beast nips my ankles, I shall forget my lines."

So we had to dress the trainer in Mr Milton's trousers and do the shot 'doubled' from ground level.

Barbara Shelley was lovely in the film and gave a most uninhibited and dramatic performance. Indeed, she was so good in it that I believe it condemned her to a long career in horror pictures. Years after *Cat Girl*, Barbara was still appearing in Hammer films with Christopher Lee, Peter Cushing and the others. I remember how, after Chris Lee had just done his third Dracula movie in a row, one critic wrote, 'It's high time Christopher Lee was given something more rewarding to get his teeth into than Barbara Shelley's neck.'

The critic was dead right. For, although he made a world-wide reputation and a good living from horror movies, Christopher Lee is an exceptionally good, multi-lingual opera-singer-actor and ought to have done more with his career than emerge with bloodshot eyes from tombs in spooky churchyards.

I made *Cat Girl* with Sydney Box as my Executive Producer. The next picture he offered me was not exactly the sort of thing I was looking for to advance my career as a director but it was a job and it was a musical.

This was a film version of the popular TV Show *Six-Five Special* and I had a cast of pop stars in it who, in 1958, were all household names: Lonnie Donnegan, Dickie Valentine, Joan Regan, Petula Clark, Jim Dale, The King Brothers, Johnnie Dankworth and Cleo Laine, Don Lang, and others including an unknown group called The John Barry Seven. These rather young musicians were slotted into the film after we had started shooting at the request of the distributors, Stuart Levy and Nat Cohen, because, as they explained, John Barry's father owned a chain of cinemas in the North. Thus, if the group were in the film, Mr Barry Senior would be sure to book the picture into his chain of cinemas. This seemed to me a dubious reason for employing the John Barry Seven but we did, and they proved extremely talented. Their leader, John Barry himself, a charming, frail, retiring young man who played sax and guitar, went on to write the music for the James Bond films, *The Lion In Winter*, *Out Of Africa* and countless major movies.

*Six-Five Special*, like the TV show, was hosted by Pete Murray and Jo Douglas. In the film, two stage-struck girls board a fantasy jazz train travelling to London, its carriages filled with pop stars, all rehearsing their acts and trying out their songs in the compartments, the restaurant car, a sleeping car, the kitchens and, in the case of John Dankworth and Cleo Laine, in the luggage van. The second half of the movie all takes place in the *Six-Five Special* Studio at the BBC. Here I had to film a number of pop acts in performance and cut away to the teenagers jigging about to the music. In order to vary the shots of the acts in action I tried to find interesting and original camera set-ups. This involved shooting through a line of saxophones like a tunnel; close-ups of fingers operating the keys of a clarinet; hands strumming guitars; the face of a bass player, the camera then panning slowly down to his fingers plucking the strings, and so on. Since that day I have always felt sympathy for the BBC cameramen covering the Proms and other concerts in their continuing search for interesting shots of musicians playing instruments.

As in the TV show, we had the set filled with real pop

fans who were not actors and therefore unaccustomed to the procedures of a film studio. One hot summer afternoon to cool the studio we had switched on the air extractors, which made a tiresome humming noise. We were about to shoot a musical number to playback. So the first assistant called out "Quiet, please. Shooting. Put the bell up and kill the fans."

Not surprisingly, this order was greeted by a roar of happy laughter from the teenagers on the set.

The awful truth was that I disliked most pop music; what I call the twanging and screeching kind; and I only directed *Six-Five Special* because I wanted to continue my career as a director.

The highest-paid star of all those pop people in the film was Lonnie Donnegan, whose presence caused more fans to swarm around the Twickenham studio gates than anyone else's. When it came to the last sequence of the picture, with Donnegan and his Skiffle Group performing a number called 'Jack Of Diamonds' in a TV Studio set, I started close on Donnegan singing, with the camera mounted on the big Transatlantic crane. As the number grew more frenzied and frenetic I craned away, up higher and higher almost into the studio roof to end on a very high top shot of the scene on the floor below as the set cleared, cameras dollied away and lights began to go out in the gantry, denoting the end of the TV show.

My producer, who knew of my dislike of that kind of music, suggested jokingly that I was trying to get as far away from the screeching, twanging group as possible. In a sense he was right, for I think I had subconsciously devised the shot for that purpose.

I had always felt that it must be rather fun to go up high on the big Transatlantic crane and the first time we used it on *Six-Five Special* we were shooting the crowded railway station scene on the big stage at Twickenham studios. The shot was to start on the station clock at 5 minutes past 6 and crane down to the crowded platform with passengers, porters and luggage trolleys milling about, ending on a close-up of one of the jazz performers boarding the train.

So I went up aloft, none to happy, on my small director's seat slung beside the camera and the operator. When, high up in the studio roof, my operator Paddy invited me to lean across and take a look at the starting set-up on the clock through the camera, I realized there was a gap and a sheer drop between us of some fifty feet to the studio floor below and I became instantly terrified and dizzy.

Desperate to get down to earth but anxious not to show fear and lose face with my crew, I murmured to Paddy "As long as you've got the clock centre frame, I'll take your word for it," and, to my relief, down we came again.

When we did the shot, I left Paddy alone up on the crane and watched the shot from *terra firma*.

MY fourth and favourite film as a director was *The Impersonator* from my own original story and script, formerly called *Pantomime*.

I'd had an idea for a rather grim little thriller in which a seedy comedian playing pantomime dame in a small provincial English town, close to a US Air Force Base, is in reality a psychopathic child-murderer. After a while I came to realize that (in those days) child murderer films, like Fritz Lang's *M*, were considered tasteless. And because I was trying to set up the film with a distributing company called Bryanston of which my old boss Michael Balcon was chairman and I knew Mick's taste, I felt it wiser to change the murder victim from a child to the child's mother. The plot hinged on the small boy coming to realize that Mother Goose was an elderly man and this led to the unmasking of the comedian on the stage by the children from the audience and the final acquittal from suspicion of the American Air Force Captain who had befriended the boy's mother.

The young school teacher involved in the story was played by Jane Griffiths, a dark, exotic actress who had a few years before starred opposite Gregory Peck in *The Million Pound Note.*

On *The Impersonator* I had an interesting experience which taught me something about actors which is useful for a director to know. There was a scene in which the film's hero, US Air Force Lieutenant Bradford, is up before his Colonel at the Base accused of misconduct. The elderly American actor playing the Colonel had to deliver to John Crawford as Bradford the line "It all adds up to lousy public relations."

For some reason the actor fluffed this line two or three times, then began to panic. We got up to Take 6 and he was still fluffing and in a state of great embarrassment. I suggested a pause to cool off. The actor went off the set for a minute or two, took some deep breaths then came back on. "Once more, please. Roll camera, mark it . . . Take 7 . . . action!"

John Crawford got to his cue line: "I understand, Sir –"

The Colonel said "It adds all up to – no – to up . . . lousy . . . oh, fuck."

Then I had an idea. I told John Crawford to allow his Colonel to say "It all adds up to . . . " and then come in himself with "Lousy public relations, Sir?" delivered with a faint smile.

One quick rehearsal and we got the scene.

It's a trick worth remembering. Actors sometimes get terrible mental blocks over a speech or just a line and nothing can free them from it them but a change of words. Either rewrite the line or have them share it.

*The Impersonator* only cost £23,000 to make and I shall always treasure Dilys Powell's review of it in *The Sunday*

*Times* in which she described it as having 'more narrative ingenuity and technical skill than plenty of British thrillers made for many times that sum.'

Much of the success of *The Impersonator* was due to my good fortune in having at my side a highly-skilled, imaginative Camera Operator in Bob Thomson. He was one of the best at Pinewood Studios, possibly in the business. With a wonderful pair of hands, he was a technician who not only operated the camera with skill and steady precision but took a deep interest in the script as well. He would discuss with me each set-up in terms of the emotional content of the scene as well as its technical aspects.

I always think a good operator is one of the director's two best friends. The other is his editor.

Again I was lucky. At Eyeline Films we had in our cutting rooms one John Bloom, brother of actress Claire Bloom. John was dark and handsome like his sister and charming to work with. I am proud that *The Impersonator* was the first feature film he ever cut, for he is now one of Hollywood's major editors.

A successful film director must be absolutely ruthless and single-minded. It requires a form of fanaticism, that relentless drive a director must have to 'get the shot' at all costs. Nothing must stand in the way of putting onto the screen the scene or image he can see in his mind's eye.

There is a grim story about a ruthless director, who shall be nameless. He was shooting on an icy winter's night in the big studio tank. It was a shipwreck sequence. Lifeboats, crammed with women and children, were being dropped down into the sea from the sinking ship's hull. In one boat an elderly woman extra, wrapped in shawls, was feeling like death. She had flu and a high temperature, she was tired and she was chilled to the bone. Let's call her Madge. After doing several takes of a set-up close on the lifeboat as it dropped over the side, the director decided to pick up the boat in the next cut as it hit the sea, again with the camera close on its occupants.

While the camera was being craned down and set up at sea level, the assistant director told the director: "One of the crowd ladies is pretty sick; old Madge. She's over seventy; couldn't we send her home?"

"Certainly not. She's continuity."

In other words, her face had been established in the boat as it went over the side, so it had to be seen in the following shot when the lifeboat hit the sea.

"She's really ill, guv. We could lose her and cheat it with Madge's shawl over another woman's face?"

"I want her in the shot and that's final."

Madge did the shot but understandably retired from crowd work soon afterwards.

Another hazard faced by members of the cast is boredom. Actors in films must often spend long hours, especially on location, standing by, all made up and ready to play their scene. At the end of a day's shooting on the complicated pantomime scenes for *The Impersonator* in the old Metropolitan Theatre, Edgware Road, the assistant director broke the news to an actor, that we were badly behind schedule and that he would not be used that day. He apologised on my behalf to the player, saying "I am afraid you have had a very boring day." The actor shrugged his shoulders and went home. As he walked away the Second Assistant Director, who had overheard this, muttered to the First: "Boring day, my foot! When I went into his dressing room during the lunch break he was stretched out on the couch with one of the pantomime chorus girls!"

In his biography of David Lean the film historian, Kevin Brownlow, relates how while Lean was filming *A Passage To India* the inhabitants of a small Indian village were asked to remove the television aerials from their roofs for one day's shooting. But the sun failed to hit a certain rock in the background at a certain moment, an effect which Lean was determined to achieve. Three days later the light was still wrong and the inhabitants complained, wanting their TV aerials back. But Lean relentlessly refused until he had got his shot and the producer was obliged to use all his tact to prevent a riot.

On location in Austria for *Heart Of a Child*, which I was producing, I went up one morning to a small Catholic chapel in the mountains where the unit was shooting, to see how they were getting on. The Camera Operator was up on a rostrum close to the side wall lining up a shot across the altar which had been set ready for evening Mass.

As I came in I heard the operator call out to the first assistant director "Frank, can we lose all those wafers and goblets and things . . ." A minute later, trying to pan the camera, he managed to put his elbow through a small stained glass window and broke it.

I am afraid that with the film maker the rule is 'get the shot at all costs'.

It all falls in line with the lack of respect felt by some directors for actors, whom they regard as necessary but tiresome obstructions to filming. Even the great William Wyler, with his reputation in Hollywood as the actors' favourite director, was once heard to say to his first assistant when the set was lit and ready and the stand-ins had been dismissed, "OK, bring on the face-makers."

On *The Impersonator* an actor asked me one day if he could be finished with by the lunch break as he had a chance to audition that afternoon for a good part in an H. M. Tennent play.

I knew I would need to do a close-up reaction shot on him, just one, when we started shooting after lunch in another part of the set. But like an idiot, I let him go, not wanting the guy to miss a chance of a good theatre job.

The actor was suitably grateful but, of course, when the editor came to assemble the material that had been shot in the other part of the set, the close-up of the departed actor was seen to be absolutely vital. Without it the series of reactions were uneven and out of rhythm. It so damaged the sequence that I had to call the actor down specially on another day – at considerable cost to the budget – so we could pick up that missing close-up.

Soon after *The Impersonator* I surveyed the movie scene and my own aptitude for directing films. I decided that I was far too easy-going and softhearted ever to be a big-time director.

IF anyone asks me now how many films I have directed I have to answer, truthfully, four and a bit. Let me tell you about the bit.

In 1959 I was asked by Sydney Box to be the producer on a picture called *Heart of a Child* from a touching novel by Phyllis Bottome. The story was about an Austrian innkeeper in the Tyrol during the Great War, his ten-year old son and the family St Bernard dog.

It was a very sentimental story in what I would call 'Lassie' territory. During shooting in the winter of 1960 the UK was hit by a severe epidemic of so-called 'Asian flu' and our director, Clive Donner, succumbed to it. During the ten days that Clive was laid up in bed, I was asked to continue directing the picture. One sequence I had to shoot was on a mountain set in the studio covered with artificial snow and prop pine trees. Large wind machines created a blizzard. In this setting the actor, Donald Pleasance, playing the Tyrolean innkeeper, was out in the storm with a lantern, following Luchs, the St Bernard. They were searching for a lost lamb.

The dog found the lamb and Donald had to scrabble about in a snowdrift and lift the frozen creature gently out, wrap it under his coat and take it home. Now most people are familiar with the problems of filming with animals. Our lamb was no exception. Every time Donald picked up the supposedly dying animal it struggled, kicked itself free and ran off, causing prop men, assistant directors and electricians to chase it round and round the studio floor until it was finally recaptured and put firmly back in its snowdrift. We went up to eight takes on that shot before we finally got it.

Later on, at lunch in the canteen, Donald and I were laughing about our awful morning when I was informed that an official from the RSPCA had arrived at the studios to see me. To cut a long story short, one of the crew on our set – nobody ever discovered who – had objected to our treatment of the lamb and phoned the local Elstree branch of the RSPCA to report us. When I conducted the official to the prop room to reassure him that the lamb had come to no harm, we found it wrapped in a blanket being fed warm milk from a baby's bottle and being petted and cuddled by all the girls from Wardrobe, Make-Up and Hairdressing who had dropped in to see it during their lunch break. The lamb was having a ball. If only animals could speak.

The pay-off to that story is that when Clive Donner recovered from his flu and came back to the picture, he insisted on reshooting every single set-up I had done in his absence with the exception of the snow sequence with the lamb.

IN 1962 I unwittingly directed a kind of love scene that would have been censored, if there had been a script.

My company, Eyeline Films, had undertaken to produce a low-budget picture for Bryanston Films of John Mortimer's short play, *Lunch Hour*, of which I thus became Executive

Producer. The stars of this piece were Robert Stephens, Kay Walsh and Shirley-Anne Field. Everyone on the picture, including the author, John Mortimer, fancied Shirley-Anne who was a very attractive, nice girl. But one day on location in Notting Hill Gate she came to me to complain that she was getting a bit tired of warding off invitations out to dinner after shooting from various people on the unit when all she wanted was to go home and learn her lines. Some days later someone told me that Shirley-Anne had declined an offer for dinner from John Mortimer and instead was going to spend the evening with Bob Stephens who had kindly offered to take her through her lines. My informant added, "Isn't it kind of Bob to go to so much trouble?" Maybe by then she knew her part by heart because from what I heard later I gathered that the evening had been no kind of trouble for Bob Stephens.

One sequence in the script of *Lunch Hour* was a montage of shots depicting London in the lunch hour on a summer day so I went out with a small second-unit crew and the Arriflex Camera to get random shots of old men eating pork pies on park benches, office girls queueing for sandwiches at coffee bars, couples lying in the grass and other forms of lunchtime activity on a warm day in the Big City.

In Hyde Park close to the Victoria Gate I found a handsome young couple lying on the grass and asked them if they would object to embracing each other affectionately while I filmed them for a movie. They would get a nominal payment and be asked to sign a disclaimer giving us permission to use the shot. The couple, who were both Australians, agreed with enthusiasm, so we set up the Arriflex, they clasped each other and I called out 'Action'.

Immediately the young man seized the girl roughly and they started to roll about, grunting and gasping. The young man pressed his lips to hers and almost tore her dress off her shoulders in a display of unbridled passion. After a while I shouted "Cut" but they went on writhing and grunting until they both fell back exhausted.

"That was fine," I said as they both staggered to their feet, out of breath, to sign the disclaimer and get a fiver each. The young man signed 'Harry J. Cooper' and then the girl signed, 'Jane Cooper'.

"Jane Cooper?" I said glancing at her signature with some surprise, "So you two are married".

"Hell no," said Jane with a hearty laugh, "he's my brother," and they strolled away across the park arm-in-arm.

# WRITING FOR TELEVISION

IN 1953, after *Laxdale Hall* was completed and I had not been offered another film by Group Three, I was living off the rather meagre royalties from my handful of stage plays that were being performed in reps round the country. At this point in my life I began to feel financially insecure. Although Jean was working regularly in the theatre and appearing in low-budget movies, I had an overdraft at the bank. In deep anxiety I called up Michael Barry, Head of Drama at the BBC, to confide to him my worry and ask him if there was a regular job going of any kind at the BBC. To my relief and joy Michael advised me to apply at once for a new post on offer in the Drama Department. He explained that he had been empowered by the Corporation to recruit four permanent script editors, 'script adaptors' to be exact, and he would like me to be one of them. They would be on salary at Lime Grove as resident staff to do the job of adapting for television plays by authors no longer living, classic or foreign plays and sometimes undertaking the editing of submitted contemporary plays, working with their authors to ensure that they were up to broadcasting standards. After I had been working in the job for three weeks I was formally 'boarded' by the BBC and passed as fit for employment by the Corporation.

My three colleagues in the new adaptors' department were Nigel Kneale, Giles Cooper and George Kerr and we had offices in a kind of temporary Nissen hut on the building site at Wood Lane where the massive new BBC Television Centre was being constructed to replace Lime Grove. Cement mixers and diggers ground away all around us as we wrestled with the texts of plays by Dürenmatt, O'Neill, Shaw, Frisch, Toller and Anouilh, preparing them for transmission on TV. The salary was modest but I was now setting off each morning from our flat in Chesham Street to catch the tube to work and felt for the first time in my life like a responsible husband bringing home the bacon.

The BBC was still a monopoly at this time and the plays were still going out live.The technique of writing a TV play to be transmitted live was quite a challenge for an author. Once transmission had started it was all continuous action, as with a performance in the theatre. The camera or cameras moved about the set following the action and piping the pictures through for transmission. So if, for example, you write a scene with two men, Smith and Jones, discussing a deal in an office and the next scene in the script is Jones arriving home to tell his wife about his meeting with Smith, you have to give Jones time, probably about two minutes, to exit from the office set, make his way across the studio by stepping over lighting cables and junction boxes to reach the set of the front door and hall of his own home. Here he will let himself in with his key and be picked up there by a waiting camera as he comes in to greet his wife.

This means adding two minutes on to the office scene after Jones has left, but it must not be 'padding'. Those extra two minutes can be added by having Smith's secretary come in and be told to take a letter to someone referring to the recent discussion we have witnessed between Smith and Jones. The dictation of this letter should be a vital scene in the plot. For example, here is the start of it.

*Smith*: Jones has just been here; he has agreed to co-operate with our scheme but is unaware of the attitude of the Chairman. I suggest we keep him in ignorance of the full facts . . .

(By now Jones has reached his home set and we can safely cut to him entering to greet his wife and enjoy the irony of their scene in the hall:)

*Wife*: There you are, darling. Good meeting?

*Jones*: Excellent. I've come to the conclusion that Smith's a man you can trust.

The playwright has built in an element to allow the audience to see that Smith has deceived Jones, while at the same time solving the problem of getting Jones from one scene to another in continuous action.

One day, at a routine meeting of the Drama Department that we adaptors were always required to attend, Michael Barry announced that he wanted each of the four of us to write a six-part thriller Serial for transmission on six successive Saturday nights at prime time. We would be paid a bit extra for them over and above our regular salaries and retain certain subsidiary rights, and were each allotted a director to work with. I was given Alvin Rakoff, a bright, young Canadian from Toronto; he had made his mark with CBC and come to London to try his luck alongside a number of his compatriots such as Sydney Newman, Silvio Narizzano and Ted Kotcheff.

Rakoff and I retired to my Nissen hut and discussed an idea I had for a thriller. I wrote it and called it *A Place Of Execution*. Alvin cast Derek Bond, Jack Watling, Catherine Lacey and William Devlin in the lead roles and a pretty blonde, Ann Hanslip.

The serial turned out to be weirdly predictive. It was about the daughter of the governor of an imaginary British colony in the Middle East called Zirdanah who is kidnapped in London by terrorists and held hostage against the hanging, authorized by her father, of a terrorist in Zirdanah's capital. I called my terrorist organization Kailak and the governor of

Zirdanah Sir John Harper. A few years later the terrorist organization Eoka emerged in Cyprus. They kidnapped a British soldier as a hostage against a hanging when the governor of Cyprus was Sir John Harding. At the time I felt that Colonel Grivas, the Eoka leader, had seen *A Place Of Execution* and copied my plot, or else that I had second sight.

Incidentally, TV history was made on *A Place Of Execution* when in the final episode we cross-cut scenes in the studio at Alexandra Palace with outside broadcast (OB) scenes transmitted live from our location in Madame Tussauds. The location scenes were piped through by GPO line into the studio and edited in by the director and P.A. in the control room.

The final denouement took place with Ann Hanslip as the governor's daughter, the noose already round her neck, being rescued by the police at the eleventh hour from being hanged on the gallows on the Charles Peace set-piece in the Chamber of Horrors. On the Sunday morning after the last episode one newspaper headline screamed: 'Millions See Girl Hanged On TV' and I was castigated for writing an unsavoury, blood-thirsty and sadistic serial. It would not seem overly sensational today.

Although *A Place Of Execution* thrilled millions and caused quite a stir, it could not compete with my colleague Nigel Kneale's effort at a six-part thriller. He had written *The Quatermass Experiment* which preceded mine. A hard act to follow.

However, Douglas Fairbanks, Jnr and his partner Tommy Clyde bought the film rights in *A Place Of Execution* and made a movie from it called *The Hostage*, directed by the veteran American actor-producer Harold Huth.

SOON after that, although I was supposed to be working for the Drama Department. I was loaned out by Michael Barry

*In an amazing manner, Susan secures . . . a Sixty-Five Guinea Wedding Dre*

AT a few minutes after six, Susan stood back and surveyed her work. Her back ached from bending down to arrange the train in a fan-shaped spread around the dummy bride's feet. The smug expression on the wax model's face annoyed her: it seemed to be alive and conscious of the beauty of the gown in whic was draped.

Sixty-five guineas' worth of v white, wasted on a papier-maché s she thought.

Outside, through the glass windo small group of pavement onlookers b

22

.B. Clarke at work on his script for *Lavender Hill Mob* with the author at Ealing Studios, 1949.

1. The Author's first short story as it appears in *Affinity* magazine.

3. James Donald and the author's wife Jean Lodge on location for *Brandy for the Parson*, with Torquay doubling for Brittany.

4. Ronald Squire, Andrew Keir and Kathleen Ryan in the film *Laxdale Hall*.

5. Fulton McKay and Prunella Scales in her first film, *Laxdale Hall*.

6. L. to R.: Richard Warner, Anouska Hempel and Eric Pohlmann, (at back Ivor Salter) in the film *Tiffany Jones*.

7. A scene from the film *Room in the House* with, L. to R, Hubert Gregg, Josephine Griffin and Marjorie Rhodes.

8. Barbara Shelley in the film *Cat Girl*.

9. Petula Clark sings 'Baby Lover' in *Six-Five Special*.

to the Light Entertainment Department to work with the producer Michael Mills. He was doing a series of quite spectacular programmes under the title of *The Passing Show* and he had just made one about George Edwardes and his Gaiety Girls with Tony Britton. Now he planned a big musical about Marie Lloyd and I was asked to write it. A young trainee writer called Christopher Barry was attached to me to do the research and together we unearthed all we could discover about the great Music Hall star who was to be portrayed by Pat Kirkwood. The show would be called *Our Marie*.

At the first read-through of the script we reached a back-stage scene between Marie Lloyd and her dresser, Bella Burge, played by Patricia Raine. Marie was telling Bella rather sadly how hard it is to dedicate your life to the public who love you and still be happy in your marriage. At this point Patricia Raine suddenly burst into floods of tears. It was a shock and quite embarrassing, but it gave me the satisfaction of thinking how effective the scene must be to get such a reaction.

I was taken down a peg when later one of the cast told me that Pat Raine was upset by the scene because her own mother, Binnie Hale, had dedicated her life too much to her public and consequently her father, Jack Raine, had walked out of the marriage.

*Our Marie* proved to be the biggest and most expensive show the BBC had ever undertaken. There were dozens of musical numbers, masses of sets and costumes, a huge cast, and a full orchestra under Eric Robinson, who had to accompany the songs by headphone from a separate studio. The whole thing was transmitted live from Lime Grove on a Sunday night and again on the following Thursday.

It was a terrific challenge for Pat Kirkwood, who had a mammoth part and over a dozen songs to learn, not to mention at least fifteen costume changes. For two hectic hours Pat was continuously playing a scene in one set then dashing across the studio floor to a big stage set to deliver a song to a packed audience of cheering extras, then off to another small set for a bedroom scene with one of her husbands, and so on. This involved her in jumping over the cables and junction boxes to get there in time, stripping as she ran, pursued by wardrobe girls trying to throw her next dress over her head. As she arrived, out of breath, in each set the actors with whom she was to play the scene would be glancing up nervously at the cue light fearing she would not make it and the scene would have to be cut. And so it went on. But Pat never missed a scene, never put a foot wrong and scored a resounding triumph in the part. In fact, when the show finally ended with Marie's death and the full chorus and orchestra singing 'My Old Man Said Follow The Van' and the green light went up, the whole studio burst into spontaneous and prolonged applause and cheering for a great trouper and a great star.

A few days after the triumph of *Our Marie* I was summoned to lunch by the impresario Jack Hylton at the Carlton Grill. I found Pat Kirkwood there. It transpired that Hylton had seen and loved *Our Marie* and wanted to present a version of it on the stage as a West End musical with Pat starring as Marie once again.

Over lunch I described enthusiastically how some of the scenes could be staged in a theatre (he had His Majesty's in mind) and found myself referring frequently to *Cavalcade*. Jack Hylton seemed to be completely set on doing the show and I went off full of hope, to await a call from my agent to start on the libretto. But not another word was heard from Hylton either by Pat or by me and it all went dead.

Late in 1954 Group Three came up again with a film for me to produce, *The End Of The Road*. It was about an old factory worker, played by that fine old Scottish actor Finlay Currie, who had appeared for me in the film *Six-Five Special*. The old man is forced to retire from work and forms a deep relationship with his small grandson. But when that picture was in the can I was out of work again and feeling the pinch, especially as Jean was now pregnant with our first child Charles. In due course Jean was obliged to give up working. She had been carrying Charlie in embryo on the stage of the Duchess Theatre while appearing in William Douglas-Home's comedy *The Manor Of Northstead,* and was now forced to relinquish her part when she became too large for her costumes. Mercifully, I managed at that exact moment to persuade Michael Barry to do *Holiday For Simon* as the BBC Sunday Night Play, which saved the situation. We were thus able to leave our small flat in Chesham Street and buy a house in Chelsea.

Two years later Jean was carrying our second son David on the stage of the Westminster Theatre where she was appearing with Griffith Jones in a thriller called *Dead On Nine*. Once again she was forced to leave the cast for confinement in the London Clinic, where David was born. It is perhaps not surprising that both our sons are now in show business, Charles as an actor in Hollywood and David also in Hollywood as a TV producer-director with CBS.

SOON the TV drama scene changed radically. VTR came in, that is to say Video Tape. From then on scenes in TV plays were recorded on tape (often out of continuity, as per film) and the tape recording of the scene may now be stopped and restarted at will – exactly as sound and picture rolls and is cut in a film studio. Today the writing of a TV script differs hardly at all from the writing of a script for a cinema film.

By 1956 we had ITV as well as the BBC and almost everybody in the land had a TV set. Gone were the days when elderly peeresses would say "We never watch television, my dear. But the servants do. Richard gave them a set for the servants' hall and they're glued to it day and night; never answer the bells."

TV drama was becoming fashionable again on a bigger scale and playwrights were in demand.

American television soon caused the producers of ITV entertainment to realize that a high viewing rate had to be guaranteed at peak hours to persuade the advertisers to pay exorbitant sums of money for air time for the screening of their commercials; and that a steady high rating for a programme could best be achieved by 'hooking' the viewer with a story and the destiny of its characters and holding their interest from week to week. Thus, benefitting from the USA's experience, UK television entered the lucrative business of making and transmitting drama and comedy series and serials. The single play was no guarantee of a wide audience. If the BBC did a Shaw or an Ibsen play on a Sunday night, they were really justifying their obligation under their Charter to provide a degree of culture and education, not to get ratings. It is true that while I was a BBC Script Adaptor Michael Barry put on O'Neill's *Mourning Becomes Electra* which, to everyone's amazement achieved massive viewing figures. But that was an exception.

As the ITV companies were in it to make money with their serials they also looked for commercial plays or groups of plays and began to make 'anthologies', a programme of plays with a theme and a collective title. Thus an ITV company would commission from different writers a batch of single plays under an umbrella title such as 'Greed' or 'Jealousy' or 'Blackmail' or just 'Love'.

100

I wrote two *Love Story* plays for ATV and another for an anthology called *Happy Ever After* which consisted of plays with a happy ending.

Some of these groups of single plays were excellent and a programme like ABC Television's 'Armchair Theatre' hit a very high standard, many of its plays winning awards. But as the '60s gave way to the '70s the single play became a hazard, a gamble for the production companies. It was harder to sell air time around a single play that was still an unknown quantity. So more and more series and serials were launched. The high-ups began to realize that a good drama or comedy series could build an audience for itself quickly and keep it watching through thick and thin.

But in the '50s the single TV play still had its place in the schedules and was an art form which attracted all the best dramatists whose work had hitherto been seen mainly in the theatre. Writing for television had become respectable.

AT this point in my life my relationship with the BBC came to an end but I still needed a secure job and it was a joy when a rather wild, brilliant but disorganized man called James Archibald became Head of Production for the J. Arthur Rank Organization at Pinewood. Nobody seemed quite clear why Archibald had been appointed, as there was a perfectly competent old showman in charge of production for Rank, Earl St John who had been in the job for years. I contrived a meeting with Archibald who was said to be looking for 'gifted writers' and my agent fixed for me to meet him. I spent a strange evening with James which consisted of motoring down to dine with him in a palatial house he had rented close to Pinewood Studios at Penn and drinking far too much of his excellent wine. We had talked about everything under the sun except a job but, as I started up my car to drive back to Chelsea, I heard him through the haze inviting me to "join the team".

I said "Thanks," and motored back to London, not quite sure what he meant.

But the next day my agent called me to say Archibald had offered me a contract with the Rank Organisation as an Associate Producer at £2,000 per year. I was in clover. This was real money. My agent was so thrilled with the deal that he took me out to an expensive lunch at the Caprice to celebrate it.

So it was, from Pinewood, that I fell in with the Sydney Box group, as already related.

Three years later James Archibald was fired from Ranks by John Davis but got himself a job as Head of Film and Television at the advertising agency, J. Walter Thompson. Into the advertising scene he brought with him a number of young film makers from Pinewood whose contracts were not being renewed, including David Deutsch, Anthony Perry, Clive Donner and me and set us all to work on making commercials for him. After a year learning about this form of film making as an agency producer, I left JWT and formed a small film company called Eyeline Films together with Anthony Perry and two distinguished directors: Charles Frend, an old Ealing colleague who had directed *Scott of the Antarctic* and *The Cruel Sea*; and Guy Hamilton, who had made *The Colditz Story* and some Bond pictures including *Gold Finger*. We also asked Kenneth More to join us on the board of Eyeline; he agreed and his name on our letter-heading helped us to look even more respectable.

For a few years we made a large number of advertising films and industrial documentaries and I personally directed over a hundred TV commercials for such products as Camay Soap, Enos, The British School of Motoring and Venos Cough Mixture. After a while I lost interest in the advertising world and became mildly disenchanted with it. I found that the clients had too much power and too little knowledge of film making. They tended to interfere in creative matters. We often had to show the rushes and rough-cuts to an audience of young and eager clients and admen anxious to make their names. After seeing the rough-cut of a commercial they would sometimes ask silly questions and make silly remarks. On one occasion in the viewing theatre a young adman asked why he didn't hear the car door slam on what was plainly a mute exterior shot. We had to explain to the lad that the film had not yet been dubbed and that the car door slam would be on the effects track and would be dubbed on later. But these young men in their well-cut business suits were 'clients' and had to be kow-towed to. After all, they were paying for their commercial and must be heeded as politely as possible.

But I did make use of Eyeline Films later to make my own feature movie *The Impersonator* and soon after that, around 1964, my agent called me one day with what turned out to be very important news.

A very bright executive lady, Stella Richman, at London's main new ITV Station, Associated-Rediffusion, was producing a high-class underworld series starring Ian Hendry as a slightly bent, disbarred barrister turned police informer. It was called *The Informer* and John Whitney, later to be Director-General of the IBA, was the Script Editor. When Stella was promoted to be Head of Series at A-R and John Whitney stepped up to produce *The Informer* they needed a new Script Editor, and my name had been put forward.

I was interviewed by Whitney and Richman and found to be suitable, so the job was mine. It was a brand new experience for me. My task was to invite writers to submit suitable storylines for *The Informer*, commission them to write the scripts then edit (or doctor) the scripts to make them fit the pattern of the series. My contract also provided for me to write a certain number of the scripts myself.

I little realized at the time that this work, story and script editing and writing for Drama Series, would become my mainstream writing activity for a number of years to come. In fact, it took me right up to that golden day in 1972 when Stella Richman, to whom I shall always be deeply indebted, invited me to edit *Upstairs, Downstairs* for London Weekend, the company which by then had the benefit of her skill and experience as its Controller of Programmes.

*The Informer* was a fascinating subject for a drama series and the stories had to depict the informer, Lambert, endlessly getting himself into dangerous situations, caught in a trap between the police and the criminal fraternity. Not unlike a secret agent or a political spy, a police informer is in constant danger of having his cover blown and, if caught, of being disowned by both sides.

In the series a convention had been established that Ian Hendry as the informer always met his police contact, a snide character called Sergeant Piper, in some secret place or setting where they could talk and exchange information. In the first script I wrote for the series, 'A Mouthful of Silver Spoons', I had Lambert and Piper exchanging their confidential information while playing squash, so that the vital words were picked up between grunts and gasps as they sloshed the ball round the court. This idea has been used a good deal since by television and movie writers.

That first episode of *The Informer* was one of many directed by Michael Lindsay-Hogg and it concerned a society girl who, being in love with an underworld villain and under his influence, arranges for her own parents' car to be held up and her mother robbed of her diamond tiara and necklace on their way to a Mansion House banquet. The girl in question was played by Tracy Reed, the tall and glamorous daughter of two old friends of mine, Penelope Dudley Ward and Fay Compton's son Tony Pelissier. I had introduced them to each other before the war, they had married and in 1940, on leave, I had dandled Tracy as a baby on my knee. Thus I was startled to find this gorgeous young woman at the read-through for 'A Mouthful of Silver Spoons'. Her mother had by then parted from Tony and married Carol Reed, so Tracy Pelissier chose to use her stepfather's surname for her stage name.

I edited two seasons of *The Informer* and was then asked to edit another series which Stella had initiated about the daily lives and relationships of a group of nuns in a convent. It was called *Sanctuary*.

The central characters of this one were the Mother Superior, a senior Nun and a much younger one. But stories were required to involve others.

We had most of the obvious dilemma-stories that can be told about nuns. One was of a young missionary nun who has been raped in the Congo by a white mercenary, returns to the convent pregnant and is given the choice of having the baby adopted and keeping the veil or keeping her child and renouncing her vows. The strong *scène à faire* was the confrontation between the wretched girl's spiritual mother and her actual mother.

Another interesting story idea that occurred to me was 'what if a nun driving other nuns around in a minibus, as they often do, has a crash, so that a motorist is killed and the nun is on a manslaughter charge?' This happened to Sister Ursula, played by the redoubtable Alison Leggatt.

During *Sanctuary* we had a bizarre and rather grim episode which gave Fay Compton, our senior nun, a fairly long part, for which she had been making constant demands. When she finally got her 'big part' she couldn't learn it and had to be given short takes. One night, just to help matters, Fay was bitten on the cheek by her own dog, a pekingese, and came to the studio next day with a massively swollen face. This necessitated allowing Fay to play her scenes with a handkerchief pressed to her dogbite and me writing in a line: 'Poor Sister Juliana has dreadful toothache today. We must pray for her in her suffering.'

A similar situation occurred years later on *Upstairs, Downstairs* when Christopher Beeny, playing the Bellamys' footman, Edward, came off his motorbike on his way to the camera rehearsal and was quite badly injured. We had just one day to cast, costume and rehearse a young actress called Jane Carr, to take Edward's place. I had to rewrite parts of the script quickly to establish that Edward had that very afternoon tripped and fallen down the basement stairs and was in hospital. Hudson, the butler had to learn a new speech to establish this and the fact that Lady Marjorie had engaged a temporary parlour-maid called Joan.

Hudson's speech ended with the comment "Those steps are badly worn; quite unsafe in my opinion."

Joan disappeared after one more episode when Chris Beeny returned to duty, limping slightly, which was consistent with his recent fall down the stairs.

WHILE I was editing and writing for *The Informer* and *Sanctuary* I was able to undertake a few other writing jobs for television. One of these was a script for the then-popular crime series *No Hiding Place* with Raymond Francis as Detective Chief Superintendent Lockhart.

It came about in a strange way. I was in my office at Rediffusion when a colleague who was editing *No Hiding Place* called me from his office along the corridor and to my surprise invited me to submit a story and do a script for his show. I was delighted and flattered and thanked him profusely. In due course I submitted a storyline which he promptly commissioned. I started work on my script. Over the next few weeks this fellow-editor appeared to be rather cool towards me and I wondered if I had in some way offended him.

Meeting him at lunch time in the canteen one day I told him cheerfully that my script for him was going pretty well, only to be greeted with a sullen look and a pretty offhand "Oh, really?"

I mentioned this to another writer, Anthony Skene, who was working for me at the time and he look puzzled. "Haven't you offered him a script for *Sanctuary* yet?"

"No. Should I?"

"My God! You've got a lot to learn about this racket," Tony Skene told me and laughed heartily.

Then I got the message. But I did not invite the editor concerned to write a script for me. I had believed that he wanted me for my talent and not as some kind of bargaining ploy and I did not need a script from him.

The script I did for *No Hiding Place*, called 'A Letter For Helga', was about a respectable Chelsea solicitor, Kennedy, who is convicted of strangling the German *au pair* who looks after his children, and burying the body under the bracken in Richmond Park. A letter for the girl from her mother in Frankfurt is found in the dead girl's room, which helps Lockhart to trap the murderer.

In my script, when Lockhart and two detectives come to the Chelsea house to arrest Kennedy, the guilty man has the line "I'll bet this is the first time you chaps have had to arrest a solicitor for murder, eh?"

The actor concerned came to me at rehearsals and asked if he need use the word 'chaps'. He said he thought it a bit old-fashioned, making the line caricature. "Could I not say 'you people'?" he asked.

If he had followed the right procedure he would have asked the director about the line and the director would have referred it to me. A golden rule is that everything should go through the director. As it was, the director was the type who wouldn't have understood the subtleties of my use of the word, so I spent ten minutes in a corner of the rehearsal room explaining to the actor why the word 'chaps' was important: here was a respected solicitor, humiliated by being charged with murder, aware of his guilt and trying to make the best of a bad moment by

(a) trying to get on top of the police by patronising them, as a country squire would call the village cricket team 'you chaps' and

(b) trying to play down the situation and make it seem everyday by the use of a friendly term, as though the police were not at that moment his enemies but in his house almost as guests.

After a while the actor saw the point and agreed to say 'chaps'. But, as often happens, he fluffed the line when he came to it at the taping, saying "I'll bet this is the first time you . . . er . . . chaps . . . have . . ." and killed it stone dead. The impact of the word I had carefully chosen was destroyed, but the hesitation was not considered serious enough for a retake and I had to let it go.

AFTER completing my work on *Sanctuary* at Rediffusion I was suddenly out of regular work and once again mildly worried, until my agent heard of an Anglo-American thriller series called *Journey To The Unknown* which was being mounted in the UK by Joan Harrison, wife of the novelist Eric Ambler and Alfred Hitchcock's right-hand woman, to be produced by the actor-director Norman Lloyd. The series was to be filmed at the MGM Studios at Elstree for Twentieth-Century Fox.

I submitted a story called 'The Last Visitor', set in a seaside resort out of season. Nothing happened for some time and I began to fret. Then, suddenly and out of the blue, I was summoned to see Joan Harrison and Norman Lloyd. Although Joan Harrison told me with a twinkle in her eye that I had written *Psycho* in reverse, I gathered that my story was liked and I was commissioned to do a script. The money was good, too. In Hitchcock's masterpiece *Psycho* Anthony Perkins assumes his dead mother's clothes to kill his victims, whereas in my story a psychopathic woman dresses up as a man to attempt a murder. That is to say a seaside landlady, a former variety male impersonator, dresses up in white tie and tails with a top-hat and monocle to stab a young woman resident in her guest house. One role is the young American girl who is recovering from a nervous breakdown in the seafront boarding-house on the South Coast of England, the other a superficially kind-hearted, jolly ex-music hall comedienne running the establishment, who turns out to be distinctly sinister.

The American girl was played by Patty Duke, who was at the time having a kind of nervous breakdown herself after a broken romance, and the landlady was Kay Walsh at her most brilliant. The producer, Norman Lloyd, and I became great friends and we always see him and his wife Peggy whenever Jean and I go over to visit our two sons in Los Angeles.

AFTER some years of script-editing on Drama Series, I finally had a taste of my own medicine when the chance came to me to submit a story for *The Saint* series, starring Roger Moore as Simon Templar. It gave me a rough ride.

I wrote a story about the theft of a top-secret vertical take-off jet or 'jump jet', a type of aircraft which was then just coming into service. A small assault unit acting for an imaginary East European Communist State break into an RAF base at night, overpower the security guards and manage to fly the jet out and across the Iron Curtain to their own country, with The Saint in hot pursuit.

The script was called 'Flight Plan' and I had discussed the

story in detail with *The Saint's* script editor, a tough Canadian called Harry Junkin.

All went well until I delivered the first draft of my script to Junkin and received his notes in the post. It consisted of pages and pages of roughly and speedily typed comment, scene by scene, some of it frankly abusive. There were notes like 'Sc. 15. Get this scene off its ass, Fred,' or 'Your dialogue makes me want to throw up . . . Templar does not talk like a poncified dandy . . .'

In one scene I had described The Saint, after a fight with some villains: 'Templar gets up, dusts down his jacket, straightens his tie and saunters off down the street.'

Junkin wrote 'The Saint never gets mussed.'

There was one sequence of which I was rather proud. Two secret agents are exchanging vital information while sitting in a rowing boat in the middle of The Serpentine in Hyde Park. Templar, from behind, cover films the two men with a long-range telephoto lens and takes the film to be blown up and then lip-read by experts at an Institution for the Deaf. Thus Templar learns what the agents were saying to each other.

Junkin questioned this whole idea, saying it was far-fetched. He marked the scene in my script with 'This is crap. Who are you kidding?'

I told him that I did not think Alfred Hitchcock would have turned down that idea. But I had to go to the producer for a final ruling when Junkin was over-ruled. The scene stayed in and it worked a treat.

'Flight Plan' was eventually finalized to Harry Junkin's satisfaction, if not to mine, and was duly filmed. I have to admit that, for all the battles and arguments with Junkin, I am eternally grateful to *The Saint*'s producers, Bob Baker and Monty Berman, for that commission. 'Flight Plan' has been shown on television world-wide several times and has earned me handsome 'residuals'.

* * *

THERE are similarities, but not many, between The Saint and the hero of my next salaried job as script editor and writer for a series. He was called Hadleigh.

The two common factors are first that both Simon Templar (Roger Moore) and James Hadleigh (Gerald Harper) are single heroes fighting for right and justice, knights in shining armour whose popularity with the ladies is enhanced by neither of them being or getting married, and second that each episode is a self-contained story with a beginning, middle and end and there are no running threads from week to week, as in a serial.

In 1968 the ITV franchises were re-offered and there was a change of companies. Associated-Rediffusion and ABC Television ceased to exist and two new companies appeared on the scene: London Weekend Television, which acquired the prized weekend franchise for the London area; and Yorkshire Television. Peter Willes, who had been doing sterling work as an Executive Producer at Rediffusion was invited to be Head of Drama at the new Yorkshire station under its controller Donald Baverstock. I remember the anxious days at Rediffusion after the announcement of the changes but, in the end, almost every member of AR's staff was posted either to London Weekend or to Yorkshire.

Peter Willes saw a chance to exercise his flair for TV Drama with more control and opted for Yorkshire.

When I told him I had heard he was going to Yorkshire TV he looked grim and said with a shudder in his voice "It's perishing cold up there . . ." as though he was being sent off to run drama for TV Alaska.

I had just finished *Sanctuary* at that time and went back to a period of freelancing with single plays for TV. But later in the year I was summoned by Peter Willes to Yorkshire's

London office. The company had made thirteen episodes of a Drama Series called *Gazette*, which was about a Yorkshire newspaper, not surprisingly since their new controller Donald Baverstock had been a journalist and current affairs chief at the BBC.

The outstanding character in the *Gazette*'s cast of newspaper people was the actor Gerald Harper, who played a local, public-school educated country squire, called James Hadleigh, the owner of a controlling interest in the *Gazette*.

There was now talk at Yorkshire of phasing out *Gazette* and phasing in a new series, a spin-off featuring Hadleigh as its central character.

Peter Willes asked me to carry out a rather delicate task. I was to travel up to Leeds, where Yorkshire TV's new studios were not yet completed, stay in the Queen's Hotel over the station in a luxury suite and read carefully the remaining scripts that had been written for *Gazette*. I was to take over as Script Editor, attend rehearsals and recordings, study the general situation and decide whether I felt *Gazette* should go on or be ended in favour of the new projected show, *Hadleigh*. It was a difficult assignment, for although *Gazette* was going fairly well, the scripts that had been commissioned by my editing predecessor were not very good.

There was also a certain unease and uncertainty among the cast and I had to exert the role of a diplomat more than once during my visit. Two well known players, Robert Harris and Adrienne Corri, were starring in an episode of *Gazette* but were unhappy with their script. They were making trouble, or rather Adrienne was. She was a great girl, exceedingly glamorous, forthright and a little mad.

I reported the situation to Peter Willes on the phone.

He said "Rewrite the script and take them out to an expensive dinner at the Queens, money no object!"

I carried out my orders to the letter and the three of us,

Bobby Harris, Adrienne Corri and I sat down in the restaurant of the Queen's Hotel to a most wonderful dinner of roast grouse and a fine claret. The next day they went to the studio and did the show without another murmur. Yorkshire Television paid the bill.

The incident reminded me of Tim Aspinall, a TV drama producer I once knew, who was asked to explain an item in his expenses account for three bottles of champagne on three different dates during the production of a series. He told the studio accounts department it was for 'conciliating difficult actors' and got away with it.

It was plain that to continue with *Gazette* was a gamble and I talked about it to Gerald Harper, who was naturally dead keen on having his own series. What actor wouldn't be?

To Peter I strongly recommended terminating the show and going ahead with *Hadleigh*.

Peter said "I hoped you'd say that."

The next problem was that a writer who had written a lot of *Gazette* episodes had been promised the opening script for the new series, which unfortunately was not very good. Peter hated its political bias and rather disliked the writer, too, so he asked me to do an opening script to get *Hadleigh* off the ground.

An amusing incident took place at this point. Peter Willes was brilliant, but he was devious. When I had finished my opening *Hadleigh* script I called him to say it was ready.

Peter lowered his voice on the phone and said guardedly "Don't let Baverstock see it yet. Let me read it and we can talk first."

I sent my script direct to Peter's private address and a couple of days later he asked me to come round to his flat in Great Cumberland Place to discuss it. He seemed happy with the script, entitled 'Thanks For The Offer', but was still insistent that Baverstock should not know that we had met over it. Our meeting must be secret, he insisted, off-the-record, or Baverstock would be offended.

During our secret session Peter made a couple of very minor suggestions and then after ten minutes or so we moved on to drinking his whisky and gossiping about people we knew. I still could not quite understand why Peter wanted to keep Baverstock out of the 'Thanks for the Offer' business but when I left him he told me to send a copy of the script to Baverstock personally.

I sent off the script. There was a pause. A few days later Peter reported that Baverstock was happy and had ordered *Hadleigh* to be scheduled.

It took someone who knew Peter better than I did to explain his curious behaviour: if, on receipt of my script, Baverstock had hated it, Peter would have pretended not to have read it and would have said to his Controller of Programmes "Oh, dear, I'm sorry. Freddy Shaughnessy's usually so reliable. I'll read it and get to work on it with him."

On the other hand, if Baverstock had said he liked the script, Peter would have said "I thought you would. I had a private session with Freddy last week and we put a few small things right. It's OK for me now."

Thus Peter Willes could hedge his bet, preserve his reputation either way and retain the confidence of his Controller of Programmes. If that is not being devious, perhaps it is being, as we have it on good authority, 'as wise as the serpent'. Peter did an enormous amount for TV Drama, introducing all sorts of playwrights to the medium, including Pinter and Joe Orton, and his taste and flair were undeniable.

Mercifully Baverstock liked my opening script:

James Hadleigh is summoned to Fleet Street by a very senior

Press Baron, Lord Shawcliffe, and offered a tremendous job as Managing Editor of an important national newspaper. It will mean shutting up his lovely house and estate in Yorkshire, left to him by his father, and going to live in London. He will be letting down his tenants and giving up his life in the country which he loves and parting from his horses and his neighbours. James has a confidante with whom he could discuss his dilemma, his late father's sister, Lady Helen Hadleigh, Aunt Helen, who lives in a small house on his estate and has been like a mother to him since his real mother died young.

This looked like a good potential running part and someone for James Hadleigh to play against, someone representing the older generation. The part was beautifully portrayed throughout the series by Ambrosine Phillpotts.

In the end Aunt Helen, and Maxwell, Hadleigh's manservant-chauffeur, were the only two regular characters in the show, apart from Hadleigh himself.

Towards the end of the opening script, Hadleigh has to ponder alone over the choice he must make between London and Fleet Street or Yorkshire and his responsibilities as a landowner.

James plays some music on his tape recorder, a piece by his beloved Delius, and looks out of the window across his broad acres. He can hear his horses neighing in the stables and a night owl hooting. It is early evening. He picks up the telephone and calls Lord Shawcliffe in London to tell him he has finally decided not to take up his kind suggestion. "I've decided that my place is here, in Yorkshire. But thanks for the offer."

*Hadleigh* got off to a good start and soon became very popular. We had an excellent producer, Terry Williams, with whom I got on well. Gerald Harper, a mannered actor but one with immense energy and style, created a fascinating character out of James Hadleigh. He was the essence of privilege but a man with the common touch, a strong sense of duty and of justice. If blunt, plain-speaking local councillors or petty Yorkshire officials who crossed his path at first called James a 'stook oop bluedy lundlord' they were soon overwhelmed by his charm and determination and came to respect him. Whatever part I see Gerald in nowadays, be it in the theatre or on the screen, he will always be James Hadleigh to me.

THROUGHOUT 1966, 1967 and early 1968, before *Hadleigh* started, I had been freelancing, and in 1965 my old friend Kenneth More had not been having too easy a time. He had quarrelled with the all-powerful John Davis of the Rank Organization and was not being offered any movies. He had just married his third wife, the actress Angela Douglas, and I had an idea for a play that I felt would suit them to do together:

A young girl film-fan wins first prize in a movie magazine competition. Her prize is an evening out on the town with a famous film star. What she does not know is that the star's last picture did not do too well: he is slipping at the box office and the whole thing is a publicity stunt to boost the star's image.

The girl is picked up from her humble home in South London by a studio limousine, taken to the studios, dressed, made-up, coiffeured and delivered to a smart restaurant to be photographed dining with the star.

Like Cinderella when midnight comes, she has to surrender the dress and the shoes to go back to the studio people when the stunt is over. But the star, with whom the girl should by now be breathlessly in love, ironically needs her company more than she needs his. It is the Cinderella story in reverse. He wants the evening to go on. She is tired, but politely agrees. So he drives her around London in his open car into the small hours. They visit an all-night coffee-stall on Chelsea Bridge, then sit in his car looking at the river. He pours out his heart to her, about his loneliness, the bitter-sweet life he must lead of worldy success and wealth but no real love and nobody to love him for himself. The girl feels desperately sorry for the star but when he suggests they might get together, she thanks him charmingly for his company and for looking after her so well during the evening, but explains she has to get up early to get to work. Sadly, as dawn breaks, he delivers her to her home in South London and they part.

Kenny and Angie More were dead keen to do the play and I told ATV so. But suddenly, when the day came for Kenny to commit to it, he became covered in confusion. He had just been offered a very big job by the BBC. It was 'a Galsworthy thing' with a nice part and lots of episodes. He couldn't do both and he felt he must go for the money. I could not blame him, so Kenny went off to do young Jolyon in *The Forsythe Saga*, which happily restored his fortunes.

Luckily my play *The Small Hours* was not dependent on Kenny and the producer Pieter Rogers came up with a sensational cast: the film star was played extremely well by Patrick Mcnee who was not for the moment doing Steed in *The Avengers*; Hannah Gordon, who gave an enchanting performance as the girl; an old friend Timothy Bateson, who made a lot out of the small but quite funny part of a tired, blasé press photographer; and an actress I had never seen or heard of before called Penelope Keith, who was quite unbelievably good as a bossy, ruthless, no-nonsense studio publicity woman.

After that I was blue-eyed boy at ATV for a while, because *The Small Hours* came second in the ratings to a popular American Western programme *Wagon Train*. This was unheard of for a single play, and they asked me for another.

I have always been intrigued by the vulnerability of people who are grieving. Especially women. When the emotions are stirred by deep sorrow, it seems that sexual urges are often aroused at the same time. Men sometimes exploit this fact, and a grieving woman will often respond so emotionally to a man's display of care and compassion that she will slip into an erotic situation with him against her better judgement. I am also interested, and have been ever since I saw John van Druten's play *Young Woodley* years ago, in the passion a middle-aged woman can develop for a young man half her age. These two elements came together in my head when ATV asked me for another *Love Story* play. The story I dreamed up this time was simple enough:

A middle-aged business man Charles Raynor and his beautiful wife Elizabeth, in her forties, live close to the golf club in the leafy Sunningdale area. They have recently lost their only son James, who was killed when his Landrover overturned in Iraq while he was working for an oil company. A colleague in the same company, Philip McKay, has flown back to the UK on leave and comes straight from Heathrow to see his dead friend's parents. He is a sensitive and charming young man who feels it his duty to visit them, give them the details of their son's death and hand over to them some of his personal effects. The Raynors are touched and invite Philip to stay with them for a few days before he goes up to Scotland to see an uncle. While Charles Raynor is commuting to the City every day, Elizabeth spends much time alone with her son's friend and a relationship develops between them. Elizabeth is swept off her feet and the attraction is mutual. She tries desperately to conceal and control her feelings but it is a strain. When at the weekend she and Charles have to go to the golf club dance, she invites a young girl neighbour to come with them as a partner for Philip. But Philip spends most of the evening dancing with Elizabeth. The short passionate affair finally ends when Philip leaves one morning. Elizabeth is certain that her husband has never guessed her feelings for their dead son's friend and when she picks Charles up from the station on his return from the City that evening, she just manages to suppress her tears. But on the way home in the car Charles says something to her which makes it clear that he has known about the affair all along but has understood and chosen to say nothing.

The lovely Helen Cherry played the wife exquisitely, and I have always wondered why she never became a very big star. Perhaps she had to spend too much time looking after her husband, Trevor Howard, to have enough time for her own career. But she was lovely in 'Sweet Sorrow' and was rightly praised by the critics.

Soon after that ATV started to make a new anthology-series of plays, under the umbrella title of *Happy Ever After*. It was really the old *Love Story* series proceeding once more under a new title, but there was an insistence on happy endings. 'Sweet Sorrow' would not have qualified.

When invited to contribute to *Happy Ever After* I came up with a bizarre little romantic comedy with the unusual title of 'What's the Matter, Darling, Can't you Sleep?'

While directing commercials during the early '60s I had made one for some indigestion relief tablets. This featured an old familiar spectacle:

> A woman in bed is woken up in the night by her restless husband who is groaning and holding his stomach.
>
> "What's the matter, darling? Can't you sleep?" asks the wife, trying to suppress her impatience.
>
> The husband says "Got terrible indigestion."
>
> The wife says "What you need is one of those marvellous new Katasodiac Tablets," and leaps out of bed to fetch them from the bathroom.

When directing those kind of commercials I always used to marvel at the coolness with which an actor and an actress who had never set eyes on each other before would come calmly onto the set, remove their dressing-gowns and climb into bed together to shoot the scene.

I used to try and alleviate any embarrassment by introducing them as at a party: "Jane this is Harry. Harry, Jane . . ."

The girl would grin wanly and murmur "How do you do?"

I would say "OK, let's rehearse it. Quiet, please . . ."

The story of 'What's The Matter, Darling, Can't You Sleep?' is about a young married couple, short of money, who both have to work. He has a night-time job; she works during the day as a model. She gets a job in a commercial and spends the day in bed on the set with a rather conceited male model. Her young husband is deeply jealous and alarmed but the model proves to be so vain and narcissistic that the little wife is glad to get home.

The wife was charmingly played by Kika Markham. Graham Crowden gave an extremely funny performance as a rather muddled, incompetent film director and Edward Fox appeared briefly as a smooth pinstripe-suited representative of the advertising agency who kept interfering with the filming. I knew the scene well from working for J. Walter Thompson and directing commercials of that sort for Eyeline.

The technique needed for the creation of tension has always been one of my special interests, especially in writing films for the cinema, with its tradition of cross-cutting from, for example, Pearl White trussed up on the railway line to the fast-approaching train, then to the car racing to her rescue.

There are few film makers in the world who have not been inspired by Alfred Hitchcock and people still refer to a suspense sequence in a movie as 'Hitchcockian'. Many books have been written about Hitch's genius for getting that edge-of-your seat tension out of small, seemingly unimportant events.

A chance came my way to exercise this craft by the emergency created at London Weekend Television when Rex Firkin, the producer of a drama series they were making called *Manhunt*, suffered a heart-attack. This happened a few weeks before the company was to start making a second batch of thirteen episodes to follow the first thirteen, which had been highly successful. To replace Firkin, the Script-Editor Andrew Brown was promoted by Stella Richman, who was now Programme Controller of LWT, to produce the second series and I was invited to step in as Script Editor.

*MANHUNT* was a good, early example of the endless *maquis* series we have had over the years about Resistance operations in German-occupied France, 1940-1944. Although David Croft has sent the whole thing up gloriously with his sitcom *'Ullo, 'Ullo*, nevertheless new, serious versions still appear to this day on our screens.

*Manhunt* followed the fortunes of an ill-assorted trio of three people on the run from the Gestapo in Occupied France: an RAF pilot who had been shot down but escaped, a French Resistance fighter, and a beautiful French girl called Nina who has secret knowledge in her head which the Germans badly want. She is a sitting duck for torture, if captured.

The series title-music was the opening bars of Beethoven's Fifth Symphony (V for Victory in Morse Code) which had been the symbol of the BBC's secret broadcasts to the occupied territories.

The three people on the run were Alfred Lynch as the RAF pilot; Peter Barkworth as Vincent, the fussy but brave academic maquisard; and the lovely Cyd Hayman as Nina.

*Manhunt* was a classy, well-made series and, although I say it, probably the best of its kind ever made for TV.

Andrew Brown, a very bright young Australian, was something of an innovator and, as the new producer of *Manhunt*, came up with two novel ideas for episodes which would be challenging but well worth a try. We discussed them in some detail.

The first was to make a whole episode silent, without a word of dialogue. A visual-only script was written, in which the Resistance manage to penetrate a German aircraft factory where a secret new type of fighter is being developed and into which Alfred Lynch as the shot-down RAF pilot, now a British agent, has been infiltrated. Silently at night the group manage to get hold of a vital component of the new aircraft, which is badly needed by British Intelligence. The sequence was very tense and was brilliantly directed by Robert Tronson.

A few eyebrows were raised at the Writers' Guild, whose Council conveyed to me as the Script Editor for the Series that they hoped I would see to it that London Weekend TV did not make a habit of using 'silent' episodes in Drama Series and so dispense with the use of those tiresome, expensive writers.

Andrew's second innovative idea was to play out a whole episode entirely in the railway compartment of a train.

The storyline, to follow the 'silent' episode, required two of our Resistance people on the run, Vincent and Nina, with an Australian cabaret singer who has joined them called Adelaide, played by Maggie Fitzgibbon, to smuggle the stolen aircraft component out of the country by train from Bordeaux to St Malo, where a fishing boat has been instructed to take them a mile offshore under cover of darkness to board a Royal Navy Torpedo Boat and so to England.

It was obvious that such a train journey, with the vital component hidden in a shopping basket, would be hazardous to say the least. Andrew suggested that I might write the train episode, to which I agreed. It would be a challenge but I could see great opportunities for tension in that claustrophobic setting. I suspect Andrew also had in mind the chance to save a little money on sets for this episode but I asked him if I could also have a small section of corridor and the *toilette*. He agreed. So in 'The Train May Be Late' we find Nina and Adelaide sharing a railway compartment with three German sailors returning from leave to La Rochelle, a Wehrmach officer, an SS colonel and a Luftwaffe captain, all in transit to St Malo.

Suspense is generated by the presence of the secret aircraft component concealed in a basket of eggs on the luggage rack. Soon after the train starts Nina is surprised and relieved to find Vincent is on the train. Having no seat, he is lurking outside in the corridor. They have not seen each other since he was captured and tortured in Paris and she went off to live with her captor, a German Army Sergeant called Gratz played by Robert Hardy. They are both overwhelmed with emotion because Vincent is in love with Nina and wants to marry her, but they must not communicate. The only safe place to talk is in the *toilette*, so Nina makes a sign to Vincent and goes out of the compartment down the corridor. Vincent follows her, making sure he is not observed.

Proposal scenes are the hardest to write, in my experience. You need more than just a man saying to a woman "Will you marry me?" and a woman saying"Yes." Sometimes an unusual setting will help, and that was certainly the case in 'The Train May Be Late'.

*Nina*: It's not safe to stay in here too long . . .
*Vincent*: Nobody saw us come in . . . Nina you're pale, you must be so tired. When we get to England you'll have a long rest, somewhere in the country away from the bombing. I don't know, Cornwall, perhaps. I'll find somewhere and then, when it's all over . . . Why are you smiling, Nina? You have such a rare, lovely smile. And I don't blame you.
*Nina*: For what?
*Vincent*: For smiling. It is pretty absurd really. Here am I, an

Anglo-French bachelor approaching forty, rattling through France in a train packed with German soldiers, locked in the *toilette* with a girl almost young enough to be my daughter.

(Nina puts her cheek to his, still smiling affectionately.)

It's not the most appropriate setting for a proposal, dearest Nina, but I do mean it. I do love you deeply and desperately. And when this horror is all over, if it ever is, I want you to marry me.

(He clutches a grip to steady himself.)

If I knelt in the traditional way to ask for your hand, I should probably land on that damned pedal and flush the thing and I refuse to drown my own words of love in that way. So, if you don't mind, I'll remain standing . . .

*Nina*: Vincent, don't. Don't say too much, not just now.

*Vincent*: I can't help it. I've lived with those words inside me for so long. All the time you were away from me. With him.

*Nina*: He wanted to marry me after the war. We were to live in Munich.

*Vincent*: I never thought I'd come to share such deep feelings with a Sergeant in the German Army. Nina, say something to me, for God's sake . . .

*Nina*: Let's just stay together and be content with that. Until we really get away. Please. Kiss me and promise not to say anymore . . . not for the moment.

(A sharp knock on the *toilette* door.)

Oh, God! What do we do?

*Vincent*: (Thinking quickly) You felt ill. I came in to help you. It's all we can say. Loosen your collar and ruffle your hair. Quickly. I'll have to open that door. Are you ready?

The Wehrmach captain outside, who is trying to get in, swallows their explanation and Vincent vanishes down the corridor. The captain notes that Nina is crying. She tries to explain that it's the strain of the war and she is very tired. She resumes her seat in the compartment. The SS officer in the corner looks up and notes that she is back but plainly upset. Suddenly the train grinds to a halt at a station. Sudden commotion and shouting is heard outside on the platform. The Wehrmacht captain comes back into the compartment to report that Gestapo agents have boarded the train. They are searching the compartments for a man they want to question. Adelaide glances up nervously at the shopping basket in the rack. Then Gestapo men come into the compartment to check passes and ask questions. They are looking for a civilian, a man of about forty. Nina is shattered. It must be Vincent and they're bound to find him on the train. The Luftwaffe officer who got out at the station to get some refreshment comes back drunk and starts molesting Nina until he is suddenly told to leave her alone by the SS officer, who questions him about his Squadron, realizes he is not a Luftwaffe officer, seizes his cap, tears off his badge of rank and denounces him as an escaped Polish worker on the run. The SS officer orders the sailors in the compartment to arrest the bogus Luftwaffe officer. He is dragged off the train and, as the train starts off again, we hear a burst of automatic fire from down the platform. Vincent suddenly re-appears. He was held in the stationmaster's office for questioning but his papers were in order and he has been released just in time to scramble aboard the moving train. They detained him because he resembled the wanted Luftwaffe Captain, whose seat he now takes. After a while the train stops abruptly once more. Air raid sirens are heard. The train is raked with machine-gun fire from RAF night fighters. The All-Clear is sounded but a stray bullet appears to have hit and killed the SS Officer who had just started to ask Nina and Adelaide awkward questions. But when the lights come on again Adelaide has a smoking gun in her hand. In the darkness and confusion of the air attack, she has shot the SS Colonel herself, but nobody will ever know. The train goes on a bit, then stops again.

The Group learn that the line ahead has been destroyed by British bombs and they will have to reverse all the way back to Bordeaux. How will they ever get the aircraft component safely into British hands?

'The Train May Be Late' was really quite a breath-taking suspense episode and shows what can be done with a fine director, James Ormerod, eight excellent players in a confined space and the right words for them to say.

The whole thing could have been done on a stage and was a perfect example of what I mean when I say, quite often and sometimes to furious opposition, that TV Drama is really 'electronic theatre'. A cavalry charge on a small TV screen looks like flies crawling across a mirror. What TV drama should be about is 'talking heads', the interplay of characters in a confined space. Alan Bennett recognized and demonstrated this most effectively. The place for big battle scenes and spectacular car chases is on the cinema screen. Television drama should be about people in an enclosed atmosphere, rather than crowds and open panoramas.

## WRITING FOR UPSTAIRS, DOWNSTAIRS

IT was while I was working on *Manhunt* that I was approached by my old colleague from *The Informer*, John Whitney, and the former film art-director, John Hawkesworth, who had been in the Grenadiers with me in the war. These two had now formed a company called Sagitta Films to develop ideas for TV Drama Series and sell them to the production companies.

The three of us had lunch one day to discuss the various series formats they were planning. One was a drama series about a bomb-disposal unit on the Home Front during the recent war. It would feature a company of immensely brave Royal Engineers whose job was to deal with unexploded German bombs that came to light in streets, parks and on beaches. I told the two Johns that in my opinion there were only two possible stories to be got out of such an idea. In one the bomb goes off, in the other it doesn't. How wrong I was. Some years later they made *Danger UXB*, which was an excellent series. They looked at the character, background and family life of each of the featured REs in turn, officers and other ranks, and you just waited for that guy to be blown up or not.

It worked very well and I watched most of the series, partly because John Hawkesworth, with whom I had by then worked for four years on *Upstairs, Downstairs*, kindly cast my younger son David as one of the subalterns in the RE company.

Sagitta had made another first-class drama series called *The*

*Gold Robbers* and soon after that they told me about an idea that had been put to them by Jean Marsh, who had been in *The Informer*, and her friend the actress Eileen Atkins. A great deal has been written and said about the origins of London Weekend's world-wide, award-winning series that John Hawkesworth and John Whitney cooked up and into which they brought me as Story and Script Editor and key scriptwriter, Stella Richman, by then Controller of LWT, having made my presence in the team a condition of giving it the go-ahead. By the time I was free to work on it, the two Johns had worked out a very viable format or 'bible', as the initial proposal document is called. I made some changes, creating the aristocratic Lady Marjorie and the Southwold family in place of Bellamy's actress second wife called Gail, and added a few other ideas. John Whitney left the day-to-day work on the writing and production to John Hawkesworth and me, and we moved into London Weekend's office tower at Stonebridge Park close to the Wembley Studios, where we started to plan and ultimately record the show.

Anyone interested in the nuts and bolts of making a world-class TV Drama Series should read an excellent American book called *Backstage With Upstairs, Downstairs* by Patty Floyd. It is published by The St Martins Press, New York. The authoress is the widow of a Tulsa, Oklahoma banker who became fascinated with *Updown* after seeing it on PBS in the States. Anxious to write a book about it, she contacted John Hawkesworth, me and others concerned before coming to London to stay at the Dorchester and gather data. She talked to the actor Simon Williams who played James Bellamy and to Jeremy Paul and Rosemary Anne Sisson, two of our best writers who contributed richly to the show, and to others. I gave her several long interviews and lent her all my notes on planning the development of the

10. Yvonne Ball as Principal Boy and John Salew as the Pantomime Dame in the film *The Impersonator.*

11. Honor Blackman and Patrick Holt in the film *Suspended Alibi*

12. The author on location for The End of the Road with, L. to R: Finlay Currie, Duncan Lamont, and director Wolf Rilla.

13. Charles Gray, Dan Ogilvey and Nicola Pagett in a scene from *Upstairs, Downstairs.*

14. David Langton and Rachel Gurney with Gordon Jackson in a scene from *Upstairs, Downstairs*

15. and with Lesley-Anne Down and the author at a summer fête.

16. The author receives a Writers' Guild Award on behalf of the *Upstairs, Downstairs* team from Sir Michael Balcon, with Susannah York.

17. L. to R.: Jeanne Moreau, Anthony Higgins and Norma West at a rehearsal for the TV play 'The Last Seance'.

situations and characters; storylines, some used, some discarded; memos and correspondence with the LWT management; and every kind of document which could help her to follow the progress of the show from its initial, germinal idea by Jean Marsh, who took the part of Rose in the series, and Eileen Atkins, right through to the final episode. By that time we had won two 'Emmies' in a row in the USA and awards from all over the world. The show was initially shown in some forty countries and had become almost a cult.

My first job as Story and Script Editor was to write the full storyline for each of the thirteen episodes that made up each batch or series and submit them to the Controller who, by the time we started Series II, was Cyril Bennett.

Throughout the whole show I liaised very closely with Martin Case, our casting director, for reasons of economy.

*Updown* was made on a very modest budget and, of all the regular characters, both family and servants, we could not afford to use every one of them in every episode. Martin was able to get actors and actresses at a reasonable rate by allowing them to do other jobs when not scheduled for *Updown*. Thus, when later in the series I began planning the episodes only a few weeks before rehearsals, I would ask Martin to tell me which characters I might use.

I would ask "Who have I got for Episode 6?"

He would consult a chart and say "You can use Mrs Bridges but not Ruby; Edward but not Daisy, James, Hazel and Richard."

I would say "Fine," and go to my office, cut out pieces of papers with those names on them and deal them on to a table like a pack of cards face up. By staring at the names and thinking of the normal relationships between the characters I could often get an idea for a story to fit them. It was a definite help. For example, an episode I wrote, entitled 'Joy

Ride', had to be planned at story stage with very few people. I was given just James, Richard, Lady Prudence, Virginia and two servants.

I started to think of the generation gap and of James as being almost the same age as his young stepmother. James was bored and missing the excitement of the war, and I thought he was the sort of chap who in the '20s would buy himself an aeroplane, keep it on an aerodrome like Stag Lane and fly it for fun. I had Lady Pru to use in the story, too. She was known to have been secretly in love with Richard for years. By thinking of those four main people an idea suddenly emerged.

James asks Virginia to come for a flip with him in his plane. But Richard wants her on that same afternoon to hear him make an important speech in the House of Lords. Virginia is torn. It is a gloriously fine day. Virginia is young enough to prefer a flight in an aeroplane with her stepson to a boring afternoon in the Lords with her elderly husband. Conflict. James wins and takes Virginia up in the Avro 504K but they get lost in bad weather over the Channel and are reported missing. To comfort Richard in his anxiety, Lady Pru volunteers to spend the evening with him and wait up for news. She sleeps on the morning-room sofa. At dawn the phone rings. Stag Lane reports James safely landed. Pru goes rather sadly home. When the lost flyers return home Richard bawls out his son – mainly out of fear – and Virginia feels very guilty and penitent. What makes things worse is that the Press have got hold of the story from the aerodrome and are running headlines like 'Peer's wife missing in airplane with stepson', which cause eyebrows to be raised among the Bellamy's friends.

That episode was written in a tearing hurry over a weekend, to replace one that had to be scrapped at the last moment. It was not the greatest story but it had a certain tension, and grew out of Martin Case's tight rationing scheme for players.

It was a little sad for me and the viewers to think of James coming between Richard and his enchanting second wife, Virginia, over this aeroplane adventure. For it had not been many years before that she and Richard had decided to marry, inspiring a more orthodox proposal scene than Vincent and Nina's in *Manhunt*.

Virginia is dining with Richard at the Hyde Park Hotel Grill, soon after arriving in London with her children from Scotland.
*Virginia*: You're being so kind, really spoiling me.
*Richard*: How, spoiling you?
*Virginia*: I didn't write and tell you our train got in at seven-ten meaning you to meet us . . . it was just by way of information.
*Richard*: How could I leave you standing on a draughty platform with two young children and a senile Nanny?
*Virginia*: The porter would have got us a taxi. And to come here first and make sure our rooms were ready and order flowers . . .
*Richard*: The flowers were to welcome you to London.
*Virginia*: I know.
*Richard*: . . . with the compliments of the Hyde Park Hotel.
*Virginia*: That's not true. Is it? (Pause) Did you really mean what you said in your last letter?
*Richard*: Every word of it.
*Virginia*: You'd be taking on three of us, you know, and a Nanny. Susan's ten now and William's six. Quite a circus.
*Richard*: Delightful. A new, young family.
*Virginia*: They'll scream and fight and rush up and down stairs . . . and invade your dressing room while you're shaving and require endless games of hide and seek . . .
*Richard*: I don't care how many screaming children you have. Or that you once nearly got me the sack from the Admiralty or that I took the most violent dislike to you the first time we met. I asked you – in writing, don't forget – to marry me, Virginia my dearest, because I have fallen deeply in love with you. I find you amusing, brave, warm-hearted and utterly adorable and I want you to think over very carefully the prospect of becoming my wife – but not to let it spoil your dinner.

*Virginia*: I won't.
*Richard*: Won't what?
*Virginia*: I won't let it spoil my dinner, Richard, because I don't have to think it over. I already have and I accept.

On *Updown*, once the storylines and thus the general direction of a new Series had been approved, I would take off my Story Editor's hat and put on my Script Editor's hat. Then, in consultation with John Hawkesworth, I would start to commission writers. I usually wrote three key scripts in each batch myself: the first, one in the middle and the last one to carry over into the next Series. This was to create what was called a 'house style' and ensure consistency. Once the scripts were delivered, John and I would both read them, discuss them and agree on what needed to be changed. I would then call in the author, go through the script line by line, and ask him or her to carry out any structural or dialogue alterations we felt necessary. If all was agreed I would then send the writer off to rewrite. There was nearly always a small amount of 'tidying' for me to do, such as minor word changes or a phrase or reference that was not quite correct for the setting or the period. Otherwise the writer's revised draft was usually satisfactory. Some of the writers we commissioned, however, were either unwilling or incapable of getting their work to a state that was acceptable and they resulted in the awkward, delicate occasions when I had to say "I think you must now leave it with me. I shall revise it to a state that is acceptable to John and myself, show it to you, then ask you to make up your mind whether you wish to keep your credit on the script or take your name off it."

This has always been normal practice on TV series. On those occasions I found that most writers chose to keep their credit. Whatever changes were made by me to a script, the original contract for it was in the writer's name so that all the residual earnings, UK and Foreign, would automatically come to him or her anyway – even if (as in some cases) the script carried no screenwriter's name on it.

I did not much relish an episode going on the air with no writer's name on it as it indicated that there had probably been trouble. At the same time I did not think it appropriate, even if the Script Editor had written four fifths of the script by the time it was recorded, to advertise the fact on the screen by putting my own name on it as author. That was just not done. One script for *Updown* actually won a Writers' Guild Award for a lady writer who had, in the end, only contributed a third of it. But that's all in the game.

There was only one case where a writer lost out altogether and I still feel bad about it, to this day. Owen Holder had been commissioned to write a script about Lady Marjorie having a secret love affair with an officer on leave from the North West Frontier.

John Hawkesworth and the director disliked Holder's script rather more than I did and John elected to rewrite the script himself. He thought I was too busy to do so. I was not, but he was the boss, and he made a fresh contract for the job with himself so Owen Holder never got a penny.

As soon as we received the go-ahead for *Upstairs, Downstairs* I realised it was immensely important that we were making a series about a household, not just about a house. If you took away the façade of No. 165, Eaton Place, Belgravia and looked into it as one looks into a dolls' house, you would see the whole life of the building functioning on every floor: the basement floor with the servants in the kitchen, scullery and the servants' hall; the Bellamy family in the front hall, morning room, dining-room and drawing-room; the family in their bedrooms upstairs and, high up in the attic, the maids' bedrooms, etc.

The secret was that whatever happened inside that house

or outside it, which involved the family, must at the same time involve the servants and *vice versa*. An early storyline, which John Harrison scripted beautifully, expressed this point exactly:

The Bellamy daughter, Elizabeth, who is a rebel, despises the 'deb season' and the marriage market implied by it. So she runs away from a grand ball at Londonderry House for which she has been dressed, had her hair done and got ready by the head housemaid Rose, acting as her lady's maid.

When Elizabeth comes back from the ball early, she gets hell from her parents. But the one person she has really let down and disappointed more than anyone else is Rose, who is furious. The head housemaid is horrified by the behaviour of her young mistress and severely rebukes her for letting down the whole household.

Rose's attitude symbolizes the curious pride a staff of servants would often take the members of the family they served.

An early episode of mine was called 'Why Is Her Door Locked'?

Mrs Bridges [brilliantly portrayed by Angela Baddeley] has a kind of nervous breakdown after her little Irish kitchenmaid hangs herself. The old cook feels deprived of a daughter figure and in her grief steals a baby from a pram in Lupus Street, Pimlico on her day off. Once the baby has been located by Hudson, acting as a sleuth, and before the police become involved, Richard and Marjorie journey down to Pimlico by car to return the child to its parents and attempt to bribe them with money to say no more about it. They are anxious to protect Mrs Bridges, who is their cook and indispensable to them. Unfortunately the baby's parents disapprove of wealthy aristocrats with servants, refuse to take the money and go to the police. So Mrs Bridges ends up in court where the butler, Hudson, finally gets her off the hook by offering her marriage in the future.

Earlier, the stolen baby's father, Webber, has sneered at Hudson for being a butler when the latter goes to intercede with the wronged couple:
*Webber*: I wouldn't stand for it, running up and down stairs, bowing and scraping and answering bells like a bleeding monkey on a stick.
*Hudson*: We all serve a master, Mr Webber, unless we happen to be King Edward himself, which we are not . . . I work for a Member of Parliament who is a man of charm and character, married into one of the great ruling families of the land with 400 years of political influence behind it . . . I know better than to seek a higher station in life than that to which I was born . . .

Of all the characters in *Upstairs, Downstairs* Hudson was for me always the most important, the anchor-man of the whole series, who held the balance between the family and the staff. He was a puritanical hypocrite, two-faced, smug and a snob. But he was real. The late Gordon Jackson, who created him, disliked the character but was magnificent in the part and richly deserved the Emmy he received in America for his portrayal of the Scottish butler. He made Hudson so true and believable that, shortly after the Series began running on ITV, a letter was received by London Weekend Television from an elderly lady in Leamington Spa who wrote to say that, since her butler, Mitchell, who had been with her for thirty years, was becoming old and deaf and would soon have to retire from service, she would be most grateful if London Weekend would ask Hudson to come and see her for an interview for the position.

English butlers as stage characters have delighted theatre audiences and many of the actors who have played them for over a century, especially those appearing in light comedy. Starting with Sir James Barrie's Admirable Crichton and on through the plays of Oscar Wilde, Frederick Lonsdale, Nöel Coward, Somerset Maugham and William Douglas-Home, stage butlers have provided a wealth of humour and entertainment. I used to tell William Douglas-Home, an old friend of mine who was a great fan of *Upstairs, Downstairs*, that in my opinion he had written one of the best lines ever written for a butler in his comedy *The Chiltern Hundreds*. In one scene the family are at dinner, discussing some intimate matter relating to a member of the family when Lady Lister, noticing that the butler, Beecham, is still in the room, clears her throat and murmurs "*Pas devant le domestique*" whereupon Lord Lister grunts "What's that mean?" and Beecham, as he refills his master's wine glass, murmurs "Not in front of the servant, m'lord."

In a Drama Series it is often possible for a good actor cast in a small one-off part to make so much of his brief chance as to earn himself or herself a lasting place in the show. An example of this was Gareth Hunt, who made a big impact in a small one-off part as Trooper Norton, James Bellamy's wartime soldier-servant. Norton comes to Eaton Place while on leave from the Front, to visit the family while James is still wounded and languishing in a base hospital in France.

Gareth played Trooper Norton with such authority and feeling that John Hawkesworth and I decided we must bring him back later. So I devised a way of Frederick Norton taking over as footman after Edward had married Daisy, the housemaid, and the couple had gone off to 'better themselves'. In the end, Christopher Beeny as Edward and Jacqui Tong as Daisy, did return to the household at Eaton Place as Chauffeur and Maid and were there at the end. By then Frederick Norton had gone off to work in films.

The episode of the King's visit to dine and play bridge at Eaton Place, 'Guest of Honour', must have been one of the most widely seen television plays ever, because in addition to the series being run and re-run many times all over the world 'Guest of Honour' has sometimes been shown on its own as a single play, as it was at the Prix d'Italia in Venice, 1973.

Having had the idea, I hesitated to put the King on the screen because in 1973 recent or current royalty were not supposed to be portrayed on television. I originally planned to show the King only from the point of view of the footman serving the vegetables at dinner. We would just see the back of his head or, later, stout fingers holding a cigar – rather as one used to see Jesus Christ in Cecil B de Mille movies as an outstretched hand or the back of a haloed head. But I was persuaded that it would be OK to show the Monarch in full, so I did. Soon after that episode, ATV did a whole series about King Edward VII, starring as the King that fine actor Timothy West, whose father Harry Lockwood West had played him in 'Guest of Honour'. Lockwood West was very good in the role of the ageing king but I could never understand why the make-up department did not stuff him with cushions to create the famous 'tum-tum' which earned him his nickname. Lockwood West was far too thin and slight for King Edward VII.

The dramatic as well as the comedy climax of the play comes when the King is about to leave the Bellamy house at the exact moment that the family doctor Foley, who has been summoned to attend Sarah, upstairs in labour, arrives on the doorstep and rings the bell.

(Hudson knows who is outside and hesitates to open the door.)

*Richard*: Open the door for His Majesty, please, Hudson.

(Hudson does so and Dr Foley comes face to face with the King, whom he mistakes for the butler.)

*Dr Foley*: You'd better take me straight to the young woman's bedroom and ask someone to fetch hot water and clean towels.

(Foley recognizes the King. His jaw drops and he scuttles quickly in and up the main stairs, clutching his Gladstone bag. Moments later Marjorie and Richard are explaining and apologizing to the King.)

*Marjorie*: One of my servants has been taken ill; sir, the doctor had to be sent for in a hurry . . .
*Richard*: We do apologize.
*King*: (Highly amused) The fellow asked me to accompany him to some young woman's bedroom . . . who do you suppose he thought I was, eh?

'Guest of Honour' ends with Rose coming down from Sarah's room where her old friend has been suddenly confined for the birth of what is in fact her illegitimate child by the son of the house, Captain James. As Rose descends the stairs slowly into the servants' hall with moist eyes, the other servants look at her anxiously. She tells them quietly "She's all right but . . . it was a little boy."

Of course, since that episode was shown we've had a free-for-all and the royal family has been portrayed mercilessly on TV, culminating in *Spitting Images*.

For 'Guest of Honour' I was greatly helped by an old friend, Mrs Roland Cubitt. She and her sister, Violet Trefusis, were the daughters of King Edward's mistress, Mrs George Keppel. In 'Guest of Honour' the Bellamys invite Alice Keppel to dine, because the King enjoys her company as a partner for bridge as well as for other activities. When I consulted Sonia Cubitt, she told me how her mother at dinner parties would watch the King across the table and, if she saw His Majesty becoming bored by a guest and drumming his fingers on the table, she would quickly intervene by saying something across the table to the King, thus encouraging general conversation. I used that ploy in my script. Sonia Cubitt also lent us a pair of her mother's earrings to be worn in the show by Mary Kenton, the actress who played Alice Keppel – an interesting touch of historical realism.

At that time Sonia's grand-daughter, Camilla Shand, as yet unmarried to Andrew Parker-Bowles, had become a close friend of the present Prince of Wales, who was still a bachelor. It looked like a case of history repeating itself. Sonia Cubitt was delighted by her then unmarried grand-daughter's close friendship with the heir to the throne but, mercifully, Sonia died before the Prince married and then separated from his wife. Sonia would have been deeply upset by subsequent events.

It is perhaps wrong to single out individual acting contributions to the show but it must be said that, after Gordon Jackson's Hudson, Pauline Collins really got the show off the ground as Sarah, and went on being miraculously good throughout the series until she and the Bellamy's chauffeur Thomas, who was her real-life husband John Alderton, finally married and went off together to set start up a garage in Kilburn.

One treasured souvenir I have of Pauline's lovely performance is a gramophone record of her singing 'What Are We Going To Do With Uncle Arthur?' In one episode Sarah was seen performing in a rather low-down, boisterous music hall-pub, and preferring to keep the Performing Rights of what she sang 'in the family', i.e. in the series, we decided to create a song for her out of Sandy Faris' jaunty, racy end-music, used over the end credits of each show, with a lyric I wrote to fit the tune:

> What are we going to do with Uncle Arthur?
> A blinkin' stallion is Uncle Arthur.
> When he goes a-strolling in the park,
> watch your step, girls,
> especially after dark . . .

Historical events such as the Great War and the General Strike in 1926 affected the servants at 165 Eaton Place who shared the tensions of the time with their employers. It was a good rule to think always of how both upstairs and downstairs would react to any given crisis in the house.

One of the major sensations during the long run of *Upstairs, Downstairs* (with sixty-eight Episodes) occurred in my script called 'Miss Forrest'. This ended with Richard Bellamy dictating to his new typist, Hazel Forrest, a radiogram to his wife, Lady Marjorie, who was on her way to New York in the *Titanic*.

I have to confess that I pinched this idea and others from Nöel Coward. One Long Leave from Eton in the winter of 1930 I had been taken to Drury Lane to see *Cavalcade*, a shattering experience which I have never quite forgotten. I was completely knocked out by the *Titanic* scene, the Wartime Station scene with the Hospital trains arriving from the Front, and the Bank Holiday Seaside scene before the outbreak of war. I have often reflected since that *Updown* took us five TV Series of 68 episodes in all, spread over three years, to tell a story which Nöel Coward told effectively in one evening. *Cavalcade* was another story of an English family and their servants living from Edwardian times through the Great War and into the Jazz age of the '20s and '30s.

Although most of the critics praised my *coup de théatre* by sending Lady Marjorie to a watery grave aboard the *Titanic*, I was pulled up short by the *Daily Telegraph* TV reviewer when I used the same technique later in the Series by letting a place name send shudders of hindsighted drama down viewers' spines. It was in the Great War and Ruby, the gormless kitchen maid, wanted to leave and do war work. So she went out one morning and returned for servants' hall lunch to inform Hudson that she had got herself a good job in a war factory. When asked where, she said "A place called Silvertown." To those who knew this name Silvertown had tragic reverberations, telling us that Ruby would be blown up in the dreadful explosion that ripped apart the big ammunition factory down the Thames Estuary, killing a large number of girl workers. But mercifully Ruby survived.

The reason why Lady Marjorie did not survive her trip to the States was that Rachel Gurney wanted to quit the series. Although John Hawkesworth and I took her to lunch to try and persuade her to stay, she was adamant. For one thing she was afraid of having to age in the Series and end up in a grey wig. But a stronger reason was that she found the character of Lady Marjorie unbearably snobbish and condescending.

One line I had written for her to say to her son was "Never apologize to a servant, James. They only take advantage." She hated that line and had difficulty in getting it out, but when she objected I reminded her that it was not the actress Rachel Gurney displaying such an attitude but Lady Marjorie Bellamy, speaking in 1912. I also predicted that waves of public sorrow and grief for her would follow that fatal name *Titanic* in Richard's cablegram to the ship at sea. It was a 'shivers-down-the-spine' word.

I once made a list of my favourite film clichés and high up on my list was a familiar 'shivers-down-the-spine' scene that graced many an early twentieth-century movie script. It is summer 1914. A wife asks her husband across the breakfast table "Anything in the papers today, dear?" – to which the husband replies "Not much. Just some Archduke has been murdered somewhere. Pass the marmalade, would you?"

IN the autumn of 1974 I sat down sadly to write the story-lines for what John and I both realized must be the final, closing series of *Upstairs, Downstairs*. It would be impossible to continue with the show any longer because we had made the mistake (or was it?) from the outset of moving the Bellamy family and their servants through history.

It is comparatively easy to make a series with its characters locked into one limited period of time: Regency,

Victorian, Edwardian, or whatever, as long as you do not refer in the text to historical events in the background and so pin-point the date. Then you can go on in that period for as long as you like. But we always felt that the running background of world events: the Boer War, the death of King Edward VII, the Great War, the General Strike, the Armistice, and the Peace Celebrations of 1919, and so on, gave the show its special socio-historical interest, and it enabled a politician's household to discuss events outside the house as they would have done in reality. It was fun to have Richard come in from the House of Commons and tell Marjorie what Austen Chamberlain had just told him at lunch, or to mention that Mr Balfour had said how much he had enjoyed staying at Southwold, or to have Richard receive a telegram of congratulations in verse on his Viscountcy from Lord Curzon. I once called the series 'an exercise in Edwardian name-dropping', which, in a sense, it was. But as the series progressed through a span of almost thirty years – from the Liberal landslide under Campbell Bannerman in 1905, to 1932 when Geogiana married Lord Stockbridge – the ages of our characters did not progress relatively. The butler, Hudson, was a man in his fifties when the series opened in Edwardian London, so that by 1932 he would have been well over seventy and becoming frail and probably deaf. Likewise, Geogiana had been a nurse in the Great War but still looked young and fresh when she married Lord Stockbridge in 1932, fourteen years after the Armistice.

Georgiana's wedding was really the last highlight of the series and Cyril Bennett, our Controller at London Weekend, was so vexed at the idea of *Upstairs, Downstairs* coming to an end that he talked John and me into making three extra episodes for the last series, Series V. Thus the whole show ran for a total of 68 episodes. John called those extra episodes 'the gussets', because they had been slotted in to fill out the show. But the show was really over.

In my last batch of storylines, written on August 22nd, 1974, I wrote:

> After the wedding is over and Geogiana has flown off to Le Touquet in an aeroplane for her honeymoon, Hudson and Mrs Bridges go to Richard and Virginia and announce that they feel the time has come for them to retire to the little boarding-house in Hastings, left to Hudson by his sister. They will have the children of the nobility to stay there with their Nannies for the summer holidays. Edward and Daisy are to go and work for Miss Georgiana and Lord Stockbridge in their new house on the Duke of Hampshire's estate. With James now dead, there is little point in Richard and Virginia staying on at Eaton Place, which is too large and expensive for them to keep up. So the house will be put on the market. The Bellamys will take Virginia's children with them and find a smaller house just outside London. Rose will go with them as Virginia's maid and to look after William and Alice.
>
> A few months later we see removal vans outside No. 165. Inside the house the hall is deserted and empty of all furniture and fittings. There are picture marks on the walls up the stairs. Rose, alone in the silent hall, hears echoes from the past, the ghostly voices of Alfred, Lady Marjorie, Sir Geoffrey Dillon, Sarah. She shudders a little, and locks the front door of the house. Then, taking one last look round, she goes down to the basement in her outdoor clothes to go out and hand over the keys to the estate agents round the corner, closing the familiar back-door on her home for the past thirty years . . . and her brainwave.

This last little in-joke was, of course, a reference to Jean Marsh's and Eileen Atkins's creative contribution to the show. The germinal idea was theirs.

# THE FRUITS OF SUCCESS

AFTER *Upstairs, Downstairs* came to an end London Weekend Television's Controller Cyril Bennett pounced on the Hudson-Bridges boarding house idea as a potential spin-off. If he could not go on with *Updown,* then at least he wanted to exploit its success with a new series. But John Hawkesworth already had other plans. He had read Daphne Fielding's book about Rosa Lewis, the famous cook and friend of King Edward VII, whom the King set up in the Cavendish Hotel in Jermyn Street. The book was called *The Duchess of Jermyn Street* and John wanted to do it as a series for the BBC about Rosa Lewis, whom I happened to know quite well before the war. I was one of a number of young men of my generation who enjoyed dropping into the Cavendish before and during the war for a glass of free champagne and a laugh with that outrageous woman in her gilt and plush *maison d'assignation*.

I could not resist teasing John Hawkesworth by pointing out that Rosa Lewis was technically an off-stage 'spin-off' character from *Updown*, because Lady Marjorie had once talked of getting her in to cook for an important dinner party at the time when Mrs Bridges was in custody for stealing a baby. Nevertheless, John invited me to join him on the new series, but I declined for two reasons. First, I felt that we would be going over the same ground all over again: Edwardian London, young Guards officers, scandalous parties and the Great War. Second, I had cooked up a series of my own which I very much wanted to do. In the event John made a great success of *Duke Street* and I managed to sell my series idea to ATV's Lew Grade, but only as an afternoon soap-opera. It was called *The Cedar Tree*.

After *Updown* I longed to do a series-serial set in the middle and late '30s, which was my own era. As a young man in my twenties I had often stayed in country houses with families where there were daughters, for some reason often three. I may also have been inspired in part by J. B. Priestley's wonderful play about three sisters, *Time and the Conways*, which I had seen in its original production at the Duchess Theatre shortly before the war. There is something appealing about three sisters. Perhaps that was why Tchekov made such a success of the subject.

By the '70s I found it profoundly moving and sad to look back to the pre-war era when my friends and I were all young and carefree. It was like turning the pages of a faded photograph album to look at snaps of young girls whom you knew and loved laughing at the camera on picnics in hayfields, paddling on windswept beaches, sailing, playing tennis or croquet; and wondering what became of them, whom they had married, whether they lived or died young, and if were they happy.

Parents with several daughters in those pre-war days had to keep their houses filled during the holidays with reasonably presentable young men, hoping that their daughters would meet and marry someone 'suitable'. So eligible young bachelors were invited to stay for the weekend to partner the girls at the pony club dance or go riding with them over the downs or play charades with them after dinner.

My series *The Cedar Tree* did not jump backwards and forwards in time as did *Time And The Conways* but I used the second world war, as Priestley used the first war, as a kind of landmark in a family's history. Remembering the houses I had stayed in during the '30s, I invented the Bournes. Commander Arthur Bourne, played by Philip Latham, had served with distinction in the Navy in the Great War and his wife, Helen, played by Susan Engel (and how good she was!) was the daughter of an old Eton housemaster, delightfully played by Cyril Luckham; Arthur Bourne's mother, Lady Bourne, was that splendid veteran, Joyce Carey. Jean Taylor-Smith was the old Scottish family nanny. And the three Bourne daughters, all named after queens of England, were Elizabeth (Sally Osborn), Anne (Jennifer Lonsdale) and Victoria (Susan Skipper). I really loved that family and therefore that cast, because they were all my own creation and really closer to me in a way than the Bellamys had been.

In one early episode of *The Cedar Tree* the middle daughter, Anne, is asked to a New Years's Eve fancy dress dance at a nearby friends' house. Her father has been in a bad mood all day because he has turned down an offer to write for a magazine his account of a famous naval action in which he had taken part during the war, feeling that he would be cashing in on the deaths of his comrades who were killed in his ship. So, to his wife's disappointment, he has declined to write the article and thus has renounced the fee, money which the Bournes badly need.

That evening Anne comes downstairs in a revealing Oriental slave costume, ready to be picked up by some friends for the fancy dress dance.

Arthur is outraged and orders his daughter to go upstairs and put on something decent. "I won't have a daughter of mine parading herself in front of half the county looking like some cheap tart in a waterfront café in Hong Kong. Go upstairs and change at once!"

There is a fierce argument, and when the car comes to fetch Anne she defies her father and dashes out of the house to go with her friends to the dance. The next day, after much sulking and an atmosphere of gloom in the house, Anne is persuaded by her grandfather to go into her father's study and apologize for her behaviour.

The resulting scene still moves me.

As *The Cedar Tree* passed through those years from 1934 to 1938 I was able, as in *Updown*, to comment on the events of the time such as the 1930 Financial Crisis, the rise of Hitler, the Roehm Massacres in 1934, the Death of King George V and the Abdication of Edward VIII, as well as Abyssinia in 1936, Munich and the Spanish Civil War.

A very early girl friend of mine, to whom I had written passionate love-letters from Eton, was one of the many daughters of the Howard de Walden family, Priscilla Scott-Ellis, known as Pip. She had rebelled against London Society when she was twenty-one and gone off with a friend to Spain to be a nurse on Franco's side in the Civil War, eventually marrying a Spanish Grandee. This provided a basis for the youngest Bourne daughter, Vicky, to do likewise.

In *The Cedar Tree* I had to perform one of the saddest acts of what I call 'character assassination' I ever had to perpetrate. It was almost worse than sending Lady Marjorie Bellamy down in the *Titanic*.

For some reason, which I have forgotten, Jennifer Lonsdale, who played the middle daughter, Anne, had to leave the serial (it was a long-running series-serial, like a soap opera) and Susan Engel, as Mrs Bourne, was also due to leave the show, for a theatre commitment.

Anticipating this sad event, I made Anne suddenly start developing bad headaches and blurred vision. The family wonder whether it could be connected with a bad fall she had earlier in the year on her beloved mare Tallulah, while riding in a point-to-point. A Harley Street specialist advises the Bournes to send their daughter to Freiburg to consult a very renowned German brain specialist. So Helen Bourne sets off for Germany via the Hook of Holland with her middle daughter and it is expected that they will be back in time for Christmas. But weeks and months go by and Anne is detained in the clinic. I am afraid I rather cruelly kept up the family's hope for the return of Helen Bourne and Anne, knowing quite well that they were never coming back. Hopeful news that Anne was responding to treatment kept filtering through and soon they were due back within a week. Then comes a telephone call late at night. Nanny is asleep in the nursery. She hurries to answer the phone. A foreign voice comes over a crackling line wanting to speak urgently to Commander Bourne. Nanny can just make out that a terrible fire has swept through the hotel where Anne and Helen are staying. Later it is confirmed that both Anne and her mother have died in the fire . . .

It was a sad time on the show. I can remember to this day writing the scene when the family return to the house after the funeral and Joyce Carey, as old Lady Bourne, sinks into a chair and says quietly "It's times like these that make it so hard to believe in God."

On the subject of Joyce Carey there was alarm early on in *The Cedar Tree* when in one episode old Lady Bourne is taken seriously ill while her son, Arthur, is somewhere abroad and they cannot contact him. Lady Bourne has been rushed into the London Clinic.

Joyce had read the script that took her into the Clinic but knew nothing about the following script which had not yet been distributed to the cast.

As I left the studio restaurant after lunch one day, I felt a frail hand clutch at my sleeve and turned to find Joycey looking up at me with great concern on her face. She said "You're not going to kill off poor old Granny, are you?"

"Certainly not," I said. "She recovers and lives to a great age."

Joyce smiled with obvious relief.

It is a terrible power you hold in your hands as a Script Editor. You can play God in deciding how people are to live or die. But the death warrant usually comes from the Front Office. Either an actor's agent has said that he wants more money for his client in the next series, which the company refuses to pay; or the actor wants to do another job; or his role has deteriorated for lack of story ideas.

For *The Cedar Tree* I again had control of the series, with full responsibility for the stories and development. This also meant being in charge of the writing team so that I was able to offer a *Cedar Tree* script to my old Ealing colleague T. E. B. Clarke, who happened to be looking for TV work after a long career spent writing Ealing comedies like *Hue And Cry*, *The Lavender Hill Mob* and *Passport To Pimlico*.

It is always good to be in a position to assist people you have admired in your youth and I had long admired the theatre director, Michael MacOwan, whose wonderful productions of *Mourning Becomes Electra* and Priestley's *Music At Night* I had seen at the Westminster before the war. Later, in Coronation year, he directed a distinguished production of Shaw's *The Apple Cart* with Nöel Coward as King Magnus and Margaret Leighton as Orinthia and had gone on to run the excellent drama school, LAMDA.

While *The Cedar Tree* was in production I heard from a mutual friend that MacOwan was looking for work as an actor and I was able to persuade the producer, Ian Fordyce, to offer him a small part as a country doctor. While he was in the series I enjoyed hearing from him about the old days of the Amner Hall season at the Westminster, which was to me a kind of golden age in the theatre.

*The Cedar Tree* did wonders for the ITV afternoon viewing figures and Lew Grade was reluctant to promote it to Prime Time in the evening, despite repeated calls from the Press and public for it to be shown at a later hour. Ironically, it was finally upgraded to an evening slot at precisely the moment that I received a huge, lucrative offer from

Hollywood. I had seen my creation through some fifty-five episodes and now willingly handed over the editorship to the highly experienced Basil Dawson, whose wife, Felicity Douglas, had been one of my principal writers throughout. I accepted the Hollywood offer and left them to get on with it. *The Cedar Tree* came to an end when I was up to my neck in my new big project but this, too, petered out, proving to be one of the great disappointments of my career.

THERE have been three major disappointments in my writing life and I will mention them, but only briefly since none of them ever hit the screen.

As a result of the success of *Upstairs, Downstairs* in the USA I was approached by two Hollywood movie producers, Arlene Sellars and Alec Winitsky, to adapt Robert Elegant's vast novel *Dynasty* into an international mini-series. They had acquired sponsorship finance from Proctor and Gamble, the soap empire, and it looked like a money-no-object kind of project.

The novel deals with Mary Osgood, the daughter of an English regimental bandmaster, who arrives in Hong Kong in 1900, soon after her mother's death, to join her father, at about the time of the Boxer Rising. Mary is so beautiful that she catches the eye of a young British officer in the Garrison who takes her to a ball at Government House. Here her father is conducting the band, and from his rostrum he can see his daughter dancing with a half-caste young man. This is Charles Sekloong, eldest son of the Irish-Chinese trading millionaire, Sir Joseph Seekloong. The couple eventually marry and found a large dynasty of descendants in all quarters of the globe. The story spans half a century of Hong Kong's and China's history, including the Sun-Yat-Sen revolution, and it highlights the clash of cultures, Oriental and Occidental.

I was paid a lot of money and worked extremely hard to

adapt this vast, sprawling novel into seven one hour episodes. After several weeks' work I delivered a full treatment and three episodes.

Soon the producers told me "P and G just love your scripts."

All seemed to be well, and there were many lunches and dinners at the Connaught and Claridge's during which there was talk about locations and directors. The name of Fred Zinneman was mentioned and Franklin Shaffner. Then it went all quiet for a while. Sellars and Winitsky didn't come over again. I delivered the balance of my scripts and got paid. My agent received a sizeable dollar cheque drawn on the Wells Fargo Bank in Los Angeles. But it was not long before I heard that Arlene and Alex had started shooting a new movie with Robert Redford and Shirley Maclaine. End of story.

The sadness is that you never hear exactly why these great projects have been abandoned. Was it the scripts or could they not get the right cast or director or was the financial backing withdrawn? One can only guess. The official explanation in this case, which might be the true one, was that someone was further ahead with a mini-series of James Clavell's *Taipan* which would cover much the same ground. Although I was paid, I had not got all my hard work onto the screen and that was also disappointing.

If *Dynasty* was a big disappointment my next one was even bigger. Granada Television, in the shape of one of its resident producers, June Windham-Davies, had asked me to adapt a period ghost story, 'Afterward' by Edith Wharton, for her spooky anthology called *Shades Of Darkness*.

'Afterward' was a clever story, with a chilling twist at the end, involving two Americans who rent an old Elizabethan manor in the Cotswolds. For this purpose Stanway, the old Wemyss home near Cheltenham, was used. It had been occupied by Lady Violet Benson since the death of her husband, 'Ego' Charteris in the Great War. 'Afterward' was very well cast and directed by Simon Langton and, pleased with the result, June asked me to tackle, again for her *Shades* anthology, an Agatha Christie story in which Granada held the rights.

This was a full-blown horror story, a far cry from Dame Agatha's usual cosy whodunnits. It was called 'The Last Seance' and the central part, of a bereaved French woman who seeks spiritual reunion with her drowned daughter, was played by Jeanne Moreau. June directed this one herself.

Then came the big disappointment. June asked me to adapt for a major mini-series Susan Howatch's best-selling novel *The Rich Are Different*. This was a larger affair altogether and I was thrilled to get the assignment. In due course I read the novel and sent in a treatment of which Granada's boss, David Plowright, evidently approved. I was told to go ahead with the scripts. By Christmas I had delivered all but three but was suddenly told by telephone to stop writing. There was a crisis.

Evidently the mini-series must be reduced in size and scale. June asked me on the phone to see how the scripts could be reduced in number and talked at the same time about meetings with the American cable company Show Time. What had plainly happened was that Granada had suddenly woken up to the reality of how much the show would cost. It was all set in and around New York and Long Island in the early '30s with scenes of the Berengaria docking, banks and stockbrokers' offices on Wall Street, polo tournaments, big parties in millionaires' homes at Newport, Rhode Island and a long sequence on the Norfolk broads in England. And that was only a part of it. Again I got paid in full for my work but *The Rich Are Different* was never made.

My third big disappointment came more recently. In 1991

a large Dutch TV company in Amsterdam called J. E. Entertainments decided to make a very large, international series of thirteen ninety-minute TV plays, each one about a colourful royal personage of Europe during the last century and a half. The show would be called *Royalty*. I was to master-mind it, first writing the 'bible' to include a list of the thirteen chosen royal personages and notes about them. I would ultimately script-edit the show. Various members of the Burke's Peerage staff were contracted to undertake the huge amount of historical research required and the plan was for each European state who had a royal personage (exiled or not) represented in the series to contribute some finance and location facilities.

Furthermore, each script would be introduced on the screen by a descendant of the royal personage portrayed, for example, Lady Douro might be asked to introduce the play about her ancestor, Kaiser Wilhelm II, the German Emperor; one of ex-King Michael of Rumania's daughters, who now lives in the UK, might be persuaded to front the episode about King Carol and Madame Lupescu; and Princess Michael of Kent would perhaps introduce the opening play about Queen Caroline of Brunswick, being herself a German Princess who married into the British royal family, and so on.

It was perhaps the most exciting and promising television project I have ever been involved with but it remains to this day just a project.

The Dutch company proposed, quite rightly, to have it produced in the UK with European actors and British writers, directors and crews. But this meant that a British 'broadcaster' must be a partner in the operation. Someone had to provide the studios, crews, etc. and be in a position to guarantee a showing on British TV for a start. This meant that without either the BBC or an ITV company as a partner, the Dutch company's ambitious project would not be viable.

J. E. Entertainments did, however, set up an office in London to launch the series, commissioned me to write the opening script about Queen Caroline of Brunswick, 'The Injured Queen of England' and made a deal with Burke's Peerage for the researching to begin. All seemed to be well. But every one of the ITV companies turned the series down. The BBC rejected it firmly and then went on to make *Eldorado*, which says quite a lot about the state of Public Sector Broadcasting today.

A FOURTH minor disappointment of my life as a writer was also something of a scandal.

Thames Television had initiated a scheme whereby writers were invited to submit a single play for a slot called *Storyboard*. The condition was that the play must have in it the makings of a series.

Someone had suggested to me a series about the famous firm called 'Universal Aunts' and I had had lunch and talks with the current head of the firm, Kate Herbert Hunting, who had given me access to all the firm's records. It was agreed that I would try to set up a series about an imaginary firm with a similar background and intentions, from which 'Universal Aunts' would derive some publicity and a share of the creative profits. This looked like a good subject for *Storyboard* so I wrote a pilot play.

The story was about three girls, all of whom had driven ambulances and nursed together in the Great War, having a reunion lunch in London in the early '20s. All three of them agree that life is dull, there is a shortage of decent men to marry and it is time they got together again to do something exciting and useful. Then the chance involvement of the girls with a small schoolboy whom one of them finds lost at a railway station, evidently the victim of a broken marriage and a cruel father, gives them a chance to rescue the boy from his unhappy home and put him on a train to his grandmother's in Scotland. This successful rescue operation encourages the three friends to set up a kind of 'solve your problem' agency with a small office over a greengrocer's shop in Paddington. After a visit from a man who mistakes the place for a brothel and a resultant visit from the Vice Squad, the girls land their first genuine job. Their client is the widow of an accountant who, the woman explains, always gave the impression in his lifetime of being a terrific 'masher', boasting to his friends in the office about his many affairs with girls. His widow tells the girls that she always knew that her husband was really sex-shy and scared of women. But he is dead now and, in order to preserve his image for the benefit of his mates, the widow hires the three girls to appear, all dressed up in black, at her husband's funeral, implying that they are three of his many conquests from the past.

The story was feminist in flavour, with scenes of the girls, while attempting to raise finance for their venture, being rejected by businessmen who tell them "Your job is to marry and have children, not to mess about in offices. Business is for men." The play went down very well and received glowing reviews, the critics predicting that Thames would make it into a series.

I was in Hollywood for my talks with Marlon Brando when my agent Cecily Ware called me from London to tell me that Thames indeed wanted to take up the option on the play, which I had entitled *Ladies In Charge*, and turn it into a Drama Series. But she added that the company intended to employ only women writers on the resulting series. I could hardly believe my ears. It is true that my agent had not been able to get a clause in the original play contract guaranteeing me my usual option to write a minimum of three out of thirteen scripts for any series arising from the play. Thames had refused to incorporate that clause but it had been implied verbally that I would most probably be asked to write at least some of the scripts for the series. Now the company was engaging in an act of blatant sex discrimination and I would have been justified in taking Thames Television to court to secure an injunction to stop the series being made, not that I was rich enough to do so. What made Thames TVs action inexcusable was that I have an impeccable track record for employing women writers. On *Sanctuary*, *Hadleigh*, *Upstairs-Downstairs* and *The Cedar Tree* I used an unusually high proportion of women writers, sometimes a majority.

I have to say that I derived some consolation from the fact that, in the end, the all-women writers' series of six episodes which Thames then proceeded to make (retaining my title) was not a success. Philip Purser, the *Sunday Telegraph* TV critic, who was kind to me over the years, wrote of it: '*Ladies In Charge* has consistently failed to rise to the promise of its last year's pilot episode written by Alfred Shaughnessy, before they turned the show over to the women.'

FROM that point on I concentrated on freelance writing for television, and was lucky enough to be invited by my old colleague from *Updown*, John Hawkesworth, to contribute one episode to his new enterprise, *The Adventures of Sherlock Holmes*, with Jeremy Brett as the sleuth and David Burke as Watson.

For this series I was asked to dramatize 'The Crooked Man', which is one of the more exciting and colourful stories in the collection, taking place at an army barracks in Aldershot and around a British garrison in India at the time of the Indian Mutiny. Conan Doyle addicts may remember the story, about a bent, broken and betrayed ex-soldier and a mongoose.

The Holmes series, made by Granada, has been a huge success world-wide and my one episode of it has earned me handsome residuals, for which I am grateful.

Next, the ever-enterprising John Hawkesworth, who is a first-class salesman, managed to persuade the BBC to let him do a series about the English Civil War, and again I joined the writing team. John, being a keen historian, saw to it that all the scripts were properly researched and checked for historical detail, and for expert military advice he engaged the services of the famous Briagadier B. S. Young, founder of The Sealed Knot Society, who is sometimes said to have 'invented the Civil War'.

My first script for *By The Sword Divided* was the third episode, in which three events of importance take place. First, the Royalist Baronet Sir Martin Lacey forms a troop of cavalry from among the tenants and estate workers at his ancestral seat Arnescote Castle, played in the series by Rockingham Castle near Corby. Second, Sir Martin's daughter Anne, whose twin brother Tom is like his father a Royalist, leaves home to marry a certain John Fletcher, a Parliamentarian whose political views she shares, and thus the family is split. Third, Sir Martin and his cavalry troop set off for the battle of Edgehill, from which Lacey's charger returns at dusk riderless with blood on the saddle. Sir Martin has been badly wounded on the field of battle.

John and the writers discussed at length which style of writing and idiom would be appropriate for the series. We all agreed to avoid 'prithees', 'forsooths' or 'oddsfish' and that kind of thing. There was a school of thought that a modern idiom avoiding modern words, such as was used by James Goldman in *The Lion In Winter*, might be best. In the end we all selected our own styles. Personally I felt that, as Shakespeare had only died about thirty years earlier, I would attempt to make my characters speak in a kind of Shakespearean metre or rhythm, using a fairly florid phraseology. I felt this form of language would fit the wigs and costumes.

At a moment when Anne had a brief political clash with her father before going off to live with her Cromwellian husband, I saw a chance to write another of my favourite father-and-daughter scenes. For some reason I seem to have a *penchant* for writing such scenes. It may be because Jean and I have just our two sons and that I have subconsciously always wanted a daughter. I do not know. I had enjoyed writing the reconciliation scene between Commander Bourne and his second daughter in *The Cedar Tree*; the tender bedside scene in *Updown* between Richard Bellamy and his rebellious daughter, Elizabeth, after she has broken up with her rich Armenian admirer; and in the play *The Heat Of The Moment* when Sir Robert Forester has a blinding row with his daughter Sarah, for taking the side of the Welsh school teacher against him, accusing her of disloyalty. Again, the daughter creeps into her father's study where he is watching television alone and makes her peace with him.

But my favourite is still the one in *By The Sword Divided* in which the Royalist Sir Martin Lacey says a sad farewell to his daughter Anne before she leaves home for good. I was lucky to have Julian Glover and Sharon Mughan (later spelt Maughan) to play this scene with such style. Both were very moving, although Sharon's performance was slightly marred for me by the wig of ringlets they had given her, which removed her lovely face a long way from those famous coffee commercials.

Here Sir Martin is attacking the Parliamentarians who have divided the country, setting family against family.

*Sir Martin*: (angrily) . . . these devils have invoked the natural passions of a hungry mob and challenged the authority of God himself . . .

*Anne*: (with feeling) Father, let us not involve ourselves in politics. I am your daughter, come to bid farewell . . . to you and to my home. I grieve enough to find this cruel, foolish war has come between us . . . let us at least part in friendship and love for one another.

(She embraces her father.)
*Martin*: Oh, Anne, at this sad parting I cannot help but think of your sweet mother on the day that you and Tom were born. The joy of twins, one boy, one girl, to grow together step by step, hand in hand, to give each other strength and friendship. Were she alive today how she would weep. Let us pray each one of us to the same God for deliverance from this hateful struggle.
*Anne*: Amen to that . . .

The thought struck me one day when a scene was being rehearsed between King Charles I and his queen, Henrietta Maria, that *By The Sword Divided* was probably the most 'aristocratic' television series ever made by the BBC. The two parts were being played respectively by Jeremy Clyde, a nephew of the present Duke of Wellington, and Marsha Fitzalan, a daughter of the present Duke of Norfolk. The scene was being directed by Henry Herbert, who is in reality the 17th Earl of Pembroke, and I heard a rumour that Timothy Bentinck who played Anne's twin brother, Tom Lacey, was a count. Whoever cast the series must have done so with Spotlight in one hand and Debrett's Peerage in the other.

SOON after I had written my first script for *By The Sword Divided* I became rather bitten with imitating Shakespeare and for fun composed an imaginary speech by the Bard.

> . . . As when the full flood
> Of tidings from the pinnacles of war
> Pour down as melted snow from the wintry peak
> Into the raging torrent of opinion
> So shall be reasoned man's intention to betray –
> Not in the name of self or God but in
> Some other craven cause –

The purpose of our noble destiny.
Now stand before the bar of time, most proud,
Embellished traitor who, as cold death
To foul poison be the sequel, shall
Be surely judged. So, when justice comes
To fruit let us be gone to sweeter climes
Where from a placid, even sea, soft winds
With many fragrant odours charged, shall to
Our baser sense make suit; and like sweet music
From some distant lyre fall on our ears
As honey to the tongue, beguiling to excess
The yielding spirit; while with lightened step
And happy mien our fortune shall be thus
Complete.
Come friends, let us away and seek
A fairer morrow . . .

I have played a recording of that piece once or twice to friends who profess to be Shakespearean experts, asking them if they can recognize from which play the passage derives.

One or two have fallen into the trap, murmuring ruminatively "Let me see . . . ah, yes, now . . . wait a moment . . . that's Coriolanus . . . no, it's not . . . it's . . . er . . . Henry Four, Part One or Two, I'm not sure which . . . or is it Pericles?"

As far as I can see, mimicking a writing style is like mimicking a person: use the same kind of words and phrases; move and walk in the same manner, which in terms of writing means keep up the lilt and metric rhythm; and, in the case of the Bard, fling in as many colourful analogies as you can think of.

Talking of language, I have always found Irish one of the richest of all. The more so since the chance came my way in 1983 to dramatize for television a number of those richly comic stories by E. Somerville and Martin Ross, *The Experiences of an Irish R.M.*

As is often the case with collections of stories some are better than others, some dramatize better than others and some are too thin to stand up on their own on the screen. In those cases elements of two different stories must sometimes be mergered into one story or the thin story must be expanded by additional invention.

There is another danger of which I have been aware ever since working in the Scenario Department of Ealing Studios in the late '40s. Film and television producers too often fall in love with something they read on the printed page; a novel, a short story or a collection of stories. They then spend money on an option and later buy the rights, hire a dramatist to adapt the work for the screen and then feel bewildered and deeply disappointed when the result fails. Sometimes this is the fault of bad casting or inept direction. But more often it is because the producer has fallen in love with pages of descriptive prose without envisaging how unreal it may seem, once translated to the screen. A notion can be very funny on the printed page that does not work on film or tape. There are certain authors, such as Evelyn Waugh and Nancy Mitford, whose humour only translates partially to the screen because much of their wit lies in the style of their narrative. Sometimes comic writing cannot be played at all.

Somewhere in Evelyn Waugh there is a description of a society woman (based on Lady Diana Cooper) who drives her car down the steps of the Green Park Underground Station by the Ritz. This is intended as a piece of characterisation, not of plot, so to film it would not contribute to the story and would be a waste of time. Nor can you film a brilliant analogy on the page by translating it into visual terms. An example would be the famous Wodehouse description of a stout girl: 'She looked as though she had been poured into her dress and forgotten to say "when",' or of Honoria Glossop, the nerve specialist's daughter: 'She had a laugh like a squadron of cavalry charging over a tin bridge.'

This truth lost for the *Irish R.M.* TV Series some of the richer passages of the source material. In one story called 'In The Curranhilty Country', which I had the pleasure of dramatizing, Flurry Knox and Dr Hickey score off the unspeakable Tomsy Flood by letting loose a pack of hounds into his house when he is out getting drunk at the hunt party in the hotel. Flood comes home and gets to his bedroom, swaying on his feet, to find several hounds lying tucked up in his bed with their heads on his pillows. This is, on paper, a very funny notion to visualize. But there are too many practical problems to make it easy to reproduce on the screen. But *The Irish R.M.* contained some glorious performances, especially from the Irish players recruited from the Abbey Theatre, such as Anna Manahan as the formidable cook-housekeeper, Mrs Cadogan (pronounced Kay-der-Gorn) and Brendan Conroy as her son, Peter.

The last Drama Series with which I became involved to any extent was the BBC's enormously successful *All Creature Great And Small*, based on the popular James Herriot stories about a Yorkshire veterinary practice.

The very able young Script Editor on the show was Joy Lale, who was later tragically killed in a car crash while on location in Ireland for the BBC. I shall always be indebted to her for my A.C.G.S. experience.

She handed me various Herriot stories or bits of Herriot stories or sometimes two different stories from the Herriot books to join together and produce one episode. Her ideas and criticisms were expert and she contributed richly to the success of the show. She was a sad loss to television.

The very first story I dramatized dealt with the amazing

subject of a cow having her calf by Caesarean Section. Being rather squeamish about such things, I did not go up to the Yorkshire location to watch that episode being filmed but remained firmly in London and left it to Christopher Timothy, playing James Herriot, to make a mess of it – literally, because in the story, not being very experienced in what was in the '50s a brand new veterinary technique, James inadvertently makes his incision in the wrong part of the cow's belly, slicing open its rumen instead of its uterus, with rather messy and smelly consequences. But the cow and her calf happily survive.

Another episode which came my way was one wherein an old and frail cottager, whom James often visits on his rounds to take the old man's dog for a walk, dies on the same night in 1952 as King George VI. The widow finds great comfort in identifying in the loss of her husband with Queen Elizabeth.

This incident helped to remind the viewers that the era of A.C.G.S. was the '50s. It also gave me the opportunity in the same episode to comment, through the character of Siegfried played by Robert Hardy, on the accession to the throne of the new young Queen, Elizabeth II.

On the morning that the news of the King's death and the succession of his elder daughter as Queen is announced on the wireless, Hardy launches off into a Churchillian speech about the new Elizabethan age which is very much in Siegfried's and Tim's character . . .

Another A.C.G.S. episode of mine was coincidentally inspired by our dear old, much loved Golden Labrador, Hudson, whom Jean and I had bought as a puppy. In the story James's much-loved black Labrador is terminally ill and James decides very reluctantly that he ought to be put to sleep. On the chosen day James is very upset and moody. Siegfried, to spare his partner's distress, offers to do the necessary for him but James gratefully refuses and takes the dog for one last walk. At some point James pauses to look at something, the dog lumbers on, then James walks on and soon comes across his Black Labrador lying dead in the field a few yards ahead of him. The dog has spared James the agony of putting him down. This had happened to us a few months earlier when Hudson, who was by then sixteen and could hardly walk or eat, was finally due to be put down. Jean and I had an appointment to see the vet one afternoon to discuss it. At lunchtime Jean came into the kitchen from a morning out shopping and found Hudson dead beside his basket. He had tried to get out of it but the strain had been too much for his heart. He, too, had spared us the pain.

The episode of James's dog caused a lot of sadness and tears among the many fans of *All Creatures* and this fact was mentioned in the Press. So Hudson, as a real dog, achieved a little bit of indirect fame by dying in similar circumstances to a fictitious dog in a popular TV series. Rather like the old cottager and King George VI.

The subject of Labradors reminds me that, in the course of writing this book, I was obliged to search through a large cardboard box containing all my old television scripts stretching back to the '50s. This was necessary to check dates, casts and even subjects of the numerous plays and series episodes I have written in my lifetime.

Among my tattered and faded old scripts I found one episode of a drama series which I had almost forgotten and glanced at the first page of my contribution. I was startled to read:

*Ext. Wood and track day*

Parked on a farm track are a Landrover and a horse-drawn gamecart. From the misty wood emerges a shooting party: six elderly gentlemen, whose faces we never see, wearing plus-fours, raincapes, shooting hats and carrying shooting sticks. Three loaders follow with guns and cartridge bags, and two keepers with Labradors on leashes are carrying the bag, pheasants and hares.

The host, a certain Lord Rushmore, points to something off-screen.

The other five gentlemen take their guns from their loaders, slip in cartridges and unexpectedly line themselves up on the path a pace apart like a firing squad. Rushmore joins them.

*Rushmore*: Safety catches, please, gentlemen . . .

(Six twelve-bore barrels are raised. Safety catches click off.)

*Rushmore*: Aim for the heart.

(Now we see the victim. A middle-aged American with hornrimmed glasses, flowing grey hair and a trendy Chelsea suit is tied to a gatepost. The keepers and loaders stand calmly by the transport.)

*Rushmore*: Fire!

(The volley echoes round the quiet woods. The American crumples, the body unmarked. The two keepers lift it up and, with a heave, toss it into the gamecart where we see it slump down among the dead pheasants, hares, woodcock, etc.)

(Rushmore turns to his guests.)

*Rushmore*: Back to the house now, gentlemen . . . for breakfast.

(The six guns climb into the Landrover and drive away down the bumpy track.)

*Fade out:*

*Run main titles.*

This bizarre opening was the so-called 'teaser' to an episode I wrote for a now forgotten series called *Spyder's Web*. From the date on my script which is called 'The Executioners', September 1971, I realize that we were all, at that time, heavily under the influence of *The Avengers* and that this off-beat and possibly underrated series, devised by the prolific Roy Clarke, creator of *Last of the Summer Wine*, *Keeping Up Appearances* and many others, was very much in the same key as Brian Clemens' masterly invention.

Shock pre-title openings or 'teasers' were also in fashion at the time but, for some reason, I find I cannot remember much about *Spyder's Web*, its format or its characters. All I do remember is that the executioners were a group of elderly clubmen who, as firm supporters of capital punishment, decide to take the law into their own hands and carry out their own executions of people they deem to be enemies of the state. That is by no means a new concept. It has echoes of Bulldog Drummond, Dornford Yates and a more recent movie by Bryan Forbes called *The League of Gentlemen*. John Buchan was slightly in that area, too, with *John Macnabb*. It is the concept of aristocrats putting themselves above the law of the land.

Lord Rushmore was played by André Morell, who at the read-through of 'The Executioners' seemed to show contempt for his role by assiduously doing the *Times* Crossword throughout, only putting the puzzle aside to deliver his lines, then resuming work on the clues until his next scene came along. I was rather distressed and not a little offended by this performance until I got to know André well enough later on in life to discover that this was his normal way of overcoming his nerves at first rehearsals. A read-through is a bit like going to a drinks party where you don't know anybody. Actors and actresses can be shy like anybody else, and a read-through or first rehearsal with a strange cast, unless you happen to know somebody, can be quite a strain. This is why directors have a kind of social responsibility to introduce casts to each other and create an easy, relaxed atmosphere – like a good host at a dinner party.

I must admit that one of the things I miss most from working as a dramatist is the social aspect of it. I like meeting actors, actresses, directors and technicians and the friendly team thing of going through the production of a play from the first tentative read of the script via the tense dress or technical rehearsals, the recording or first night to the relief when it's all over, the drink in the bar with the cast and the sense of achievement. You do not get that writing books except, perhaps, at a book launch party. But books are my life now and nervous read-throughs of what I have written for actors to battle with is a thing of the past, warmly remembered.

There is one enormous advantage in writing for Television over the theatre and that is 'residuals'. Because TV reaches such a vast audience anyway, and most good plays and series are sold abroad, a TV writer can enjoy the knowledge that his work is being performed world-wide from San Francisco to Saudi Arabia, from Iran to Iceland.

A friend of mine, back from a business trip, reported seeing one of my episodes of *Upstairs, Downstairs* on the TV set in his hotel room in Istanbul. "There was Mrs Bridges," my friend told me, "babbling away in Turkish."

And at the height of the Gulf War, I received via the BBC a payment of £54 from Kuwait for two Episodes of *All Creatures Great And Small,* which had been running there shortly before the Iraqis invaded them.

I once worked out that a single play of mine, *The Small Hours,* had been seen (theoretically) by about ten million people in the UK and overseas. To reach such an audience in the form of a stage play, it would have had to run for seven years at the Theatre Royal, Drury Lane, playing to capacity at every performance. The normal royalties at 10% of the gross box-office takings would in that case earn me something like fifteen times more money than the original television fee plus foreign residuals, but of course not many stage plays run for anything like so long. Also, it must be remembered that a lot of the millions of viewers who are watching your play according to the Ratings, are probably asleep with the TV on, or washing up or having an argument in the living room, totally unaware of your work being screened for their benefit. I often imagine the hurried switch off that suddenly interrupts your best-written scene, because the husband has said to his wife "Come on, Elsie, turn that bloody thing off, time we were going".

And your actor is rudely cut off in mid-sentence so that Elsie and her husband can get into the car and drive over to Auntie Flo's.

But, at least as a TV writer your work can go on earning you money for years after you have forgotten what it was you wrote in the first place.

# WRITING STAGE PLAYS

AS a schoolboy and in later years I saw a large number of plays in the theatre that were contemporary. That means that they were written and produced between the late '20s and the late '50s, when styles changed.

The plays I saw with breathless excitement and fascination during my impressionable years were mostly well-made plays that observed the unities of time and space, had a beginning, a middle and an end and were often confined to one set. The mainstream British dramatists of that period such as Shaw, Coward, Novello, Priestley, Emlyn Williams, Dodie Smith, Van Druten, Ronald Mackenzie, Rodney Ackland and others were all to some extent under the influence of Ibsen. The technique was difficult and the aim was to introduce a handful of characters into a setting and bring their inter-relationships gradually through conflict to a climax and a surprising conclusion. The curtain fall of each act, be it two or three, would normally consist of a punch line or twist in the situation – a cliff-hanger, I suppose, leaving the audience anxious to see what happened next.

This conventional form of dramatic craft requires a great deal of technical imagination and ingenuity. Plausible reasons have to be invented to get the characters on and off stage in order to leave it clear for important duologues or to avoid people overhearing things they should not, if the plot is not to be ruined. Casual references and odd remarks must be devised by the dramatist to inform the audience from the start of what they need to know about the situation and characters, without appearing to ram it down their throats. This is usually called 'exposition,' and imagination must be used to set atmosphere by the use of words.

But it must be done with subtlety. It is far too bald to have a character on a tea estate in Malaya come out on to the verandah and declare "God, I hate this damned heat".

Better to let him come out buttoning up a clean shirt while his wife says "Have you changed your shirt again, Norman?"

And the tea-planter says, "Had to, my dear. Ten minutes out there and, by Jove, one is wringing wet."

Lecturing about the theatre to literary groups I have sometimes given the following as an example of creating an atmosphere with words:

The curtain rises on a darkly lit room. A woman in a shawl sits by the fire. A man is peering out of the window.
*Man*: I can hardly see the church clock now. It's getting thicker every minute.
(He shudders, rubbing his hands together, and returns to the fire.)

A fog has been created and there is no need to spray the stage with dry ice.

For the same lecture I invented as an example of 'exposition' an imaginary opening scene for a play and invited my listeners to hear it and then tell me what they had learnt about the characters.

The scene is a London drawing room. It is dusk. A young woman, Kate, comes in to join an older woman, Helen.
*Helen*: (Looking up from her needlework) Has he settled?
*Kate*: Hope so. He'll take time to get used to that old cot.
*Helen*: It was yours, darling.
*Kate*: I know. (She moves to window) Daddy back yet?
*Helen*: He may be late. There's a division in the house tonight.

(Looking over to window) This damp weather's not good for his lungs.
*Kate*: You mustn't worry. (Kate crosses to the fireplace.)
*Kate*: He does agree I was right, doesn't he?
*Helen*: Well. He agrees you had no alternative.
*Kate*: "That's something I suppose."
*Helen*: And he is going to inquire about a flat for you.
*Kate*: Good.

What should have been established by these opening lines is that we are in the home of a Member of Parliament who has weak lungs, that the MP's married daughter has just left her husband and brought her small child to live in her parents' house until her father, who disapproves of the break-up but must support his daughter, will help with a flat for her to move into with her child . . .

Critics of plays sometimes use the word 'contrivance' in a pejorative sense but, in truth, a certain amount of contrivance must be undertaken to allow important things to happen on stage in what seems to be a natural way. A good example of inventive contrivance was achieved by Terence Rattigan in *The Deep Blue Sea*. How was Rattigan to have Freddie Page discover, on his return from playing golf, that Hester Collyer has just attempted to commit suicide?

Alone in the flat after recovering from the attempt, she quickly removes the suicide note which she has left for him on the mantelpiece and stuffs it into her dressing-gown pocket. Freddy returns, cheerfully unaware of what has happened. Later she goes off to have a bath, hanging her dressing gown on a door. They continue to chat naturally. Then Freddie finds he's out of cigarettes and asks 'Hes' if she's got any. Without thinking she calls through, "There are some in my dressing-gown pocket." Freddy finds the packet of cigarettes but he also finds the suicide note which he sits down to read slowly with mounting horror as the curtain falls.

This is a great curtain and it is theatrical skill of the first order, the stuff of well-made drama.

Rattigan was a master of what is called 'planting'. That is, feeding the audience with small, seemingly unimportant facts, incidents and remarks which will assume significance later in the play.

Another theatrical skill which Rattigan possessed was the use of the oblique, indirect line of dialogue to conceal emotion. Englishmen meeting in the village street invariably greet each other with a comment on the weather. It stems from a desire to be friendly or neighbourly but not too intimate, and the weather is always safe common ground for communication. Thus:

*Jones*: Good morning.
*Smith*: Morning. Warm isn't it?
*Jones*: Bit of thunder about though. Might get a drop of rain.
*Smith*: We could do with it.
*Jones*: We could.
(They go their separate ways.)

But Rattigan also knew that shy, inhibited Englishmen often communicate with each other through sport, especially cricket, as he demonstrated in *Separate Tables*:

The old schoolmaster in the hotel, Fowler, disappointed that an old pupil has not come to see him, needs to share his sense of rejection with Major Pollock, the disgraced bogus army officer who is being ostracized by the other guests. So, leaving the dining room and passing Pollock's table, Fowler pauses to say "Hampshire did pretty well today, did you see? Three-hundred and eighty-odd for five . . . I wish they had more bowling . . . well." And he moves on.

That line catches me by the throat as firmly as does a scene in another Rattigan play when a schoolboy, Taplow, presents his dreaded teacher Crocker-Harris with a copy of the Browning version of the Agamemnon by Aeschylus, inscribed with a translation from the Greek, 'God from afar looks graciously upon a gentle master.'

THE year 1951, which marked my *début* as a screenwriter and film producer, also saw the first stage production of my first-ever play written for the theatre. I was thirty-five.

*Release* is a social drama, inspired by the Mrs Duffy case, about a young woman who has been in prison, serving a life sentence for murdering her brutal husband.

The play opens on the day of Catherine Bailey's release and her arrival home in the company of an after-care officer at the suburban house where the Bailey family live. The girl's mother, ashamed of having a convicted murderess for a daughter, has lied to the neighbours about the girl's absence, making out that she has come home after an unhappy marriage in Canada. When a young man, who as the lodger has been occupying Catherine's room, inevitably meets her, he falls in love with her and proposes to her, unaware of her past. Catherine rejects him for she has been poisoned against the idea of marriage by her jealous, possessive mother who tells her she can never have children or lead a normal life because of the stigma of her prison term. Thus the mother creates a new prison for Catherine in her own home. But Catherine's father defies his wife by telling the young man the truth about his daughter's past. The young man feels nothing but pity and sympathy for her and they go off to start a new life together.

It was usual in those days for a play to be seen on the stage first, then to be filmed or televised and later broadcast on radio. With *Release* it was the reverse. The play was first broadcast by the BBC in a short version for Wednesday matinée. Soon after that it went out at its full-length as Saturday Night Theatre. Eventually it was offered to and accepted by Michael Barry, Head of BBC Television Drama, to be televised 'live' as the Sunday night play from Alexandra Palace. I was especially thrilled when I heard that the part of Catherine had been offered to Wendy Hiller who had eagerly agreed to do it, and that she and the producer-director Harold Clayton and I were to have lunch at the Café Royal to talk about it.

We had a delightful lunch and I went home very happily, until a call came two days later from Harold. We were within three days of starting rehearsals and Wendy Hiller had dropped out. It seemed that her agent had made an error and she was suddenly required to do post-synching for some 'film people' who had a prior claim on her services. The film people turned out to be Carol Reed for whom she had just done *Outcast Of The Island* and they had first call on Miss Hiller, so we had to think again. I was desolate until London Films' casting director, Bill O'Brien who had incidentally fixed Miss Hiller in Carol's picture, felt guilty and decided to help us. He called Harold Clayton and mentioned that Margaret Leighton had never done a TV play and was free for a few months. The upshot was that I was sent scurrying round to Miss Leighton's flat in Albany with a script of *Release* under my arm. Here I explained the plot to her over a gin and tonic and left it with her to read. She would let us know tomorrow. I went to a movie with friends that night but could not concentrate on the screen. I kept thinking through the script of *Release*, wondering how Miss Leighton would react to each scene. The next day Harold Clayton called me to say she was happy to do it and my cup of happiness overflowed.

Margaret Leighton was a very big star indeed at that time. She had played opposite Ralph Richardson, Laurence Olivier, Rex Harrison and Nöel Coward and there was no actress with a greater degree of quality and prestige.

She turned up for the read-through draped in furs,

wearing a glamorous Dior dress, high-heeled court shoes, earrings, jangling bracelets, a huge necklace and a big hat. By day three of rehearsals she was wearing an old skirt and jersey, flat shoes and no make-up.

Her father in the play was that fine old character actor from Yorkshire, Julian Mitchell, who had also played her father in the original 1946 production of J. B. Priestley's *An Inspector Calls* at the New Theatre. On that occasion Ralph Richardson played the mysterious Inspector Goole from another time plane who symbolizes the collective conscience and guilt of the well-to-do family. Alec Guiness was in it, too, and the play was a good deal better done and easier to appreciate than a certain recent production of the piece in which exploding bombs, billowing smoke and part of the set collapsing, together with the cast rushing about in a dark street shouting out their lines, made it almost impossible to hear Mr Priestley's absorbing and disturbing play. In the same production the chilling second telephone call from the Infirmary about the girl's death came through rather implausibly on a wrecked telephone kiosk in the street, which almost destroyed Priestley's theatrically effective ending.

When *Release* went out on TV live from Alexandra Palace it caused quite a stir. Leighton received rave reviews for her performance, for which she also won an award, and the play was also praised.

What I did not realize at the time was that up in Birmingham, Maggie Leighton's home town where she learned her trade at the famous Repertory Theatre on Station Street, a group of her friends, her mother and the great Sir Barry Jackson were all glued to a TV set.

A few days later, to my joy, I received a letter from Sir Barry saying that he had loved my play and would like to stage it as the second production of his new autumn season at the Birmingham Repertory Theatre.

A note here about directors and authors. I was a young, green dramatist and it was my very first play. In the second week of rehearsals I received in London a four-page letter from the director, Douglas Seale, in Birmingham. In it he told me that all was going well but there was one small point about time needed for an exit or some such technical detail and asked my permission for the insertion of two simple lines of dialogue into the text in order to get round the problem. I sent Douglas Seale a telegram back saying 'Please make change. Thanks.' I remember thinking at the time 'This is the real theatre, where directors treat authors with respect and courtesy.'

I cannot see that happening with some of today's young directors who believe themselves to be creative artists not beholden to authors, whose texts they use merely as material to show off their clever staging gimmicks.

*Release* received more good reviews and T. C. Kemp of the *Birmingham Post* called me 'a young dramatist with a great future' while according to *The Times* critic I 'had a flair for dialogue and characterisation and an eye for a popular theatrical situation.' All very heady stuff. The young Birmingham cast were excellent and Catherine was portrayed beautifully by Rosalind Boxall, who was married to Paul Rogers. Playing the Bailey family's teenage son, Johnny, was Paul Daneman who was about twenty-five at the time but, as a good rep. player, he accepted the challenge and brought his age down to sixteen most convincingly.

One or two West End managements turned down the play on the grounds that it was 'kitchen-sink stuff' and therefore not commercial. This was 1951 and the world had not yet heard of John Osborne. Only one London management was interested, but only on condition that Margaret Leighton repeated her TV performance on the stage. This she regretfully declined to do and I could not blame her. With her impeccable good manners, she wrote me a charming letter pointing out that she had already played Catherine to millions of people and did not feel tempted to go on doing it every night to a few hundred people in a theatre. In due course the play was published and proceeded on its career in repertory theatres and amateur groups all over the UK and abroad. In Germany it was entitled *Die Entlassung* where it was a success.

Seven years later the BBC Television Drama Department decided to revive it. This time the mother, Mrs Bailey, was Freda Jackson and Catherine was played by the earthy, superb Welsh actress, Rachel Roberts, who unfortunately got entangled later in her life with Rex Harrison and ended tragically as a gin-sodden suicide case.

IT is an interesting mental exercise and not too bad for combatting insomnia to lie abed in the small hours and cast your mind back on how and exactly when the first spark of an idea hit you that later developed into a play for the theatre.

I have always found that one idea is not enough. The germinal idea may be a relationship between two of your friends, a chance remark overheard in a bus or a situation involving two people you know. But that germinal idea needs to be joined by, or fertilised by, a secondary idea. Often the secondary idea will be a development of the first, preferably an unexpected twist on it. Suppose a man comes home from abroad to find his wife is living with a sailor. So what? The play has to be about what he does about it. That is the secondary idea. So make the husband fall in love with the sailor and you have a play. *Release* was an example of this. The germinal idea was: how does a suburban family in South London conceal the fact from their neighbours that their daughter, ostensibly home from living in Canada, is really a murderess just out of prison? That in itself was plainly not enough for a play. So the secondary idea was: What happens if the young man who has been boarding in her room during her absence in gaol falls in love with her, believing in the Canada story, but as the girl's mother tells her daughter that she cannot ever marry with her past. There you have the makings of a play.

MY next play for the stage, although in a very different key, had similar origins to *Release*. It was first written for the theatre and the idea that took hold in my mind was germinated curiously enough, at a dinner party at Windsor Castle just after the end of the war. I was sitting next to a young widow, Pam Hore-Ruthven, whose husband Pat had been killed in the war. She was living in the Governor's Tower with her in-laws, Lord and Lady Gowrie. Pam mentioned that she was taking her schoolboy son abroad for his summer holiday and that she had hired a tutor to coach him for his exams. Further, she informed me with a mischievous smile that the tutor she had hired was rather attractive. That was the germinal idea for my second play, *Holiday For Simon*, so the model for the schoolboy Simon was the present Lord Gowrie, then aged sixteen,who later became a Tory Minister for the Arts.

Then I began to remember being taken as a schoolboy by my mother to stay at a villa in the South of France with an old friend of hers, the famous Canadian opera *diva* Louise Edvina, whom she had known in Montreal. As these two ideas began to lock into each other a third element forced its way in. My mother had a friend called the Countess Heiden, a Finnish woman who had married a Dane, divorced and became a top Paris *couturière* working for Schiaparelli. Hating the Communists, Irene Heiden and her husband had collaborated actively during the occupation. At one time Irene was making dresses for the wives of the senior German Generals: "Madame von Stulpnagel has telephoned and wishes to change her fitting to Wednesday. The General has to go to Berlin and she is to accompany him."

When the Germans marched out of Paris in 1944 Irene's husband Doric Heiden marched out with them. The marriage was finished, and not long before the dinner party that gave me the idea for my play, Irene had found herself a sympathetic 'walker' in the shape of a penniless White Russian who lived with her in her flat in the Rue Christoph-Colombe and gave singing lessons.

*Holiday For Simon* is about the ageing Comtesse de Vernay, an Englishwoman and former opera singer, thrice married, who has ended up in a villa near Cannes with her White Russian 'walker', Alexis Mouranoff. He is a failed painter who has collaborated with the Nazis in Paris during the war and been denounced by a jealous rival artist.

Out from England to stay with them in 1950 comes a sad but beautiful English divorcée, Angela Dale-Adams, accompanied by her sixteen year old son, Simon. She has hired a tutor 'blind' from an agency in London to come out to the villa and coach Simon for his exams and they are expecting some fussy old pedant in pince-nez to arrive by the next train. But in walks a very handsome young prep. schoolmaster, Charles Latimer, who has taken the job because he is anxious to earn a little extra money during the holidays. He is, however, married, with a wife and two little girls on holiday in Folkestone. Everybody falls in love under the Mediterranean moon: Alexis with Angela as he paints her in his studio; Angela with her son's tutor, Charles; Simon with the Comtesse's little French maid, Nicole. In the end, when everybody has left, the Comtesse and Alexis are left alone in the villa where we found them, an elderly couple playing Canasta as the sun sets and the evening grows chilly. They are facing the autumn of their lives.

Binkie Beaumont of H. M. Tennent's evinced some interest in *Simon* as a vehicle for Diana Wynyard but went cold on it. So, after my experience with *Release,* I swiftly sent it to Michael Barry at BBC Television.

He accepted it at once and, just as *Release* had before it, *Simon* went into production as the Sunday Night Television Play.

Angela, the English divorcée, was played by Rachel Gurney and the tutor was Robert Flemyng. They were charming together, and Olga Lindo played the old opera singer with great authority and wit. Gerhardt (later Gerard) Heinz played Alexis Mouranoff with just the right amount of cunning and unctuous charm, but the miracle performance was the boy actor, Jeremy Spenser, who was brilliantly touching as Simon. There is a scene when the tutor has sent himself a telegram in order to escape from the threatened love affair with his pupil's mother, an affair which he knows must end. He tells Angela he must go before things get out of hand.

As his taxi leaves for the station in Cannes, leaving Angela alone, staring out to sea with moist eyes, Simon comes quietly on to the terrace and takes his mother gently by the hand, saying, "I've put the tennis net up, Mum; shall we have a game because I don't want you to be alone today . . ."

That line always brings the tears even when Simon is below par, as some of the rep. ones have been. With Jeremy Spenser it was devastating.

The TV production of *Holiday For Simon* was by Barbara Burnham and went down very well. Peter Black, the Daily Mail TV critic ended his notice with 'we are left to compare Mr Shaughnessy with Tchekov . . .' I must admit I rather liked that.

Then something rather sad happened. It was one of those mistakes that were 'well meant'. My agent received an enquiry first thing on the Monday morning for the film rights of *Simon*. Not stopping to consider its implications he called me at once and recommended me to accept the deal offered. Hammer Films wanted to acquire the film rights in the play and to commission me to write a screenplay at once. The money was good.

I, too, failed to think to myself 'What the hell do Hammer Films [who make bloodthirsty X-cert 'Dracula' and 'Frankenstein' movies] want with a gentle, romantic comedy like *Holiday For Simon*?'

But the Hammer producer, Michael Carreras, was evidently keen to film *Simon* so I agreed.

A few days later, after the Hammer deal had been signed, the theatre producer Peter Saunders called my agent and said he wanted to put on *Holiday For Simon* in the West End rightaway, with the original TV cast: Bobby Flemyng, Olga Lindo, Jeremy Spenser and Rachel. But it only took Peter Saunders three minutes on the phone to discover from my agent that the film rights in the play had already been sold to a film company. End of message. Peter Saunders was no longer interested. But the play was eventually published by Samuel French and produced in a fair number of repertory and amateur theatres around the country. Hammer Films did nothing with *Simon* until years later when Mike Carreras took me out to lunch one day to ask me if I could turn it into a grim, dramatic movie about a woman and her son on holiday on a Greek island with strange rituals, witchcraft and sexual orgies in a cave. I could not.

In fact, I had always thought the story slight but charming enough to make a romantic play with music; something in the Coward idiom, like *Private Lives* or *Shadow Play*. For this purpose, in 1991, I wrote some songs for it and tried it out as a musical with a gifted local amateur cast at the little Kenton Theatre in Henley. One performance was a Gala for the St John Ambulance Brigade and the Royal National Lifeboat Institution. So *Simon* raised some funds for charity and at the same time proved to me that the show works as a small musical.

I cannot remember where the idea for my next play, *Light Fingers*, came from. I only know that I hesitated to start writing it for some time because I had an idea that it might be considered in bad taste to write a comedy about kleptomania. I would be getting laughs out of a rather sad, mental condition or affliction which usually needs psychiatric treatment. I suppose at the back of my mind there was that fine play, *Black Chiffon*, by Lesley Storm who was herself married to a psychiatrist and might have got the idea from her husband's casebook.

*Black Chiffon* was a serious play about a jealous mother who steals a chiffon nightdress from a shop on the eve of her son's wedding. The nightdress represents to the mother a subconscious symbol of her son's forthcoming sexual experience with a person who will come between them and take him from her.

On the other hand, *Light Fingers* is essentially a comedy and the woman is not really a kleptomaniac at all; she merely allows her husband to believe she is, in order to punish him for his selfishness:

A pompous MP, looking for something in his wife's handbag, discovers a number of silver coffee spoons, unaware that she can't stop buying things in sales and concealing them from her husband who would accuse her of extravagance.

Confronted with the spoons by her husband, the wife panics and says she has no idea how they got there. He jumps to the conclusion that she has become a kleptomaniac. He fears she will be caught shoplifting and that the story will hit the headlines and damage his political career, so he secretly hires a paid escort to go everywhere with her and prevent her from pinching things. When the escort, a handsome young ex-officer turns up, she takes one look at him and decides to keep up the pretence for as long as she can.

Looking at it today, the plot seems more suitable for an eighteenth-century opera bouffe than a modern stage comedy. But I managed to get *Light Fingers* produced in 1954 for one week at the Richmond Theatre, which was in those days a weekly repertory house. It went quite well and the notice in *The Stage* said 'there is little doubt that this delightful new comedy will prove a success, for it has all the necessary ingredients.' This gave me hope for a West End transfer, but it was not to be. *Light Fingers* took its place, with two other light comedies of mine, *Serenita* and *Love En Suite* together with a more serious play, *Parting Day*, in my bottom drawer where I keep scripts of plays which have been staged only once in a theatre and never seen again.

One compensation was that *Light Fingers* was seen during its brief run by a film producer who bought the rights and made it into a movie. In the film version the part of Humphrey Levenham, the pompous MP, was played by Roland Culver and his flighty wife Rose by Eunice Gayson. The wife's handsome escort was played by a tall dark film actor called Guy Rolfe who had already caused ladies' hearts to flutter in a number of British films. Had he not been cursed with poor health Rolfe could have been a very big star and enjoyed a similar international career to that of Stewart Granger.

*Serenita* was produced at the Little Theatre in Bristol in 1962.

Two married couples, the Hornbys and the Challoners, share a holiday at a *pensione* called the Casa Serenita overlooking the Bay of Naples. The Challoners, who are young, poor and in love, have been persuaded to accompany the Hornbys, who are rich, older and quarrelling, on a holiday to Italy. But the young

Challoners soon start to quarrel themselves about the Hornbys, wife siding with wife, husband with husband.

One night, after a blinding row, the Hornbys tumble into bed and make love for the first time for months. Next morning they are sublimely happy while the young Challoners are no longer on speaking terms.

My wife and I got caught up in precisely that situation once in the South of France. A couple we knew whose marriage was strained begged us to share a holiday with them to Cannes as peace-keepers. We would always be around to suggest a swim or change the subject if their conversation became heated. Like the Challoners', our holiday would have been ruined by our friends' bickering if events had not saved the situation.

The play is now dated, having been written when the Currency Regulations were still in force:

When the Hornbys decide to dump the Challoners and move on to Capri without them, the Challoners are left without enough currency to get them home. So Michael tries to get a loan from a bored English bank manager, also on holiday with his wife in the *pensione*, who jumps at the opportunity to practise his trade. So with Michael sitting opposite him at a wrought-iron table on the patio, the bank manager questions him about his finances while Michael desperately makes out his case for a loan.

Because Vesuvius was visible in the distance as a smouldering symbol of marital eruption one review was headed, 'Warmth Beneath The Volcano.' The same notice went on to mention that the characters were 'astutely drawn' and that 'middle-aged tranquillity was represented by James Fairley and Wendy Errol' who played the bank manager and his wife.

I have always been amused by stage reviews in regional

newspapers when the reporter, obliged to mention everyone, has to vary the verbs and adjectives to avoid repetition. Thus a review will end by saying:

> The cast acquitted themselves admirably. Sheila Booth triumphed as Mrs Wainwright while Harriet Plum scored as the Maid. Arthur Gates hit the target as the clumsy Police Sergeant while Susan Bachelor struck exactly the right note with her portrayal of the Grandmother. John Fuller was a confused Vicar to the life and the play was efficiently staged by Derek Lineham. Clare Davidson's setting was apt; the lighting was professionally handled by Harold West and the costumes by Sarah Wells fitted the occasion perfectly.

Something important happened for my playwrighting career about this time which started badly but was to have fruitful results later.

A personal friend, Judith Truman, who was running the play publishers, The English Theatre Guild, suggested that two of my single TV plays, 'Breaking Point', recently screened by Associated-Rediffusion, and 'The Tea-Cosy', a former Sunday night play for the BBC, would make a good double-bill for reps. and amateurs if published together. The plays were well contrasted; one a rather sad play about a bachelor girl in love with a married man; the other a black comedy-thriller about a Kensington teashop and a body in a trunk. They could be cross-cast, i.e. a leading part in one play would also suit the player of a smaller part in the other. I was delighted to achieve yet a third play publication.

'The Tea-Cosy' had actually been one of the first of a small number of plays to be written specifically for television. After the success of *Release* Michael Barry had suggested I should write another Sunday Night Play for the BBC so I cooked up this black farce:

Two old sisters run a dainty teashop in Kensington. One foggy night, overhearing their furtive whisperings, they become suspicious of a young couple who habitually meet at a corner table in the café. Believing them to be spies, they call in the police. But all the while a respectable old clockmaker who lives over the shop, Mr Salusbury, who also has his tea regularly on the premises, has been busy upstairs cutting up Mrs Salusbury, whom he has poisoned, and putting her remains in a trunk, telling people "the wife's gone abroad". At Mr Salusbury's request the old ladies have innocently agreed to store the trunk for him in their basement.

The mood of the play is summed up by the curtain line when the police inspector finally opens the trunk, the old sisters look into it with horror and one exclaims "Oh, my dear, it's Mrs Salusbury."

The second sister starts "And . . ."

And the first sister finishes "And with our carving knife!"

'The Tea Cosy' was later bought for production by Rome Television and transmitted as 'Il Copriteiera'.

Almost unanimously the critics compared 'The Tea Cosy' with *Arsenic And Old Lace* and I could hardly blame them. The plot was different, of course, in that my old ladies, played by Jean Cadell and Katie Johnson, were innocent dupes, not murderesses. All the same, it was a black comedy about murder with two 'respectable' old ladies as the central characters and I suppose the comparisons with Mr Kesselring's American classic were inevitable.

Talking of *Arsenic And Old Lace,* that world-famous black comedy, reminds me it contains the perfect example of how one line of ordinary dialogue can produce a tremendous effect in the right place, when it becomes what John van Druten once called 'the line crackling in the situation.'

In *Arsenic* the nephew says to his two elderly aunts "Do you realize there are six dead bodies buried in the cellar under this house?"

And one of the aunts delivers the simple reply "Yes, dear, we know," and brings the house down.

My double-bill did well in the UK but a production of it abroad proved to be one of the most comic tragedies of my writing life. In the winter of 1964 Judy Truman of The English Theatre Guild called me to say that she'd had an offer for the double-bill to be produced at the Theater der Courage in Vienna around Christmas. Soon I heard that an Austrian translator was at work on the script and that the Austrian publishers, Universal Edition, hoped I would fly to Vienna to attend the *première*. Thrilled beyond measure and imagining a glittering first-night in some plush and gilt rococo playhouse of Hapsburg days, with chandeliers and plush boxes filled with smart Viennese society ladies, I boarded an Austrian Airlines Caravelle at Heathrow and settled in my seat. A stewardess came down the aisle selling copies of the *Wiener Tageblatt*. I bought one, opened it and saw my photograph prominently displayed on the Arts page with a write-up about me and my plays. My pride knew no bounds. I was Ibsen himself on his way to a production of *The Wild Duck* in Berlin.

We landed at the Schwechat Airport in deep snow; Christmas in Vienna – romance, excitement! At the hotel I was interviewed for the Austrian Radio. What was my opinion of current English drama? How did I rate Osborne, Wesker, Whiting? I replied with tact. I had a bath and changed. The translator of my plays came to the hotel to take me to the Theater der Courage, a venue which Peter Brook, whom I had met at lunch a fortnight earlier, had assured me was immensely prestigious.

We drove in a taxi along the Franz Josef's Kai and stopped outside what looked like a small shop. I imagined my translator wanted cigarettes but he opened the door for me to get out.

We entered the premises and went down some stone steps; a slight smell of cheroots and fresh paint; then a tiny room with a little stage at one end; faded, shabby drapes. The room was full of people sitting on hard chairs: most of the men were scruffy and bearded, some looked like university professors; all the Vienna drama critics were there. An added attraction, I learned later, was the fact that both plays had been directed by the famous Viennese actress, Helene Thiemig, the widow of Max Reinhardt. In fact Thiemig herself later appeared in the Austrian TV production of 'The Tea Cosy' as one of the old ladies. 'Breaking Point' was also produced on TV with an excellent cast and went very well. But the plays fared less well at the Theater der Courage.

The evening, which had been given the overall title of 'Gaste Zum Tee' (Guests For Tea), was a disaster. The audience had come to see what they imagined would be a pair of *avantgarde*, experimental plays by a new, young English playwright. What they got was a couple of simple middle-brow entertainments written for television. I was roasted by most of the critics, one notice describing the event as '*eine Tasse weicher englischer tee*'; 'a cup of weak English tea –'

Only the critic from Linz was kind. '*Ein erfolgreicher Abend* [a successful evening],' he wrote, bless him.

I flew back in a blizzard, low and depressed, masochistically translating my awful reviews with the help of a pocket German dictionary and wishing I had never learned the wretched language.

It is bad enough for a writer to read a damning review of his work in any language but in his own language when every word strikes home it can be painfully shaming and thoroughly discouraging. Reference to 'The Tea Cosy' and its reception in Vienna reminds me that the original television production of that particular little play inspired one of the worst reviews I have ever had for anything. The *Evening*

*Standard* critic on that occasion, noting that the play was billed as a 'mystery', wrote as his headline 'The only mystery – why was it staged?' The review went on: 'the players went through this dispirited and childish affair with an air of indifference . . .'

A writer must develop an immune system to survive bad reviews. The best consolation is often commercial success and 'The Tea Cosy' achieved respectably high ratings. Sometimes a glance round a packed auditorium can alleviate the pain of bad notices. But the best cure, after a 'stinking review' in one paper, is to buy another and read in it immediately a total contradiction of the first.

This differential can often apply to the opinion of producers to whom you submit a play. On one occasion I received letters from both Binkie Beaumont and Henry Sherek on receipt of the same play. Beaumont told me it was 'well constructed but weak on characterisation' while Sherek said 'Fascinating characters but the play is a trifle shapeless.'

No two individuals ever react exactly the same way to a play, either reading it in script form or seeing it acted on a stage. Three people can be sitting in adjoining seats in a theatre, Row F3, 4 and 5, watching a play about a suffering wife threatening to divorce a cruel husband. In F3 is a woman on her own whose attitude to men, marriage and sex is coloured by her own traumatic marriage to a brutal husband. Next to this woman, in F4, may be sitting a young man of twenty-four in love for the first time, holding hands with his fiancée, next to him in F5. He is unlikely to respond in the same way to that play. The events unfolding on the stage belong to a different world from the one he inhabits and are so alien to his experience that he has probably given up listening and is wondering where to take his girl friend to supper afterwards and how much it will cost him. His fiancée is probably thinking 'Geoffrey would never behave like that;

he's gentle and kind. . .' Refusing to be upset, she will perhaps relax in her seat, noticing that the wife on stage is wearing a jersey just like one she saw yesterday in Marks and Spencer. But the mysterious magic of the theatre is that a whole audience of individuals with their varied ages, backgrounds, lifestyles and experience, do in the end respond as one mass of people to the overall emotion generated by the play, be it curiosity, fear, suspense, laughter or absorption in a human situation. I am inclined to believe that the majority lead the way and the rest follow.

# THE ELUSIVE WEST END

IN 1990 I wrote another light comedy called *Monsieur Fragonard*, set in a hotel in Paris, but failed to find a producer for it. But that year, soon after we moved from London to live near Newbury, my thriller *Double Cut* was produced at the charming little dinner theatre, The Mill at Sonning, not too far away. Thus I was able to meet the gorgeously attractive actress and Artistic Director of the theatre, Sally Hughes.

*Double Cut* did very good business at the Mill, so I offered *Monsieur Fragonard* to Miss Hughes, who accepted it for production but thought audiences might think it was a biographical play about the eighteenth-century French painter. It was not. M. Fragonard was a French businessman in the story. However, Sally rightly asked me to find another title so I did, and it went on in the summer of 1993 during a heatwave with the title of *Love En Suite*, and had a considerable success, playing to 86% capacity for five weeks, with excellent reviews in the Reading press. But nobody picked it up and it, too, remains in my bottom drawer.

Like most modern theatres, the Mill at Sonning has an open stage and no house tabs, so that the audience are able to see the set as they take their seats. I deplore this new convention and would still prefer scene changes to take place behind a curtain. For me, it destroys the illusion of the theatre to see stage hands in black cat-suits moving furniture and trays about on the dark stage between scenes. But some directors now make an art form of it. In *Love En Suite*, for example, a supper table for two had to be set in a Paris hotel suite with cutlery, glasses, champagne on ice, lit candles, etc. Sally Hughes directed this necessary operation like a ballet. The hotel manager and a waiter, both characters in the play, assisted by a stage-hand dressed as a waiter, set the scene swiftly and neatly, accompanied by romantic French songs by Maurice Chevalier, Charles Trenet and Jean Sablon. When the stage was finally set they went off to a burst of applause; it had provided a few minutes of extra entertainment that was not in the script.

In this play I learned a sharp lesson about funny lines. An older woman is discussing with a younger woman the possibility of someone coming into the hotel suite while the younger one is having a fling with a lover. The younger woman says, "You mean sort of coitus interruptus" to which the older woman says, "Do you know, an aunt of mine thought coitus interruptus was a Roman Emperor."

Of course the big laugh came on *coitus interruptus* and killed the follow-up joke about the Roman Emperor. If the aunt's naive ignorance had been under discussion in general terms, the older woman could have said, "Dear Aunt Maud, so naive. She thought coitus interruptus was a Roman Emperor." Just like that, all in one piece, it would have been better.

*PARTING DAY*, written in 1978 and in my view to be one of my best stage plays, had such a long, frustrating history that I feel inclined to describe it in detail, if only as an example to aspiring playwrights of the painful business of getting a play produced anywhere.

It concerns two middle-aged brothers. The elder, a civil-servant called Evan, is married with grown-up children and commutes to London from a country house made over to him by his mother, a famous novelist who has just died in a London flat aged eighty. The younger brother, Peter, is a rich and successful author, unmarried and living for tax reasons in the South of France. When Peter arrives in Hampshire to stay with his elder brother for their mother's funeral in the village church, Evan and his wife Marion are put out to find that Peter has brought with him from France his English boy friend, a former cabin steward called Geoff. Evan's son and daughter are modern and liberated young people who take it all as a matter of course and make Uncle Peter's boy friend feel welcome. But over the weekend of the funeral Peter's relationship with Geoffrey reaches an emotional crisis and they have a blinding row. Geoff stages a walk-out and Peter makes a grand gesture of attempting suicide. The storms and dramas created in the house by Evan's brother and Geoff cause Evan and Marion great embarrassment and they sigh with relief when the couple finally depart for France, leaving the young generation to explain to their old-fashioned parents what Uncle Peter's gay marriage is all about.

After Peter and Geoff have left Marion reveals to Evan that she was once attracted to his brother Peter years ago when they were all young but that she changed her mind one weekend at breakfast after a dance at their house:

*Marion*: . . . I saw Peter as he really was. He had a slight hangover; we all had. But he was in a waspish, rather unkind mood. He made the most horrid remarks about some of the girls at the party and the dresses they were wearing; made everyone laugh, of course, but it was cruel and mean and, you know, like a woman. He said the band must have come off a third-class Cruise ship on its way to the Canaries. Then he made fun of your mother's books. I thought to myself 'What a nasty young man he turned out to be! How could I have found him attractive last night? Evan's the one for me. Good solid, loyal Evan who says little, but never anything unkind or malicious.'

Peter Harcourt, the lead role, is a sharp, witty, rather camp part and for a start I sent the play to a number of stars in an attempt to get it going. Extremely polite and often complimentary letters were received back from John Gielgud, Frank Finlay, Paul Scofield, Alec Guinness, Ian Richardson and later Ian McKellen and Peter Barkworth, all declining the part for various reasons:

*Gilegud*: 'The play is very well put together and should act effectively but . . . this kind of play has already been done by Nöel Coward in *Suite In Three Keys* and is no longer shocking . . .'
*Frank Finlay*: '. . . a smashing play with beautifully drawn characters. Peter is a meaty, attractive part and I'm positive it would interest many actors but I don't think I would be able to play him truthfully.'
*Alec Guinness*: 'It's lively to read and I was intrigued but it is not, I feel, a play for me . . . do please let me know when it is done somewhere, in case I can get to see it.'
*Paul Scofield*: 'I much enjoyed your play but have already filled 1979 to the brim . . .'
*Ian Richardson* was honest enough: 'I successfully stemmed the flow of crusty soldiers that came my way after Montgomery; almost sank under the weight of spies on offer following *Tinker, Tailor* . . . declined the Morecambe and Wise show after *Private Schultz*; and agreed to Pebble Mill at One only to prove I wasn't really the senile old queen I played in *Woman In White*. Recently I undertook Pandit Nehru (in dark makeup, shaved head and tinted contact lenses) and daily expect to be fighting offers of a remake of *Gungha-Din*. This sounds flippant for which I apologize and for returning your excellent play for which I wish you all the luck it deserves.'

It was 1978 and some of those actors may have feared playing an outrageous old queen at that time. There was no point in sending the play to West End producers without suggesting a star for Peter, so in the end I turned to my good friend Roger Clissold at the Salisbury Playhouse and he agreed to do it.

For Peter he cast a marvellous actor I had never seen before, Philip Voss, who is, to this day, the only actor ever to play Peter Harcourt in *Parting Day* and probably the last. But he was quite excellent in the part and could not have been bettered by anyone.

As an illustration of how risky it was considered to stage this play at the time, Roger was forced to make a note in the Salisbury playlist and on the posters warning the patrons that *Parting Day* was 'perhaps not suitable for children.'

All the same, it opened at the Playhouse to the kind of reviews a playwright dreams of. The *Salisbury Times* called it 'absolutely spellbinding . . . a delicate situation which Mr Shaughnessy handles so well and so delicately that there is nothing to which offence can be taken . . . in fact a feeling of deep sympathy is built up . . .'

The *Stage* wrote: 'It deserves to succeed . . . a touching and very powerful climax . . .'

The *Western Daily Press* called it 'a gentle tale of near-tragedy . . . the reunion of two long-separated brothers almost ends in disaster but the problems are resolved with compassion and gentle humour, typical of the author's work . . .'

There were a number of fan-letters from members of the audience during its five-week run at Salisbury and one evening I was accosted in the bar at the interval by an elderly couple who seemed to know who I was. They told me that they had a son who was 'queer' and that the play had helped them to understand him a little better.

Some time before *Parting Day* opened at Salisbury Roger Clissold had been asked by the joint-committee of the Hampshire and Wiltshire St John Ambulance if he would give them a Gala Performance at the Playhouse to raise funds and he had suggested a random date which they accepted. When it transpired that *Parting Day* would be on that evening and the St John Committee were told of the nature of the play, there were some misgivings and questions were asked. But they decided to go ahead. The Gala Evening was a very dressy affair with most of Hampshire and Wiltshire society present, got up to the nines, the women in evening dresses and jewellery, the men in dinner jackets. Tickets cost from £15 upwards. But word had got round that the play was 'a bit unsuitable' and some elderly matrons whom I knew personally came up to me in the foyer before the show wagging their fingers at me and saying things like "Now then, Freddy, are you going to shock us?"

In the event the play went well and was warmly received. When the curtain finally fell, a uniformed senior St John official came on stage to thank the Playhouse and me for providing the evening's entertainment and ended by saying "I think we must all agree that, after what we had all heard about the play, it came as a great relief and we are grateful to Mr Shaughnessy for not causing us any embarrassment."

Another little play of mine, 'Never Walk Alone', vanished into oblivion after only one performance, one of a number of new plays tried out by the Salisbury Playhouse on Monday evenings at special prices.

This is a three-hander about a young German *au pair* girl on the run from an unhappy situation; a middle-aged doctor who has been struck off the Medical Register for misconduct; and a young tearaway just out of prison. This oddly assorted trio meet up by chance while sheltering from a storm in an old burnt-out and deserted wreck of a country house. Suspicious of each other at first, they gradually make a home for themselves in the empty shell of the house and become a kind of family unit, dependent on each other for their restored self-confidence. The storm ends, the sun shines again and the three 'lost souls' go their separate ways with new hope and courage to face the future.

It was a somewhat allegorical but quite moving little play with three excellent acting parts; it had its one night airing at Salisbury and retired to the bottom drawer.

I coupled 'Never Walk Alone' to make a double-bill with a short, sharp and quite shocking little play called 'The Bitter

End'. This one starts off as a comedy and suddenly turns 'black' in the Ayckbourn manner.

A group of ordinary suburban men and women meet at a house on New Year's Eve, dressed in fancy costume, ready for a ball at the Town Hall. Before going on to the ball they have sandwiches and drinks and dance to a CD.

But a piece of classical music is put on and underlying sexual passions and jealousies, stirred up by the drink and exotic music, begin to surface. The six friends begin to speak and act as the characters represented by their costumes. A normally shy office secretary, who reluctantly removes her mac to show she is scantily dressed as Salome, later loses all her inhibitions and executes a lasciviously provocative dance for the benefit of one of the husbands present who secretly fancies her. A vicious fight breaks out and at its climax one of the men stabs his rival with his make-believe pirate's dagger.

Suddenly blood spurts and a woman screams. The orgy comes to am abrupt halt. They all come back with a bump to reality and freeze with horror.

The shy secretary crouches half naked in a corner with her veils torn off; the rival husband lies dead in a pool of blood; midnight strikes outside and distant cheering is heard as someone phones for an ambulance. The group never get to the Town Hall to celebrate the new year.

'The Bitter End' was performed for two weeks in a small fringe theatre upstairs over a Dulwich pub and was remarkably well acted by a good cast under the direction of the talented Peter Benedict. But nowhere else, so far.

One play I wrote actually had three separate existences. In other words it was produced three times in three different versions, over the space of thirteen years. This was *The Heat Of The Moment*.

If my kitchen-sink play, *Release*, by anticipating *Look Back In Anger* by five years, was that much ahead of its time then *The Heat Of The Moment* by preceding Mrs Thatcher by fourteen years, did likewise. Let me explain.

The year 1965, when John Counsell accepted the play for his autumn season at The Theatre Royal, Windsor, was well into the permissive '60s. A Labour government was in office under Harold Wilson and the class war was raging. The theatre establishment of the day had set its face against almost anything that was not palpably left-wing in tone and the comedies of playwrights such as Frederick Lonsdale, Nöel Coward, Terence Rattigan, and William Douglas-Home were despised as creaky, dated, upper-class, Tory rubbish.

John Counsell, however, whose famous theatre standing in the shadow of Windsor castle, was an oasis of gentle middle-class, non-political, traditional drama. Running one of the only theatres in the country that was entirely self-financing and receiving not one penny of Arts Council subsidy, John stuck his neck out and announced in *The Times* and other national newspapers that he was going to present an autumn season of what he called 'normal plays' by which he meant conventional, well-made plays with a beginning, a middle and an end and a curtain to go up and down on each scene.

*The Heat Of The Moment* was to open the season and be followed by a new comedy by William Douglas-Home called *A Friend Indeed* and two others. Unfortunately, my play was by no means a gentle 'Anyone for tennis?' light comedy. On the contrary it was a controversial, fairly political drama about the class war, set in the country seat of a baronet. I suspect that the critics' pencils were being sharpened well before it opened. The story is indeed provocative and Frank Lawton, who was in it, likened the play to Galsworthy's *The Skin Game*:

Sir Richard Scott-Carey [the name was to reappear years later as the family name of the Earls of Southwold in *Upstairs, Downstairs*] is a country squire and a Master of Foxhounds. One winter evening Sir Richard Scott-Carey, his wife Marjorie and their daughter Sarah who works in London, plus Sarah's boyfriend Tony, who is in advertising and staying for the weekend, are dining before the Hunt Ball. The front door bell rings and a very angry Welsh teacher called Lewis from the local school demands to see Sir Richard. It seems that two boys from the school have that afternoon climbed a wall into Richard's stableyard and thrown a thunder-flash into one of the loose boxes, almost causing a brood mare to lose her foal. Evidently Sir Richard arrived on the scene, caught one of the boys and, in a blind rage, thrashed him with his riding crop. The schoolmaster, Lewis, has come to demand an apology for the boy and his widowed mother. Sir Richard tells Lewis to get out of his house. A furious row develops. The incident gets into the newspapers. Richard has a brick thrown at his car in the local town and is called a 'fascist pig' but the local community is split down party political lines; Richard tries to enlist the support of the Chief Constable whom he knows personally. Sarah is torn between her father's cause and her younger, more liberal attitude to class differences and can see Lewis's point of view.

In the end the young generation, Sarah and Tony, manage between them to broker a kind of face-saving cease-fire. Lewis comes to like and respect Sarah; Tony secretly takes the thrashed boy and his mother to a cinema and buys the boy an ice-cream, so that eventually the boy writes in his childish handwriting a letter of apology to Sir Richard. The latter is very touched and promptly invites the boy and his mother to come up to the stables one day soon to see the mare and her foal.

Because I told that carefully balanced story from the point of view of the baronet's family, the critic from Slough saw it as Tory propaganda. Although Sir Richard was played by Frank Lawton, whom John Counsell cast purposely to set Frank's quiet charm against the rather blimpish part of Sir Richard, the role does contain a number of angry speeches about the state of the country at the time.

It is shortly after Lewis's first visit and before they go off to

the Hunt Ball.
*Richard* (wearily to his wife): Have you ever thought about it, Marjorie? From the age of three you and I were taught by our nannies to believe in God and the Royal Family . . . we obeyed our parents even when we didn't agree with them and we respected our elders. Now, it seems God is a joke, the churches are empty, the very existence of Jesus Christ is being challenged by the scientists. The Royal Family can be mocked with impunity by any cheap cartoonist looking for an easy victim who can't hit back and the Tories are rich people without brains who trample on the poor and the underprivileged. We're living in an age when any long-haired lout who can strum a guitar and make noises like an animal in pain can earn ten times more money than a Cabinet Minister . . .

In another scene Lewis talks about the thrashed boy having his 'rights', to which Richard replies:

*Richard*: Children have too many rights these days, in my opinion. That's why we have blocks of concrete on the railway lines and parents suing teachers for assault when they slap a child for bullying on the playground.

Those sort of sentiments were so out of fashion in 1965 that two managements who came down to Windsor to see the play confessed to my agent that they would not dare to present such a play in the West End. The public would love it, they said, but the critics would tear it to shreds.

The English Theatre Guild, however, did publish the play in an acting edition and it was performed in half a dozen repertory theatres, including Colwyn Bay (because Lewis was a Welshman?) and for some extraordinary reason by a Drama Group at Lampeter University. A production was also mounted at the St Martin's Theatre in Melbourne, Australia too and, to my amazement, BBC Radio broadcast it as Saturday Night Theatre. That radio production drew several 'fan' letters from viewers who deplored the current undisciplined, permissive society and agreed with a lot of Richard's arguments. But *Heat* never made it to from Windsor to London.

By 1977 I was feeling more confident after the success of *Upstairs, Downstairs* and I had a new agent, the enterprising Richard Stone. One day I discussed with him the possibility of reviving *The Heat Of The Moment*. To update it, I made a few minor alterations, changing Richard into Robert, probably so as not to confuse him in my mind with Richard Bellamy of *Upstairs, Downstairs* who was of the same mould. In the revised version the family were not on their way to a Hunt Ball but to a Charity Function in a nearby big house, the dress having gone down from white ties and tails to dinner jackets, and the tickets up to £25. Otherwise the thrust of the play was unchanged.

In 1977 Richard Stone packaged *The Heat Of The Moment* with his client Richard Todd, who was a star name, a country squire himself, with a most distinguished war record. A try-out production was arranged at the Connaught Theatre, Worthing with a view to a West End transfer.

For the part of Sarah the daughter, Richard Stone suggested another of his clients, Delia Lyndsay, an excellent actress who had played an important part in *Upstairs, Downstairs* extremely well. So *Heat* opened for its second chance in Worthing and was an instant success. The houses were packed, albeit mostly with elderly, retired seaside residents but some younger people were to be seen in the audience.

The reviews were more than encouraging: 'A finely balanced play with both sides of the argument being skilfully represented . . .'

. . . 'the beauty of this play is that it shoves the hard facts of the class-war brutally down the audience's throats but at the same time maintains a level of gentle sophisticated humour throughout . . .'

But one notice pleased me especially. The young girl critic of a Sussex newspaper wrote: 'Alfred Shaughnessy's new play at the Connaught recalls the work of Terence Rattigan but should not be dismissed on those grounds for there is still room for a play that can deal absorbingly with matters which are all too contemporary . . .'

Richard Todd himself was so confident that the play would transfer that after every performance he made a short curtain speech thanking the audience for their wonderful reception, adding with a wave, "see you in London."

But the country was again under a Labour Government, that of Jim Callaghan, and the 'winter of discontent' that put Mrs Thatcher into Downing Street was two years away. In this political climate Richard Stone persuaded the West End manager John Gale to come down to Worthing and see the play. Gale brought with him a director who happened to be a resolute Labour supporter, Frith Banbury. Yes, they said, it was definitely a West End play. But Frith said he wanted some changes to the script.

To cut a long and painful story short, I had a number of meetings with Frith at my house in Hampshire where we argued bitterly. He wanted to slant the play to the left and had ideas for the characters which would achieve this. Anxious to see the play reach London, I foolishly agreed to let him have his way. But Frith at least had the courtesy to ask me if I could think of a suitable writer to make the revisions. I suggested the powerful left-wing playwright David Pownall because I knew and greatly respected him. He had done good work for me on my TV Serial *The Cedar Tree*. But David Pownall had a brief to fulfil and what came out was a rather unpleasant, charmless play with no humour and a strong political bias, the one thing I had tried so hard to avoid.

Banbury and Gale cast Jane Baxter as the wife, Lucy Fleming as Sarah and, with Richard Todd in his original but rewritten role of the baronet, the piece opened at the Churchill Theatre at Bromley. At Frith's instigation it was renamed *Assault*. I took my name off it and the whole thing was a total disaster. If only John Gale had hired a less political director in the first place and left the text as it was at Worthing, I am convinced the play would by 1979 have slipped into the West End when Mrs Thatcher slipped into Downing Street . . . and prospered.

Within two years Maggie Thatcher, for all her faults, had made respect and discipline fashionable again and attempted to re-establish old British traditions. In that climate the play might have run for years.

# ADAPTATION

IT has to be admitted that the three most commercially successful and best known of my plays for the theatre were all adaptations of someone else's brainchild. One was the dramatization for the stage of a feature film. Then came an adaptation of a French hit-comedy which had run for years in Paris. And the third was based on a short novel by Reginald Arkell.

Neither of the first two plays mentioned made it to the West End but both were widely toured around the country and published by the prestigious play publishers, Warner Chappell Plays, who grew out of Chappells' take over of The English Theatre Guild and then from Warner Brothers' take-over of Chappells.

*Double Cut* has one of those odd histories which may be of interest to readers.

My old friend Thomas Clyde, in partnership with Douglas Fairbanks Jnr, had made a movie for Warner Brothers called *Chase A Crooked Shadow*. It was a thriller directed by Michael Anderson and starring Richard Todd, Anne Baxter and Herbert Lom. The story was derived from a TV play by two American authors, one of whom wrote the screenplay for *Crooked Shadow.* The film was a moderate success at the box-office but won no awards and made no film history. However, years later, Tommy Clyde asked me if I thought his movie would make a stage play. I had seen the film some years before but now refreshed my memory by having a look at it on video and studying the original movie script. The story had a most ingenious plot.

At a Spanish villa, recently bought by an attractive young South African diamond heiress, a young man arrives, claiming to be her brother and evidently able to prove it. She denies this, declaring her brother to be dead – she saw him die in a car crash. She denounces the man as an impostor after her fortune and calls in the local Spanish police inspector. The audience are never sure who is lying and there are many twists and turns before a shock denouement explains everything.

Some of the action of the movie was, naturally, set against the sunny Spanish landscape: in the grounds of the exotic villa, beside the swimming pool and on a mountain road. But it was clear that, for a stage play, the main action could be contained inside the villa with some events happening offstage. So I told Tommy that, in my opinion, it could be turned into a play for the theatre and he asked me to write it. This I did on spec.

The plot of *Crooked Shadow* was complicated and full of twists so I used a device which I had perfected once when working on a whodunnit and always find useful. All down the right hand margin of the script I draw a thin line which breaks at certain points when what I want the audience to believe at that point in the play has to change. For example, the audience have from the start believed that my imaginary heroine, Julia, who found her husband murdered in the potting shed, had a normal happy childhood. She has spoken of it. So down the margin line I note 'No real suspect here, possibly a business rival, but we'll see.' Then Julia's long lost younger sister, Kate, arrives from abroad and reveals that, far from having a happy childhood, Julia was bullied and ill-treated by their father who always preferred and favoured his younger daughter. Julia had a mental breakdown and once attacked Kate with a pair of scissors. At this point the audience are being coaxed by the author into suspecting Julia of the murder of her husband. She is unstable and has attempted to kill before. The margin note reads 'Here they think Julia did it.'

Then, after a while, the plot takes another twist. Another character in the play is found murdered but Julia, who was on stage at the time, could not possibly have done it. She has a watertight alibi. At this point I alter the marginal note to show suspicion is now off Julia and write down 'audience to think it was that tramp who was seen near the house in Act 1. Scene 1.'

Then, a few pages later, Julia in an angry scene accuses her sister Kate of having been in love for years with her murdered husband and jealous of her all her life. At this point the margin note says 'Now the audience suspect Kate.' And so on. It is essential at all points to be absolutely clear of what the audience believes at that moment, or what you want them to believe, so that you can, if need be, add an ingredient to strengthen that required belief until the next twist alters it.

The play version of *Chase A Crooked Shadow* worked pretty well and we embarked on a series of discussions with a West End producer, Robert Fox, and Allan Davis who, if we could cast it satisfactorily, would co-present and direct the play. After a long frustrating period of waiting for various stars to read the script and accept or reject the leading roles, Allan became entangled in a scheme to revive *Dial M for Murder* in some regional theatre somewhere and lost interest. But Allan and I had by then worked together on my script and he had made a number of valuable suggestions including that of a new and, as it turned out, final title, *Double Cut*. Eventually Simon Williams, whom I knew well from *Upstairs, Downstairs*, agreed to do the play co-starring with Lucy Fleming as the diamond heiress. But Robert Fox had no theatre fixed for a try-out. At this point I suggested approaching Roger Clissold whom I had worked with at the Salisbury Playhouse but was now in charge at the Thorndike Theatre in Leatherhead. Fox agreed. Roger liked the play and it was resolved that it should be launched from the Thorndike with Roger directing, and in the hope of a West End transfer.

Unfortunately I had to miss the opening night because I had been stricken with an arthritic hip so when the curtain went up I was in Sister Agnes' Nursing Home recovering from a hip replacement operation. Before I could walk on two sticks I heard that Robert Fox had told Tommy and the cast that, despite good reviews, he would not be taking *Double Cut* into London after all.

His given reason was that the cast was not strong enough in name value. But my belief is that he had been relying on Allan Davis to back the piece and wasn't sure enough of the package to risk his own backers' capital.

It was a blow, but there was some consolation to be derived from a new offer from Clissold's successor at Salisbury, David Horlock, to present the play at the Salisbury Playhouse. This proved to be a very good production and our hopes were raised once again.

As a result of Salisbury Tommy Clyde secured an extensive tour of the play by the producer Mark Furness, who launched it from the Wyvern Theatre in Swindon. It was very well directed this time by the Wyvern's resident Artistic Director, Charles Savage, and the tour was a distinct success. The play was published by Warner-Chappells under whose banner it is to this day, doing pretty well with the regional theatres and amateur groups.

Soon after that I was approached to go to Paris and see a hit comedy called *Coup De Soleil* by Marcel Mithois, which was packing the Antoine Theatre. It was a modern, very funny comedy vehicle for a popular Parisian star. On my return to London I did a quick synopsis and a literal translation and the agent for the play, Eric Glass, approached Mark Furness, who had just done *Double Cut*. Mark agreed to use Swindon again as a launch pad and I started talks with Charles Savage. He had reservations about the play but felt it would work if it was set back in the '20s. It was a brilliant idea and made all the difference, so I got to work on a final script. It was not easy to translate the title *Coup De Soleil* properly. In French it means the kind of 'sunstroke' a person feels when falling in love. In the end the play was called *Love Affair.*

The central character is a smart Parisian woman Valentine, in her forties who is a 'nose' for a perfume firm and is working on a new scent called *Love Affair*. She has for years enjoyed the gentle attentions of a middle-aged lover, but is suddenly *bouleversé* by a charming, bubbly young man half her age who delivers, ironically, some flowers which her middle-aged lover has sent her on his return from a business trip abroad. In the end a *mènage á trois* develops and Valentini gets the best of both worlds, for her two lovers agree to share her favours on a weekly basis with friendship and understanding.

The script was sent to and accepted by Sian Phillips who had appeared in my TV play *Breaking Point* years before with Griffith Jones. I was thrilled because I believed that with Sian's name and that of the incomparable Moray Watson, who was to be the middle-aged lover, we could make the West End.

The author, Marcel Mithois, came over from Paris for the opening night at Swindon and I had the uncomfortable experience of sitting beside him in the stalls, praying that plenty of laughs would come, although his English was so limited that I knew he could not possibly argue with my actual translations. The laughs did come, and with each one

18. Margaret Leighton and Anthony Forwood in the TV production of *Release*.

19. Paul Daneman and Christine Finn in the Birmingham Repertory production of *Release*.

20. The German version of 'The Tea Cosy', 'Die Teepuppe'. Left is Helen Thiemig, actress wife of Professor Max Rienhardt.

21. Roger Hume as Old Herbaceous.

22. L. to R.: Michael Davis, Frank Lawton, Elizabeth Counsell and Marjorie Stewart in the Theatre Royal, Windsor première of *The Heat of the Moment* in 1965.

23. Robin Sachs, Sian Phillips and Moray Watson in the play *Love Affair*.

24. Working at home.

Mithois grinned with pleasure, not really quite sure where we were in the text. The next morning I took him for an excursion down to Bath where he bought expensive presents as he put it '*pour les comediens*'. That is, I gather, the normal way in France of referring to the cast of a play. To me it sounded as though Sian Phillips, Moray Watson and the others were a troupe of clowns.

The tour of *Love Affair* was successful everywhere, received good notices, especially at the Theatre Royal, Brighton, and ended up 'pre-West End' at the Yvonne Arnaud Theatre in Guildford. Here it did three weeks of near-capacity business. Mark Furness hired a composer to do some special music for the West End production and was talking about going into Wyndham's Theatre in London. But no more was said. The run at Guildford came to an end. Then we heard that Wyndham's management had been offered a choice of *Love Affair* or a musical version of Sue Townshend's *Adrian Mole*. Of course, they chose the latter.

I was beginning to despair by now of ever seeing my name in lights outside a London theatre. Much of my work had been seen over the years in West End revues but a couple of sketches and a song do not warrant billing. To achieve this you must either have a hit on Shaftesbury Avenue or at the Royal Court in Sloane Square, a playhouse with the most commendable respect for playwrights.

My third and possibly most successful play did make it to London although my achievement of West End-status as a playwright was very late in coming. When it came it was roundabout, indirect and not wholly satisfying. But it did happen, at last, in the winter of 1979. And this is how. While we were living in Hampshire and I was closely involved with the Salisbury Playhouse Roger Clissold gave me a small book to read, a short novel by Reginald Arkell. It was called *Old Herbaceous*. I read it with delight. Then he asked me if I thought I could convert it into a one-man play.

Patrick Garland had recently had a signal success with his very skilful adaptation of the diaries and sayings of the eighteenth-century wit and chronicler, John Aubrey. This had been performed as a soliloquy by Roy Dotrice under the title of *Brief Lives*. Roger saw *Old Herbaceous* as something along those lines: a one-man play about an old gardener in his potting shed talking about his life. I said I'd have a crack at it but couldn't be sure that I could produce anything with which an actor could hold an audience in a theatre for two hours with an interval.

I need not have worried, but had it not been for Roger's vast experience of actors over the years and his immediate certainty of the right actor for the job, the piece might never have seen the light of day. He offered *Old Herbaceous* to an actor who was unknown to me at the time, Roger Hume. When I arrived at the rehearsal room and saw this quite young actor in his forties or early '50s, I could not envisage the thing working. Then Roger Hume began to read. He put on a pair of old steel-rimmed glasses. He introduced a Gloucestershire 'burr' in his voice and chuckled and grunted, and gradually aged as the text progressed. Bit by bit this crusty, lovable curmudgeon of an old gardener, whom Reginald Arkell had skilfully created, came to life . . .

I remember thinking that the best one-woman show I'd ever seen in my youth was that of the American *diseuse*, Ruth Draper, who could hold an audience spell-bound for a whole evening all by herself. She also had the ability to make you see the other characters in her life as she appeared to speak to them. This same talent was passed on by Ruth Draper to the daughter of her friend Mrs Nora Phipps, the brilliant Joyce Grenfell. So in *Old Herbaceous* the gardener Herbert Pinnegar encounters various people such as his employer Mrs Charteris, who gave him his first job in her garden as a schoolboy. And there is George Honey the station master, young Sophie the little underhousemaid, a few elderly village characters, and Lord Gratton who invites him to be a judge at the County Show. All these characters Roger Hume brought to life on the stage as vividly as though they were actually there.

Over the years Bert Pinnegar is promoted to head gardener at the Manor and Mrs Charteris is still his employer when she grows old and a little ga-ga and has to sell up and go into a residential hotel in Torquay to be looked after.

Near the end of the play old Herbert Pinnegar describes a visit to see old Mrs Charteris in the Torquay hotel:

*Herbert*: . . . I saw her sat there, all pale and shrivelled up, with a shawl over her shoulders. She looked up and said, "Good morning. I hear you want to see me. What can I do for you?". . . I put the basket of strawberries on the table . . . then she started to tell me about this old gardener she'd once had at the Manor House, Fairfield, and how he had the knack of forcing strawberries early . . . and how stubborn he could be at times, she could have smacked him. When I said he sounded an odd sort of chap, this gardener, she said "Odd? Not at all. Pinnegar was a gardener. Just a gardener and all gardeners are a little bit like that." We had a cup of tea and talked about flowers and shrubs till the nurse came in to say Colonel Widford was back with the motor car to drive me home. I never let on to Mrs Charteris that she'd had tea with that funny old gardener she'd once employed . . .

*Old Herbaceous* was first performed in the small 100-seater studio theatre, The Salberg, at Salisbury, where it was a complete triumph. After that it was repeated for five weeks in the Main Theatre and again sold out. A West End management then took it up and managed to get it transferred into the Mayfair Theatre in London. Here it opened to fantastic reviews. All the critics praised to the skies both the play and Roger Hume's performance; Jack Tinker of *The Mail*, John Barber of the *Telegraph*, *The Times*, *Financial Times*, all of them. But nobody came to see it and it was off in four weeks. The trouble was that we had had virtually no pre-publicity. Nobody knew who Roger Hume was and, I suppose, the title was a mild put-off. And it was a cold and foggy winter.

Then, thank God, a producer, Dudley Russell, told us that he thought he could organize an extensive tour of *Old Herbaceous* in Australia. Roger Hume was as delighted as Roger Clissold and I were, so he packed his bags and went off with the show down under. There followed over the years a tour of Zimbabwe and a production at the Spoleto Festival in Charleston, South Carolina. After that Roger gave numerous performances at regional theatres in the UK: The Redgrave at Farnham; the Haymarket at Basingstoke; the Connaught at Worthing; the Thorndike at Leatherhead; The Watermill at Newbury three times; and many other smaller venues at local Arts Festivals and even performances in churches. On Boxing Day, 1979 Roger Hume played *Old Herbaceous* as a sort of Command Performance to the entire Royal Family gathered for Christmas at Windsor Castle. The Queen wanted *Old Herbaceous* to be presented as a little surprise for The Queen Mother and it was performed in the Green Drawing Room (recently destroyed in the fire) between tea and dinner. Roger Hume, Roger Clissold and I and our respective wives were invited to stay on afterwards for dinner with the very extended royal family. It was clear there would not be time between tea and dinner for the entire play, so I had to cut down the text, with Roger Hume's co-operation, to about seventy-five minutes.

It had been an icy cold day outside and by contrast it was rather warm in the drawing-room. During the performance Prince Charles, understandably sleepy after a long cold afternoon out shooting in Windsor Great Park, nodded off for a few seconds and Roger Hume saw the Queen tap her son tactfully with her programme, whereupon the heir to the throne woke up with a start and a grunt and sat up to watch the play. Later, at drinks before dinner, HRH made a point of going over to Roger and congratulating him on his superb performance. At dinner the Queen and The Queen Mother were most complimentary and both admitted to shedding a little tear at the rather sad ending of the play.

Over the next fifteen years Roger Hume continued to perform *Old Herbaceous* in various theatres and was granted the exclusive right to do it professionally, although it is published in an acting edition by Warner-Chappell plays and may also be licensed for performance by amateurs.

After the Australian tour Roger Hume acquired the set and props for the potting shed setting and kept them in the garage at his home on the Cotswolds, so that whenever he was clear of other work such as recording *The Archers* for Radio 4 and his agent could fix up a venue, off he would go with the set, his stage manager and electrician in his van, like a snail carrying his home on his back, to perform *Old Herb* somewhere, often to audiences who had seen it before and to whom it had become almost a 'cult'. But it was Roger Hume's one-man play until the sad day when, after a succession of strokes, he died in the autumn of 1996, and in a sense I felt that *Old Herbaceous* died with him. His performance of Herbert Pinnegar, the old head gardener, was a 'tour de force' which will be long remembered. It was a perfect example of the right ingredients being brought together by chance and resulting in something special: a wonderful little book, a competent adaptation, a superb performance and a fine director with a passion for gardening. That is how hits are born. But I still wish it had run a bit longer in the West End.

* * *

ONE small writing job that I was asked to do rather late in life was the libretto for a musical of Frances Burnett Hodgson's classic childrens' story, *The Secret Garden*. Two women, a very talented American composer from Seattle called Sharon Burgett and an English poetess, Diana Matteson, wrote a whole score of songs, solos and ensembles, for a musical version of the story and invited me to do the book. The songs were quite magical: Sondheim-style, tuneful music and excellent lyrics. A book needed to be crafted to accommodate the musical numbers.

When it was ready I suggested that we should offer the show to David Horlock, who was then Salisbury's new artistic director, for a try-out at The Playhouse and this was accomplished. David directed it, and *The Secret Garden* broke box-office records in that theatre. As usual, the Press predicted an immediate transfer to Shaftesbury Avenue but nothing happened.

Shortly after that production David was tragically killed in a car crash while returning from a visit to his mother. It was a disaster for the Playhouse at the time. David was an ideal artistic director, one of the very best, and a lovely person to work with.

Soon, alas, Frances Burnett Hodgson came into the public domain. A whole spate of productions of *The Secret Garden* appeared; one at the little King's Head pub Theatre in Islington; another on Broadway. Then a major film. It was too late.

I still have three or four unproduced plays in my bottom drawer which may or may not ever see the light of day. But they are there as part of my output for the stage and I am always imagining that one of my grandchildren will pick one of them up some day in the distant future and find it quaint and 'period' enough to promote so that, who knows, it could end up as a newly discovered masterpiece.

On reflection I have to say that, of all the pleasurable moments provided by writing over the years, I have derived most kicks from sitting anonymously in the stalls of a crowded theatre and watching one of my own plays in performance. It is always instructive to feel and hear the minute reactions, the intake of breath, the small or heavy laughs on the same line or situation that vary from house to house, theatre to theatre. The same applies to quiet, emotional moments in a play. The zenith is quietness. A tense or tender scene that plays to a hushed silence in which you could hear a pin drop has come off, 100 per cent. You might find yourself remembering what a pain the scene was to write. You may recall the long hours you spent on that particular scene or passage, wondering whether it would work or not. You also may remember 'taking the scene for a walk'. This is an activity which I know for a fact is practised by many playwrights. You are about to write a difficult scene and you are indulging in a bit of what some writers call 'pencil sharpening'. In other words, you are putting off for as long as you can the awful moment of sitting down to write the scene. You fear it will not work so you delay starting it. Once you have started, it may not come off and you will be disappointed and demoralized. But as long as it is still unwritten, there is a chance that it will finally work. So you say to yourself 'I'll go for a good walk in the park and think hard about that scene. When I get home, I'll get down to writing it.'

One foggy winter's afternoon, when we were living in our small flat in Chesham Street, Belgravia, I was stuck with a scene for *The Heat Of The Moment* and decided to 'take the scene for a walk.'

Entering Hyde Park by the Household Cavalry Barracks, I struck out in a northerly direction towards the Marble

Arch, across that vast open space, beyond which is Park Lane and Grosvenor House. The park was evidently empty, with not a soul in sight. As I proceeded along the path, thinking about my troublesome scene, I became aware of a small distant figure, emerging from the fog and heading towards me. It was a man, walking alone as I was, and as he came nearer I could see that he was wrapped in a heavy overcoat and had long flowing grey hair. We approached to within a couple of yards of each other and I saw that it was Emlyn Williams, evidently also 'taking a scene for a walk'. I had met him a few times before the war and longed to stop to say 'hullo' and ask him if he was doing what I was doing. But I feared he wouldn't remember me and anyway I was reluctant to break into his thoughts, so I passed on. I long to know which scene in which of his wonderful plays he was taking for a walk that winter afternoon in Hyde Park.

Another pleasure that emanates from seeing your own plays performed in theatres can also be a source of shock and unhappiness. Given the merciful anonymity of the author whom few people recognize, it is very easy to follow members of the audience out to the bar in the interval and eavesdrop on their conversation. If you can get close enough to a party of, say, two couples, you may hear something useful or pleasing about your play. But it is more likely to be:

A: Are you enjoying it?
B: Oh, yes, we're quite enjoying it, aren't we, Jack?
C: Yes. We're quite enjoying it.
(Embarrassed pause. )
A: She's good.
C: Yes. She was in that . . . er . . . on the telly, you know, about the hospital.
A: That's right. She was good in that.
C: Well, what's everybody going to have. I'm in the chair. Doris?

A: Small gin and lime, please.

And that is the sum total of their assessment of your work.

But eavesdropping in theatre bars can be quite entertaining, especially if it's somebody else's play.

I shall never forget overhearing a party of American tourists in the bar at the Criterion Theatre during the interval of *Waiting For Godot*. They were discussing who Godot was supposed to be and one lady said "Why God, of course"; another blue-rinse matron suggested "No, dear, he's a symbol of peace in a devastated world." Then a man in the party said "In my opinion Godot is definitely Marshall Aid."

I wish Beckett could have heard that. On that very night I went backstage afterwards to see Peter Bull who was playing Pozzo, as we were going out to supper together. After I tapped on his dressing-room door it was suddenly flung open and Peter, still half made-up as the monstrous bully said "What was it all about?"

"I was hoping you were going to tell me," I said.

One sad thing from a playwright's point of view, until recently, was that he or she could never again see the first or any other past performance of a play. Great performances remained buried in the past, as theatrical history, hearsay to be written about and passed down from generation to generation but never experienced again. But the comparatively new technologies of sound recording, film and video tape, all movies, TV shows and radio shows can in theory be preserved for posterity. On any evening, if there's not much to watch on telly, I can go to my video library and get out any of my old TV shows or movies that I have taped and I can indulge in a bout of egotistical nostalgia.

We also have a number of old movies, taken from TV, in some of which Jean appeared in the '50s and '60s. I find it fun to see her again as a beautiful young screen actress of twenty-three, but she finds it all a bit sad. She just mutters, "I don't look like that now."

But old movies can bring back happy memories of the actors and actresses, some of them long since dead, with whom one enjoyed working. A particular sequence in an old film can remind you of a beautiful, enjoyable day on location when everything went right; or of one when the weather was terrible and everything went wrong. But you can afford to be amused now in retrospect or, perhaps, sigh for the good old days.

But that exciting first night of your new stage play in a theatre that took place forty years ago is only a hazy memory now and all that is left of it is a collection of faded reviews and a partly torn photograph in a scrapbook. That evening is as dead now as the first night of Sophocles's *King Oedipus* in Athens in 498 BC.

# WRITING BOOKS

IN 1978, because the success of *Upstairs, Downstairs* had given me a somewhat high profile and I felt I had reached a climax in my life, I wrote an autobiography called *Both Ends Of The Candle*.

The title was supposed to express the dichotomy of my adult life which I had spent with one foot in show business and the other in what is sometimes known as 'society'. However, as the book progressed and I realized increasingly how privileged my early life had been before the war when I was a young, irresponsible, pleasure-seeking playboy, the title began to make more of its usual sense. From the day I left Sandhurst in 1934 until 1939 when I went off to the war I certainly burned the candle at both ends.

I offered *Both Ends Of The Candle* to the courageous and very independent publisher, Peter Owen, who agreed to do it. The book was a success and went into a second impression, so that, encouraged by the reviews, I decided to try my hand further as an author of books.

I had inherited from my mother a diary and several bundles of letters which she had received throughout her life: some from her father and mother in Nashville, Tennessee, when she was an American girl being educated in Paris in 1906; some from my Canadian father before she married him, and others from the trenches in France shortly before he was killed in 1916; and some from my stepfather, Sir Piers Legh, while he was touring the world with his boss, the Prince of Wales, later King Edward VIII.

My mother's handwritten diary and letters were extremely difficult to decipher but gradually, by getting them in the right order and into print, a picture began to emerge of her life that I found fascinating. Apart from descriptions of the multitude of famous people she met and knew and her relationships with them, my brother, sister and I were able to learn a great deal about our mother's experiences, attitudes and characteristics as a young woman, of which we had all been in total ignorance during her lifetime.

I set about putting the material together, and the result was published in 1989, again by Peter Owen, under the title: *Sarah: The Diaries and Letters Of A Courtier's Wife. 1906 to 1936.*

Because some of my stepfather's letters to my mother, written during his royal tours with the Prince, contained some 'delicate' material, especially some not too complimentary remarks about the Prince himself and about Lord Louis Mountbatten, I felt it prudent to get the blessing of the Queen's Private Secretary before allowing the book to be published. In the event, Sir William Heseltine gave me his OK. I cannot help comparing my caution with the recent explosion of confidential gossip about Mountbatten and almost every other royal personage, and revelations that have shaken the monarchy to its foundations and triggered off republican talk which, not so long ago, would have been considered High Treason.

After years of writing stage plays, TV and movie scripts the publication of *Both Ends Of The Candle* and *Sarah* enabled me to experience the novelty and excitement of seeing my writing in print between the hard covers of a book. Now I thought it was time to try my hand at fiction, so I wrote a novel *Dearest Enemy*, which was published by Tabb House in 1991. This was followed by a second novel, *Hugo*, published in 1994, again by Tabb House.

I must say I find it extremely pleasant in the twilight of my life to sit in my house in the country in front of a word-processor and write books and the occasional play for the theatre. But movies, TV and revue material belong to my past and have become for me subjects for reminiscence rather than projects for the future.

I decided to call my first novel, published in 1991, *Dearest Enemy* without any idea that the title had already been used for a Rodgers and Hart musical back in 1926. With an interest in musical shows of the past, I ought to have known this, especially since I have been a dedicated Rodgers and Hart fan ever since I was taken to see *The Girl Friend* at the Palace Theatre, Shaftesbury Avenue as a child. It became an even stranger coincidence when I discovered that the 1926 Broadway show, which was set at the time of the American War of Independence, had opened with a British redcoat officer of King George III's army coming across an American colonial girl swimming in the Potomac river in 1776 and falling in love with her. My novel opens with a British officer in battledress coming across a German girl swimming in the Rhine in 1945 and falling in love with her. The other more tenuous link between my novel and the Broadway show, *Dearest Enemy*, is a song called 'Here In My Arms' by Rodgers and Hart and a 1927 London show produced by my old friend Jack Hulbert for his wife Cecily Courtneidge, called *Lido Lady*.

Because I am such an ardent fan of Rodgers and Hart I am tempted to use the title of my novel *Dearest Enemy* as an excuse to relate a curious story about those two brilliant song-writing partners. In the summer of 1926 Richard Rodgers and Lorenz Hart were in London, having rented a flat in St James's Street, when they were approached by Jack Hulbert and contracted to go to Venice, soak up the atmosphere, and come back with a number of songs for *Lido*

*Lady* which he was then planning.

One morning, strolling down to the Lido, Larry Hart spotted a bar and predictably dived in to get himself a drink, while Dick Rodgers carried on walking along the beach.

Suddenly a voice hailed him. "Dick, what on earth are you doing in Venice?"

Rodgers spun round to see a very young, bronzed Nöel Coward in a bathing costume grinning at him.

The two men had met in New York a few times and Coward was quite a fan of Richard Rodgers' music, so he invited Dick to come along to meet some Americans he was staying with. He took him by the arm and led him over to a cabana where a couple were sitting on deck chairs, a pretty woman and a short, sallow man with popping eyes like a pekingese, wearing a white linen cap and smoking a cigarette.

"This is Richard Rodgers from New York, my host and hostess, Cole and Linda Porter," Coward said.

The upshot was that the Cole Porters invited Rodgers and Hart to dine with them that night and sent their private gondola round to the songwriters' hotel to fetch them. It paddled them to the landing stage in front of a large building on the Grand Canal called the Palazzo Rezzonico which the Cole Porters, who were immensely rich, had rented for the summer.

Here they dined in style, waited on by servants in white gloves, and after dinner, when Linda Porter excused herself to go off and write letters, the five men went into the music room to 'fool around' on the piano. To most people the Palazzo Rezzonico, now a picture gallery, is known as the place where Robert Browning died while visiting his son in 1889, and a plaque on the building commemorates the fact. But there is no plaque to commemorate what must have been a riveting evening in 1926 when Cole Porter, Nöel Coward, Richard Rodgers and Lorenz Hart all sat round a piano swapping songs until three o'clock in the morning. I would love to know what they played to each other: my guess is that Nöel Coward, who was always an assertive, ambitious young man, probably took the piano first to regale the others with a number he had recently completed for Gertrude Lawrence to sing in the André Charlot revue, *London Calling*, called 'Parisian Pierrot'. Perhaps Richard Rodgers played and Larry Hart sang a chorus from 'Manhattan'. I'm not sure what Cole Porter might have played for the others but it could have been that terrible thing called 'Hitchy-koo.'

When Rodgers and Hart finally returned to London to play over their songs for *Lido Lady* to Jack Hulbert he pointed out that they had not written enough of them. The show would need another love song. So they added to the score of *Lido Lady* a number from their *Dearest Enemy* show, which had been produced on Broadway but not in London the year before. The song was called 'Here In My Arms'.

I have to admit that a large percentage of my novel *Dearest Enemy* is autobiographical. Some of the incidents in Jack Hamilton's idyllic sojourn on the Rhine as Entertainments Officer and his deep involvement with the lovely German girl, Karin Freidl, and, through her, with the early postwar German concert and opera scene, actually happened. And like Jack's latter-day search for news of Karin after forty years, my own return to Germany in 1990 in search of the real girl – Hildegard Hammes was her name – was successful.

When I found Hildegard living in Baden-Baden she was still unmarried, although she had lived much of her life with a man whose wife had refused to divorce him. Her lover had died a few years before. But Hildegard was the proprietor and director of an alternative medicine clinic in Baden-Baden, rather than rich widow of a hotel-owning Baron, living in a *schloss* in the Black Forest as was the fictional Karin. And while I was very happy to meet Hildegard again, it could only be for friendship's sake.

After the publication of my novel *Dearest Enemy* and its good reviews, I was convinced that I would have no difficulty in getting it set up as an Anglo-German co-production TV mini-series. With 1995 approaching and much talk of Anglo-German reconciliation, which I guessed there would be, it seemed like a snip. But nobody picked it up. My agent told me that one or two German publishers and TV companies had turned the book down, saying in effect, 'We are more interested in stories about the new united Germany within the European Community, not the old Germany of the past'. In other words 'Don't give us stories about defeated Nazi Germany on its knees under Allied Occupation in 1945 but stories of Germany today, East and West, mergered into one country again.'

I could understand that. But what I was trying to do was to compare the amazing recovery of defeated Germany and the courage and determination of its shattered people working to rebuild their country and in due course to achieve their 'economic miracle', with Karin Freidl's and Jack Hamilton's joint efforts to revive German music as a symbol of Anglo-German reconciliation. But unfortunately nobody saw it like that.

An episode in the novel that represented Jack Hamilton's final separation from his idyll on the Rhine was his burning of a little model theatre with miniature sets for *La Bohème* which had been presented to him by the Bonn opera company, because it was too bulky for him to take back to the UK. In reality, I am glad to say, I did not burn the miniature theatre but found a home for it by giving it away to a local school.

*Dearest Enemy* sold better in hardback than many first novels and has performed surprisingly well in the public libraries. With the Public Lending Right system and its Loan Sampling scheme in full swing, an author can get a pretty good idea as to how his work is going down in the libraries. He may get only 2p a borrowing or some such minor sum but it is not the money that matters, it is the knowledge gained from his book's inside page full of dated borrowing stampings, which show him how many people are reading it. That is very rewarding. After all, the main motivation for a writer is a desire to communicate with people, to share his or her views and experiences with others.

To spot one lady in the corner of a crowded railway compartment or in the Tube, deep in one of my novels, is every bit as pleasing, if not more so, than to see an auditorium in a theatre full of people waiting for the curtain to rise on a performance of one of my plays, or to have friends ring up immediately after one of my television plays has just been on the air and tell me how much they enjoyed it.

To get *Dearest Enemy* published I needed and had a bit of good luck. My half-sister, Diana Colville, was High Sheriff of Cornwall in 1988 and, staying with her at Penheale, we went over to Bodmin one day to watch her take part in the ceremonial opening of the Assize Court, processing through the streets to the Court with the police, the robed Judge and his Marshal and other dignitaries. At an official lunch in a hotel afterwards I found myself sitting next to a Mrs White who told me that she was the wife of an Officer of the Devon and Cornwall Light Infantry, the famous DCLI, and that she was a publisher. Her firm, Tabb House, was sited in Padstow. By the time lunch was over I had persuaded Caroline White to read my new novel and within a week or two she wrote to say she had read it and would like to publish it. I was delighted.

Two years later she published my next novel, *Hugo*, which was in no sense autobiographical. Admittedly, the central character of Hugo, a sensitive boy who has been orphaned soon after the Great War and who grows up in a large country house in Dorset in the '30s, is my contemporary and would have been at Eton when I was and involved in the Second World War when I was. But there the similarity ends. Hugo Mayne is clever, and knowledgeable about furniture, paintings, architecture and historic houses, and in the course of time becomes Curator of the house in which he grew up, now run by the National Trust.

The novel ends with the elderly Hugo mourning the death of his life-long male companion.

I was pleased to get a favourable review for *Hugo* in the *Gay Times*, because the point of the novel was to trace sympathetically and with understanding the emotional development of a young man of my generation whose life resembled that of so many of my friends and contemporaries who in those days were forced to conceal their sexual leanings from family and friends.

I was also anxious to point out, through Hugo's wartime exploits in Albania with the SAS and his extremely well-deserved Military Cross, the simple fact that homosexuals are often just as brave in battle as anyone else, if not braver. The absurd arguments of today about homosexual people in the Armed Forces does seem quite ludicrous to someone of my generation who went through a major war in the company of a number of gay brother officers and other ranks. But nobody ever mentioned it. Of course there were raised eyebrows on occasions but usually people were discreet, accepted it and got on with the job.

One 'raised eyebrow' situation did, sadly, end in tragedy when two brother officers in the Grenadier Guards, who were close friends of mine, fell in love in 1941.

The story really began at the OCTU at Sandhurst where, in the winter of 1939, I found myself in the same company as my friend and solicitor, Ralph Howard, who had been in peacetime a partner in the firm of Frere, Cholmeley and Nicholson. Also in my company was a fair-haired, blue-eyed young man, the Hon. Charles Standish Vereker, who was the only son of Viscount 'Tiger' Gort, VC, Commander-in-Chief of the British Expeditionary Force in France.

Sandy Vereker was the exact antithesis of his distinguished father; he was gentle, sensitive and effeminate and he hated being in the army, disliked wearing heavy boots and rough battle-dress, and resented being bawled at by Drill Sergeants on the square.

As the OCTU term wore on Ralph Howard and Sandy Vereker became drawn to each other and the three of us would escape of an evening to sit in Sandy's room and drink quite a lot of gin, of which Sandy had a fair supply in his locker, and talk about aesthetic matters such as painting, ballet, music and theatre – anything but the war – as an escape from our brutish daily routine of bayonet-drill, rifle-shooting and physical training.

One icy winter evening the three of us, having obtained leave passes, went up to London in my small Ford Prefect where we dined at the Savoy Grill with Hector Bolitho and Terence Rattigan, who were both in the RAF. Later, driving my two friends back to Camberley with enough port in my bloodstream to earn me a stiff gaol sentence under today's laws, my car skidded on the icy road coming down the hill into Camberley and we went into a ditch. Here we remained, uninjured and giggling helplessly, until Ralph extricated himself and went to a nearby garage for help.

When in February, 1940, we passed out of the OCTU, it happened by chance that the three of us were posted to the 1st Battalion of our regiment, which pleased Sandy and Ralph particularly, for they had by then fallen in love.

As we moved from one camp to another this relationship

blossomed, until we found ourselves in the winter of 1941 in billets at Swanage in Dorset. Here, in the relaxed atmosphere of a seaside resort, Sandy and Ralph unwisely let their guard drop and when off-duty were often to be seen by senior officers and others walking hand-in-hand along the cliffs. It came as no surprise to me, but as a shattering bombshell to Ralph and Sandy, when Ralph was suddenly and unexpectedly posted to the 3rd Battalion of the Regiment, which was stationed many miles away up at Louth in Lincolnshire.

I remember the shock to both of them at this plainly deliberate separation. Then, only a week or so after Ralph's departure, we learned at breakfast one morning in the Officers' Mess that Sandy Vereker had shot himself dead with his own revolver in his billet the night before.

There was much speculation among the officers of the Battalion as to the true cause of the tragedy. I remember thinking at the time, as I have always believed, that suicide is usually brought about by an accumulation of factors adding up to uncontrollable depression, rather than one single cause. Sandy's marriage to his wife, Yvonne, was for obvious reasons not very happy; in addition to that he had money worries and it was also thought that, although no military figure himself, he had been upset by his father's humiliating dismissal as C-in-C by Winston Churchill after Dunkirk, to become Governor of Malta. But to my mind there is no question that Sandy's parting from Ralph was the final straw that shattered him and caused him to take his own life.

After Sandy's death Ralph soldiered on with the 3rd Battalion in North Africa and Italy and showed a degree of heroism and bravery in battle that was almost unmatched in our regiment. He was wounded in the arm and lost both legs at Monte Camino but stayed with his troops under fire to encourage them, and won a very well-deserved DSO.

In the years after the war Ralph was to be seen in his much loved club, Boodles, sitting in his wheel-chair, grown stout from lack of exercise, downing dry Martinis and chatting to his many friends. But to me he was always a tragic figure and I suspect that he never quite got over the death of his friend Sandy, whom he survived by just ten years.

ONE technical device, which is more suited to novel writing than to drama, is the use of the written letter. I have always found the reproduction of letters which people write to each other – especially in historical biography – more revealing of character and inner thought that any other source. In a play or movie the reading out loud of a letter by either its sender or its recipient can be a *longueur*. At all events it must be short. But in a novel, you can make two characters write to each other in such a way that their letters become as entertaining, revealing and literarily interesting as a two-handed scene or a long descriptive passage about their respective characters in the main text. You can demonstrate the current writing style of a period of history and show character by the kind of phraseology your characters use, how they abbreviate, how they date their letters and the degree to which they can or cannot let themselves go on paper. A shy man can often write the most sensitive, deeply felt, expressive letter but stammer and stutter in confusion when engaged in conversation.

My two novels *Dearest Enemy* and *Hugo* demonstrate clearly my affection for the letter as a means of characterisation and the reporting of off-stage events through the eyes of the writer.

An early glimpse of the orphan Hugo Mayne, in *Hugo,* is provided by his first letter home from his first boarding-school, in which he writes:

Dear Aunt Celia and Uncle Richard,

I am liking school very much and yesterday we played football and I am going to be inside left for the new bugs team.

There are some very rough boys in my dorm and one of them got the hairbrush on his B.T. from the matron for throwing water over another boy's head called Spencer. I have a friend called Maidment he is very nice and I sit next to him in form and we send funny messages to each other when Chappo who is really called Mr Chapman isn't looking. Please send me some sweets and my book on famous paintings to show to Maidment.

Love Hugo.

I seem to have come round in a full circle now, because my publisher is at present considering a collection of my short stories under the umbrella title of *Tapestry*. They have been written at intervals throughout my life – some published in magazines, some not. And it all began with that short story in the magazine *Affinity* called 'Shop Window Bride', which I wrote as a cadet at Sandhurst in 1934.

Undeniably, Life and my pen have been kind to me.

# INDEX


ABC Television, 91,101
Ackland, Joss, 47
ACT Films, 48,67-8
Addison, John, 37-8
*Affinity* magazine, 4,220
'Afterward', 141
Alderton, John, 129
Alexander Palace, 86,164-5
*All Creatures, Great and Small*, 152-4,157
American International Films, 69-70
Anderson, Michael, 194
Anderson, Lindsay, 35
Anglo-Amalgamated, 69
Antoine Theatre, Paris, 197
April, Elsie, 11
Archibald, James, 91-2
Arkell, Reginald, 194-9
Ashton, Sir Frederick, 6
Aspinall, Tim, 103
Asquith, Hon. Anthony (Puffin), 68
Associated-Redifusion, 93,98, 101,175
Atkins, Eileen, 118-9,133
Attenborough, Lord, 31
ATV, 90,107-9
Austrian TV, 78

Baddeley, Hermione, 5,27
Baddeley, Angela, 124
Baden-Baden, 213
Baker, Robert, 100
Balcon, Sir Michael, 17-20,29, 34-6,38,74
Banbury, Frith, 192-3
Barkworth, Peter, 111 *et seq.*, 183
Barr, Patrick, 48
Barry, Christopher, 87
Barry, John, 72
Barry, Michael, 83,90,163,170,175
Bateson, Timothy, 107
Baverstock, Donald, 101-4
Baxter, Anne, 194
Baxter, Jane, 193
Baxter, John 34
BBC *c.f.* ITV, 90
BBC, Lime Grove, 87
BBC Television Centre, Wood Lane, 83-4
BBC Television Drama, 163,175
Beaconsfield Studios 70
Beaumont, Hugh (Binkie), 170, 179
Beckett, Samuel, 207
Beeny, Christopher, 96,126
Benedict, Peter, 187
Bennett, Cyril, 119,132,134
Bennett, Alan, 116
Benson, Lady Violet, 142
Berman, Monty. 100
Between Ourselves, 13
Birmingham Repertory Theatre, 165-6
*Bitter Sweet*, 12
'Bitter End, The', 186-7
Black, Peter, 170
Black, George, 23
*Black Chiffon*, 172
Blackman, Honor, 68
Bloom, Claire, 76
Bloom, John, 76
Bolitho, Hector, 217
*Boltons Revue, The*, 20
Bond, Derek, 85

Bonn, 16-17
*Both Ends Of The Candle*, 209
Box, Muriel, 57
Box, Sydney, 57,69,71,79
Box, Betty, 57
Boxall, Rosalind, 166
Bradley, Buddy, 6
Brando, Marlon, 55-7
Brando, Christian, 56
*Brandy For The Parson*, 36-8
'Breaking Point', 175
Brett, Jeremy, 146
Brisson, Frederick, 32
British United Artistes, 55
Britton, Tony, 87
Brook, Peter, 177
Brown, Andrew, 111-2
Brownlow, Kevin, 77
Bryanston Films, 74
Bull, Peter, 207
Burge, Hugh, 14-15
Burgett, Sharon, 204
Burke, David, 146
Burnham, Barbara, 170
Bushell, Anthony, 53-4
Buxton, Judy, 50
*By The Sword Divided*, 50
Byng, Douglas, 26

Cadell, Jean, 176
Cambridge Theatre, 25
Capek, Karel, 9
Carey, Joyce, 136,138
Carisbrooke, Marquess and Marchioness, 6
Carr, Jane, 96
Carreras, Michael, 46,171
*Carry On, Nurse*, 58-9
*Carry On, Sergeant*, 58-9
Carstairs, John Paddy, 44
Case, Martin, 119-20
*Cat Girl*, 70
CBC, 85
*Cedar Tree, The*, 135-140,192
Chappells Ltd, 194
*Chariots Of Fire*, 19
Charles, Prince of Wales, 202-3
Charlot, André, 23
*Chase A Crooked Shadow*, 194-6
Cherry, Helen, 109
Churchill, Sir Winston, 34
Clark, Petula, 71
Clarke, Roy, 155
Clarke, T.E.B., 18
Clayton, Harold, 164
Clissold, Roger, 184-5,197,199
Clyde, Thomas, 44,86,194-7
Clyde, Jeremy, 149
Cochran, Sir Charles, 6,23-4
Cohen, Nat, 72
Cole, George, 43
Colin, Jean, 39
Collins, Pauline, 129
Columbia Pictures, 43
Colville, Mrs Norman, (author's half sister), 215
Comedy, Theatre, 13
Compton, Fay, 94-6
Connaught Theatre, Worthing, The, 191
Conroy, Brendan, 152
*Conversation Piece*, 12
Cooper, Duff (1st Viscount Norwich) & Lady Diana, 6
Cooper, Giles, 83
Copley, Peter, 44
Cornelius, Henry, 19-20
Corri, Adrienne, 102-3
Cortese, Valentina, 35
Counsell, John, 188-9
Courtneidge, Cecily, 211
Coward, Sir Nöel, 5,15,23,28, 32,69,130,139,212-3
Crawford, John, 75
*Crescendo*, 46-7
Crichton, Charles, 38
Croft, David, 111
Crowden, Graham, 110
Cubitt, Roland, Mrs, 128-9
Culver, Roland, 173
Cunard, Lady, 6
Currie, Finlay, 89
Cushing, Peter, 71
Cusick, Peter, 43

Dale, Jim, 71
Daneman, Paul, 166
Dankworth, Johnnie, 71

Davies, Betty Ann, 13
Davis, Allan, 196-7
Davis, Sir John, 92,106
Dawson, Basil, 140
Day, Frances, 5-8
*Dead On Nine*, 89
Dearden, Basil, 34
*Dearest Enemy* (musical), 211,213
*Dearest Enemy* (novel), 210,213-5
*Deep Blue Sea, The*, 161
Delderfield, R.F., 58
Deutsch, David, 92
Devlin, William, 85
Dickinson, Thorold, 34-5
Dickson, Dorothy, 9
Dighton, John, 18
*Diverson*, 13
Dixey, Phillis, 13
Donald, James, 37
Donnegan, Lonnie, 71,73
Donner, Clive, 58,79-80,92
*Double Cut*, 181,194-8
Douglas-Home, Hon. William, 89,125-6,188
Douglas, Angela (More), 106-7
Douglas, Felicity, 140
Douglas, Josephine, 72
Draper, Ruth, 200
*Duchess Of Duke Street, The*, 135
Dudley Ward, Penelope, 94-5
Duke, Patty, 99
Dunne, Irene, 30
*Dynasty*, 140

Ealing Studios, 18-20, 34 *et seq.*
Eden, Sir Anthony, 12
Edvina, Louise, 168
Edward, Prince of Wales, 209-10
Eldridge, John, 34-8
Elegant, Robert, 140
Elizabeth II, Queen, 202-3
Elizabeth, Queen Mother, 202-3
Ellison, Robert, 8-10,17
Elstree Studios, 67
Elvey, Maurice, 48-9
Emery, Betty, 29
Empire Cinema, 37
*End Of The Road*, 88
Engel, Susan, 136-7
English Theatre Guild, 175, 177,190,194
ENSA, 13
Errol, Wendy, 174
Eton, 3,19
Evans, E. Eynon, 48
Evans, Dame Edith, 13
Eyeline Films, 76,80,92
*Experience of An Irish R.M., The*, 150-2
*Eyes Have It, The*, 16-17

Fairbanks, Douglas, Jnr, 86
Fairchild, William, 54
Fairley, James, 174
Farjeon, Herbert, 23
*Fascination*, 67
*Fiddlesticks*, 10-13,27-9
Field, Shirley Anne, 81
Fielding, Daphne, 134
Finlay, Frank, 183-4
Firkin, Rex, 110-11
Fisher, Bertie, Major General, 5
Fitzgibbon, Maggie, 112
Fitzalan, Marsha, 149
Five Ocean Films, 54
Fleming, Lucy, 193,196
Flemyng, Robert, 170-1
*Flesh And Blood Show, The*, 47
*Floodlight*, 5-8,11
Floyd, Patty, 118-9
*Follow That Horse*, 45
Forbes, Bryan, 156
Fordyce, Ian, 139
Fox, Robert, 196-7
Fox, Edward, 110
Francis, Raymond, 96
Frankel, Benjamin, 6
Fraser, Bill, 13
Frend, Charles, 92
Frere, Cholmeley and Nicholson, 217
Furber, Douglas, 23
Furness, Mark, 197-8

Gale, John, 192-3
Garland, Judy, 69
Garland, Patrick, 200
Garson, Greer, 31

Gaumont State Cinema, 44
Gayson, Eunice, 173
Gershwin, Ira, 28
Gibbons, Carroll, 13
Gibson, Alan, 46
Gielgud, Sir John, 183-4
*Glamorous Night*, 14
Glasgow Citizens Theatre, 38
Glass, Eric, 198
Glover, Julian, 148
*Godot, Waiting For*, 207
Gordon, Hannah, 107
Gort, Field-Marshall Viscount, V.C., 217
Gowrie, Lord, 168
Grade, Lord, 135,139
Granada Television, 141
Gregg, Hubert, 48
Grenadier Guards, 2,13-16,216 *et seq.*
Grenfell, Joyce, 200
Grierson, John, 34,39
Griffiths, Jane, 75
Group Three, 34 *et seq.*, 88
Guiness, Sir Alec, 31,183-4
Gurney, Rachel, 48,131,170-1

*Hadleigh*, 101-6
Hale, Binnie, 87
Hammer Films, 46,71
Hamilton, Guy, 92
Hammerstein, Oscar, 28
Hammes, Hildegard, 213
Hammond, Kay, 67
Hampshire, Susan, 46-7
Hanslip, Ann, 85-6
Hardy, Robert, 153
Harper, Gerald, 101-6
Harris, Robert, 102-3
Harrison, Joan, 98
Harrison, John, 124
Harrison, Rex, 53-4,167
Hart, Lorenz, 27,211
Hawkesworth, John, 117-8, 122-3,126,131-2,134,146-7
Hayman, Cyd, 111-5
*Heart Of A Child*, 58,78-80
*Heat Of The Moment, The* 187-9, 205
Heiden, Count & Countess, 168-9
Heinz, Gerard, 170
Hempel, Anouska, 47
Hendry, Ian, 93-4
Hepburn, Audrey, 36-7
Herbert, Sir A.P., 23-4
Herbert Hunting, Kate, 144
Herriot, James, 152
Heseltine, Sir William, 210
Heslop, Charles, 10-12
*High Terrace, The*, 52
Hiller, Dame Wendy, 164
Hitchcock, Alfred, 18
Holder, Owen, 123
*Holderness*, HMS, 15-16
*Holiday For Simon*, 89,168-172
Hollywood, 55,89
Homolka, Oscar, 9
Hore-Ruthven, Pam, 168
Horlock, David, 197,204
*Hostage, The*, 86
Household, Geoffrey, 36
Howard, Ralph, 217-9
Howard, Trevor, 109
Howatch, Susan, 142
Howerd, Frankie, 41-42
Hubert, René, 6
Hudis, Norman, 53
Hudson, Hugh, 19
Hughes, Sally, 181-2
*Hugo*, 210,215-6
Hulbert, Jack, 23, 30-31,211,213
Hume, Roger, 200-3
Hunt, Gareth, 126
Huntley, Raymond, 39
Huth, Harold, 86
Hyde-White, Wilfrid, 43,59
Hylton, Jack, 88
Hyson, Dorothy, 9

*Idiot's Delight*, 69
*Impersonator, The*, 74-7,79,93
*Informer, The*, 93,117
*Inspector Calls, An*, 165
*It Always Rains On Sunday*, 19
*It's All Laid On*, 14-15

Jackson, Sir Barry, 165

Jackson, Freda, 167
Jackson, Gordon, 125,129
Jacques, Hattie, 59
Jeans, Ronald, 23
J. E. Entertainments, 143-4
John Barry Seven, The, 72
Johnson, Katie, 176
Johnson, Nunnally, 53-4
Johnston, Brian, 14,16
Jones, Griffith, 89,198
*Journey To The Unknown*, 98-9
Junkin, Harry, 100
*Just My Luck*, 26,44,48

Kazan, Elia, 57
Keith, Penelope, 107
Kemp, T.C., 166
Kent, Jean, 30
Kenton, Mary, 128
Kenton Theatre, Henley, 171
Keppel, Mrs George, 128
Kerr, George, 83
Killanin, Lord, 5-6
Kilmuir, Lord, 54
King Brothers, The, 71
Kirkwood, Pat, 87-8
Kneale, Nige, 83,86
Knight, Esmond, 9
Kotcheff, Ted, 85
Kydd, Sam, 46

Lacey, Catherine, 85
*Ladies In Charge*, 144-6
Laine, Cleo, 71-2
Lale, Joy, 152
Lang, Don, 71
Langton, Simon, 142
Lapotaire, Jane, 47
*Last King, The*, 55
'Last Seance, The', 142
Latham, Philip, 136
Lawrence, Gertrude, 213
Lawrie, James, 34
Lawson, Mrs Derek, (author's sister), 2
Lawton, Frank, 189
*Laxdale Hall*, 38-41,83
Lean, Sir David, 66,77-8
Lee, Belinda, 68-9
Lee, Christopher, 46-7,71
Leggatt, Alison, 95
Legh, Lady, (author's mother) 209-10
Legh Lt. Col Hon. Sir Piers, (author's stepfather), 2,209
Leigh, Vivien, 13,30,49
Leighton, Margaret, 139,164-7
Lesley, Cole, 8
Levy, Stuart, 72
Lewis, Rosa, 134
*Lido Lady*, 211-2
*Light Fingers*, 172-3
Lindo, Olga, 170-1
Lindsay-Hogg, Michael, 94
Linklater, Eric, 38
Lipscombe, W.P. (Bill), 18
Lister, Moira (Vicomtesse, D'Orthez), 31
Little Theatre, 23
Little Theatre, Bristol, 173
Lloyd, Norman, 98-9
Lloyd, Peggy, 99
Lodge, Jean, (Mrs Alfred Shaughnessy), 37,89,154,207
Lom, Herbert, 194
*London Calling*, 213
*London Life*, magazine, 4
London Weekend TV, 94,101, 110-2.132,134
*Long Dark Hall, The*, 53-4
Lonsdale, Jennifer, 136-7
*Love Affair*, 198
*Love En Suite*, 181-2
Lowe, Arthur, 45
Loy, Myrna, 30
Luckham, Cyril 136
*Lunch Hour*, 80
Lynch, Alfred, 111
Lyndsay, Delia, 191
Lyon, Ben, 31

MacDermott, Robert, 23
MacNee, Patrick, 107
MacOwan, Michael, 139
MacPhail, Angus, 18
Macquitty, William, 58
Manahan, Anna, 152
Mander, Miles, 67

*Manhunt*, 111-5,117,121
Mankiewicz, Joseph, 57
Mann, Christopher Ltd, 10
*Manor Of Northstead, The*, 89
Markham, Kika, 110
Marsh, Jean, 118-9,133
Maschwitz, Eric, 13
Massey, Raymond, 69
Matteson, Diana, 204
Maughan, Sharon, 148
Mayfair Theatre, The, 201
Maxwell, Lois, 53
Mayo, Virginia, 30
McKellen, Sir Ian, 183-4
*Melody That Got Lost, The*, 9-10
Melville, Alan, 23
Metropolitan Theatre, 77
MGM, 31,98
MGM Studios, 47
Mill Theatre, Sonning, The, 181
Mills, Sir John, 5-8,39
Mills, Michael, 87
Milton, Billy, 20
Milton, Ernest, 70-1
Mitchell, Julian, 165
Mithois, Marcel, 197-8
Monkhouse, Bob, 26
Monte Carlo, 11
Moore, Roger, 99
More, Kenneth, 37,92,106-7
Moreau, Jeanne, 142
Morell, André, 156
Morgan, Diana, 23
Morley, Robert, 43
Mortimer, John, 80-1
Mountbatten, Lady Iris, 53
Murray Anderson, John, 23
Murray, Pete, 72

Narizzano, Silvio, 85
Nathan and Rosselli, 6
Neale, Patricia, 30
Nesbitt, Cathleen, 44
Nesbitt, Robert, 23
'Never Walk Alone', 186
*New Faces*, 13
Newman, Sydney, 85
NFFC, 34, 37
Nichols, Beverley, 5,11
*Nine Sharp*, 23
'Ninth Knife, The', 4,19
*No Hiding Place*, 96
Novello, Ivor, 14

O'Brien, Bill, 164
O'Brien, Guardsman, 14
*Old Herbaceous*, 199-203
Olivier, Lord, (Laurence) 13,30
Olsen, James, 47
Opera House, Blackpool, 6
Operation Overlord, 15-16
Ormerod, James, 115
Osborn, Sally, 136
Osborne, John, 166
*Our Marie*, 87
Owen, Peter, 209-10

Palazzo Rezzonico, Venice,
Palmer, Lilli, 53-4
Parker-Bowles, Mrs Camilla, *see* Shand
Parker, Cecil, 45
Pascal, Gabriel, 49
Parsons, David, 9
*Parting Day*, 173,182-6
*Passport To Pimlico*, 19
Paul, Jeremy, 118
Payn, Graham, 8
Peach, Mary, 45
Peck, Gregory, 31
Pelissier, Anthony, 94
Pellissier, Tracy, 94
Pembroke, (Henry Herbert), Earl of, 50,149
Perkins, Anthony, 99
Perry, Anthony, 92
Philips, Sian, 198-9
Phillips, Leslie, 44
Phillpotts, Ambrosine, 105
Phipps, Nicholas, 23
Phipps, Mrs Nora, 200
Phoenix Theatre, 9
'Pick Up', 12-13
Pidgeon, Walter, 31
Pinewood Studios, 43,57-8
*Place of Execution, A*, 85
Playhouse, The, 13
Playhouse, Salisbury, 184-6,

127,199,204
Pleasence, Donald, 79-80
*Pleasure Of Your, Company, The*, 10,26
Plowright, David, 142
Porter, Cole, 28,212-3
Powell, Dilys, 75
*Power And The Glory, The*, 9
Powers, Stephanie, 47
Pownall, David, 192
Price, Dennis, 42-3
Priestley, J.B., 135,139
*Punch Revue, The*, 24
Purser, Philip, 146

*Quatermass Experiment, The*, 86

Raine, Jack, 87
Raine, Patricia, 87
Rakoff, Alvin, 85
Ramage, Jennifer, 44
Rank Organisation, 43,57-8, 68-9,91-2
Rattigan, Sir Terence, 161-3, 192,217
Reagan, Ronald, 30
Reed, Sir Carol, 67,95
Reeves, Michael, 46
Regan, Joan, 71
Reggiani, Serge, 34-6
*Release*, 34,163-7,175
*Revuedeville*, 29
Rhodes, Marjorie, 44,48
*Rich Are Different, The*, 142
Richardson, Ian, 183-4
Richardson, Sir Ralph, 31
Richman, Stella, 93-4,118
Richmond Theatre, The, 173
RKO (USA), 52
Roberts, Rachel, 167
Robertson, Dale, 52
Robinson, Eric, 87
Robson, Dame Flora, 46-7
Rockingham Castle, 147
Rodgers, Richard, 211-13
Rogers, Paul, 166
Rogers, Peter, 57-9,69
Rogers, Pieter, 107
Rolfe, Guy, 173
*Room in the House*, 48,67
Rose, Richard D., 7
Ross, Martin, 150
Royal Festival Hall, 21
Royal Film Performances, 29
RSPCA, 80
*Royalty*, 143
Rusoff, Lou, 70
Russell, Dudley, 202
Russell, Rosalind, 31-2
Rutherford, Margaret, 9,43
Ryan, Kathleen, 39-40

*Saint, The*, 99
Sagitta Films, 117
*Sanctuary*, 95
Sandhurst, RMC, 1,2-5
    OCTU, 216
Sangster, Jimmy, 47
*Sarah*, 209-10
Saturday Night Theatre, 163
*Sauce Piquante*, 25
Saunders, Peter, 171
Savage, Charles, 197-8
Saville Theatre, 5,13
Savoy Theatre, 9
Scales, Prunella, 41
Schepisi, Fred, 55
Scofield, Paul, 183-4
Scott, Margaretta, 47
Scott-Ellis, Hon. Priscilla, 137
Seale, Douglas, 166
*Secret Garden, The*, 204
*Secret People, The*, 34-6
Sellars, Arlene, 140
*Separate Tables*, 162
*Serenita*, 173-4
Shand, Camilla, 128-9
Shaughnessy, author's relatives:
    Capt. Hon. Alfred (father), 209
    Charles (son), 89
    David (son, 89,117
    Thomas (brother), 2
    *See also*: Colville, Lawson, Legh, Lodge
Shaughnessy, Alfred, *writings of*:
    Books
        *Both Ends of the Candle*, (autobiog.) 209

*Dearest Enemy*, (novel) 210,213-5
*Hugo* (novel), 210,215-6
*Sarah: The Letters and Diaries of A Courtier's Wife, 1906-1936* (ed.) 209-10
Film scripts
*A Touch Of The Sun*, 42
*Brandy For The Parson*, 36-8
*Crescendo*, 46-7
*Flesh And Blood Show, The*, 47
*Follow That Horse*, 45
*Impersonator, The*, (director) 74-7,79,93
*Just My Luck*, 26,44,48
*Laxdale Hall, (Scotch on the Rocks*, USA), 38-41,83
*Room In The House*, 48,67
*Suspended Alibi*, (director) 19,68
*Tiffany Jones*, 47
One act plays
'Bitter End, The', 186-7
'Breaking Point', 175
'Never Walk Alone', 186
'Tea Cosy, The', 175-9
Plays for the stage
*Double Cut*, 181,194-8
*Heat Of The, Moment, The* 187-193,205
*Holiday For Simon*, 89
*Light Fingers*, 172-3
*Love Affair* (from the French), 197-9
*Love En Suite*, 181-2
*Old Herbaceous*, 199-203
*Parting Day*, 173,182-6
*Release*, 34,163-7,175
*Serenita*, 173-4
Plays for TV
'Afterward', 141
*Ladies In Charge*, 144-6
'Last Seance, The', 142
*Our Marie*, 87
*Small Hours, The*, 107,157
'Sweet Sorrow', 109
'What's The Matter, Darling, Can't You Sleep?', 109-10
Short stories
'Shop Window Bride', 3
'Ninth Knife, The, 4,19
TV Series Editor for:
*Cedar Tree, The*, (creator) 135-140,192
*Hadleigh*, 101-6
*Informer, The*, 93,117
*Manhunt*, 111-5,117,121
*Place of Execution, A*, (creator), 85
*Sanctuary*, 95
*Thomas and Sarah*, (NMT)
*Upstairs, Downstairs*, 94,96, 117-133
TV episodes for:
*All Creatures Great and Small*, 152-4,157
*Alleyn Mysteries, The*, (NMT)
*By the Sword Divided*, 50
*Fourth Arm, The* (NMT),
*Irish R.M., The*, 152
*Journey To The Unknown*, 98-9
*No Hiding Place*, 96
*Saint, The*, 99
*Sherlock Holmes*, 146
*Spyder's Web*, 155
Shaw, Peter, 55-6
Shelley, Barbara, 70-1
Sherek, Henry, 179
*Sherlock Holmes, The Adventures of*, 146
Sherwood, Robert, 69
'Shop Window Bride', 3
Simmons, Jean, 31
Sisson, Rosemary Anne, 118
*Six-Five Special*, 71
Skene, Anthony, 97
Skipper, Susan, 136
*Small Hours, The*, 107,157
Somerville, E., 150
Sothern, Ann, 31
Spender, Sir Stephen, 17
Spenser, Jeremy, 170
*Spyder's Web*, 155

Squire, Ronald, 39-40
St James's Theatre, 20
St John, Earl, 91
St Martin's Theatre, Melbourne, The, 190
*Stage, The*, 185
Stephens, Robert, 81
Stewart, Hugh, 43
Stone, Richard, 191-2
Storm, Lesley, 172
Stross, Raymond, 41
*Suspended Alibi*, 19,68
'Sweet Sorrow', 109

Tabb House, 210,215
*Tapestry*, 220
Taylor, Elizabeth, 30
Taylor, Robert, 30
Taylor-Smith, Jean, 136
'Tea-Cosy, The', 175-9
*Telescope*, 28
Tennent, H.M., 170
Tennyson, Penrose, 19
Thatcher, Lady, 32
Theater der Courage, Vienna, 177-8
Theatre Royal, Brighton, The, 199
Theatre Royal, Windsor, The, 188
Thiemig, Helene, 178
*This Year Of Grace*, 5-6
Thomas, Gerald, 58
Thomas, Ralph, 58
Thompson, J. Walter, 92
Thomson, Bob, 76
Thorndike Theatre, Leatherhead, The, 197
*Tiffany Jones*, 47
Timothy, Christopher, 153
Todd, Richard, 30,191-3,194
Tomlinson, David, 44-5
Tong, Jacqueline, 126
*Touch Of The Sun, A*, 42
Tree, Sir Herbert Beerbohn, 9
Tree, Viola, 9-10
Trefford, Michael, 23
Trefusis, Violet, 128
Tronson, Robert, 112
Truman, Judith, 175,177
Twentieth-Century Fox, 98
Twickenham Studios, 72-4

*Up and Doing*, 13
*Upstairs, Downstairs*, 94,96, 117-133
Universal Aunts, 145-6
Universal Edition, 177

Valentine, Dickie, 71
van Druten, John, 176
van Thal, Dennis, 8-10
Vereker, Hon. Standish (Sandy), 217-8
Voss, Philip, 184

Walker, Peter, 47
Walsh, Kay, 81-99
Ware, Cecily, 145
Warner Brothers, 46,194
Warner-Chappell Plays, 194,197
Waters, Ronald, 39-40
Watling, Jack, 85
Watson, Moray, 198-9
Wattis, Richard, 45
Waugh, Evelyn, 151
Welles, Orson, 66
West, Lockwood, 127
West, Timothy, 127
Westminster Theatre, 89
Wharton, Edith, 141
What's The Matter, Darling, Can't You Sleep?, 109-10
White, Caroline (Mrs W.H.), 215
Whitehall Theatre, 10-13
Whitelaw, Billie, 48
Whitney, John, 93,117-18
Wilding, Michael, 30
Willes, Peter, 101-4
Williams, Emlyn, 206
Williams, Simon, 118,196
Williams, Terry, 105
Williamson, Malcolm, 47
Wilson, A.E., 26
Wilson, Sir Harold, 188
Windham-Davies, June, 141-2
Windmill Theatre, 29
Winitsky, Alec, 140

Winter Gardens Theatre,
Eastbourne, 10,26-7
Wisdom, Norman, 26,43-4
Wodehouse, P.G., 151-2
Worth, Irene, 35
Writers Guild of Great Britain,
62-6,112
Wyler, William, 78
Wyndham's Theatre, 13,199
Wynyard, Diana, 53,170
Wyvern Theatre, Swindon, 197-8

Yorkshire Television, 101 *et seq.*
Yvonne Arnaud Theatre,
Guildford, 199

Note: NMT: Not mentioned in text.